Fresh Fruit Desserts

OTHER BOOKS BY SHERYL AND MEL LONDON

The Fish-Lovers' Cookbook
Creative Cooking with Grains & Pasta
The Herb & Spice Cookbook

BY SHERYL LONDON
Eggplant & Squash: A Versatile Feast
Making the Most of Your Freezer
Anything Grows

BY MEL LONDON
Bread Winners
Bread Winners Too: The Second Rising
Easy Going
Second Spring
Getting Into Film
Getting Into Video
Making It In Film

Fresh Fruit Desserts

CLASSIC AND CONTEMPORARY

Sheryl and Mel London

PRENTICE HALL PRESS

1990

NEW YORK LONDON TORONTO SYDNEY TOKYO

SINGAPORE

PHOTOGRAPHER: Dennis M. Gottlieb
ART DIRECTORS: Amy Barison Cohen, Patricia Fabricant
FOOD STYLIST: Rick Ellis
PROP STYLIST: Adrienne Abseck
PROP CREDITS: Star Spangled Bananas and Cherry Dumplings: courtesy L. S. Collection, N.Y.C.; Two-toned Terrine, Chocolate Tartlets, and Mango, Strawberries and Kiwi in Passion Fruit Sauce: courtesy New Glass, N.Y.C.; Sicilian Orange Expresso Cheesecake: plate courtesy A Show of Hands, N.Y.C.; utensils courtesy Sointo, N.Y.C.

Prentice Hall Press
15 Columbus Circle
New York, NY 10023

PRENTICE HALL PRESS and colophons are registered trademarks of Simon & Schuster, Inc.

Library of Congress Cataloging-in-Publication Data
London, Sheryl.
    Fresh fruit desserts : classic and contemporary / Sheryl and Mel London.
        p.   cm.
     ISBN 0-13-136896-6 : $22.95
  √ 1. Desserts. 2. Cookery (Fruit)   I. London, Mel. II. Title.
    TX773.L585   1990
    641.8′6—dc20   89-16221
                                                                         CIP

Designed by Barbara Cohen Aronica
Manufactured in the United States of America

10 9 8 7 6 5 4 3 2 1

First Edition

It is only fitting that a
dessert book be dedicated
to two of the
sweetest people we know and love:
Gerald Holmes
and
Jim Reed
of Grove Street Café

Acknowledgments

No cookbook is ever a solitary endeavor. Rather, it is the summation of the work of all the people who contribute their talents and who influence the authors in the realization of the final result. We would like to thank everyone who made it possible.

We created and tested many of the recipes during the winter on Fire Island, which is for the most part a summer community, except for the few hearty souls who are year-round residents. During the winter, our village is almost completely deserted. Our one store, owned by the gracious Whitney family, closes down for the season. Thus, in addition to finding various ingenious ways of obtaining fresh fruits and other ingredients when we ran out, we also had to round up our neighbors and tasters. As delicious and tempting as desserts are, two people could never (and *should* never) consume three desserts per day (meant to serve 6 to 8 people!)—and we certainly were not going to discard our efforts, since we abhor waste.

We must admit that we met with no resistance. Rather, we found a group of discriminating palates, who tasted and critiqued our desserts most seriously and carefully. Our chief taster was Jean Kolars, a cultured, refined woman "of a certain age," who has eaten many a dessert in her lifetime and whose opinions we value greatly.

Jim LoDuca, our village Police Chief, left empty plates and cryptic notes such as "Yum Yum" tacked to our door. Sadat and Marija Beqaj, who both love to cook and eat. Lee and Dana Mehlig, who received only a few samples (since they were on a diet), but who graciously made some mainland runs through the snow in their trusty jeep, in order to get emergency supplies at the supermarket. Tina and Mark Bain spent the Christmas and New Year's holiday with us, at which time we created an impromptu "Pie and Tart Festival," in which they prepped, helped clean up, and then ate the results. We are grateful for their expertise, good humor, and sense of joy, all of which helped to make it a true festival.

After that, we moved back to the city and away from our island dampness in order to test meringues and tropical fruits. Tom Schwab and Robert Brascomb took over the testing, and we dubbed Robert "El Excelente," after the South American coffee TV commercial, for he just won't eat any old thing. He nibbles. Doesn't comment. He tastes again. Maybe he frowns. Maybe he turns his eyes skyward. If he breaks out in a big grin, we don't change a thing in the recipe! To please him is a challenge.

Madeleine Morel, our friend and agent, was another taster whose opinions on food, life, and business we treasure. Marilyn Abraham contributed greatly to the final results by her complete faith in us.

And last, but indeed not least, our gratitude to our editor, Toula Polygalaktos, whose competence, intelligence, warmth, and charm, made our hard work finally seem effortless.

Contents

Introduction

For the most part, we have always tried to practice what we have preached. In the seven cookbooks that we have written over these past years, our readers have certainly become aware of the fact that we eat whole grains and that we bake our own bread so that we are quite certain of just what ingredients go into the loaves. We consume vast quantities of fresh vegetables, some of which we grow in our own garden, others eagerly purchased as they reach our city from states that boast extended growing seasons. We lavish our food with redolent fresh herbs that come from right outside our kitchen door, many of which we dry or freeze for use during the winter months. We are both addicted to a healthful diet: low in fat and relying mostly on fish and chicken for our protein needs. So—*why have we written a book on desserts?*

During all of our working and travel lives, we have been lucky enough to have visited over 60 countries, both as filmmakers and as cookbook authors. And never have we lost our fascination and our curiosity about how people live and what they eat. Children forever, we hastily unpack our bags in a foreign country, find the nearest marketplace, and then hurry to feast on the carousel of colors, textures, and perfumes.

We want to know just what people dine on throughout the world. Thus, the markets become irresistible to the eye as well as to the palette, and we have been especially seduced by the displays of fruit in those marketplaces. This has held true for all the years, whether they are the bustling, municipal, covered marketplaces such as those near Las Ramblas in Barcelona, the noisy, busy mid-city ones in Porto and Lisbon, or the hot, canvas-covered displays along the klongs of Bangkok. The colors, the voluptuousness, the aroma, and the *promise* of fresh fruit has always filled us with delight.

Possibly another, less obvious—yet, more practical—reason for our love of fresh fruit is that, in many countries, it becomes the only *safe* method of feeding our film crew in outlying areas where the water and meat are less than acceptable.

In thinking back to some of those trips, we realize with amazement just how many of our fondest memories have to do with fresh fruit! We found that we knew very little about bananas until we wound our way down from Quito in Ecuador to the jungle villages near Santo Domingo de los Colorados, buying from a choice of *twenty* varieties, stacking the stalks in the film van for future lunches.

Apricots were truly undiscovered until our film crew traveled through the Peloponessos in Greece and the bounty of a roadside fruit stand filled the van with a perfume that we have never been able to forget. No apricot anywhere has ever lived up to the promise of those incredible fruits.

The most memorable pineapple came to us not in Hawaii but in Nigeria, where a trip up country out of Lagos brought us to a lush, tropical cocoa plantation. When we stopped to admire the cocoa pods, still on the trees, a large, rather fierce looking man jumped out, brandishing a wicked machete. We were a bit startled and even frightened, when he leaped back into the bush, only to reappear carrying a pineapple in his hand and wearing a large, open smile. With several swift strokes of the machete, he hacked the peel from the fruit and handed us the dripping, sensual, fleshy gift of friendship. The juice ran down to our elbows as we devoured it.

Peaches have been our weakness in many places, even in our own country, when we happened to travel through the state of Delaware during the height of the season. The perfumed Verona peaches of Italy were offered to us by a farmer whose grapes we had been photographing for a film on food and wine. We merely admired his peach orchard and he filled the back seat of the car with the harvest.

The durian in Thailand is a notorious fruit, for its odor is so severe that it is banned on all public transportation, yet inside lies the most delicious of tastes. Passion fruit was first offered to us in Australia, carambola (star fruit) in Hong Kong. The surprising cherimoya (custard apple) was actually a part of the food service on an airplane down to Santiago in Chile, and we remember our delighted reactions when the dark, leathery skin was broken to reveal the most luscious of fruit custards.

The cherries in the south of France were taken in the car to keep us sustained until lunchtime at the next two-star family-run restaurant, still three hours away, and we seem to remember leaving a trail of pits from the gold and red fruit all the way from Lyons to Paris. Plums were a way of life in Yugoslavia, and autumn in the north of Portugal supplied us with sun-ripened grapes and the freshest of large figs. The huge intake of citrus during a film we produced for Sunkist Growers caused us to break out into hives, all the way from Fresno and down into Yuma, Arizona.

Certainly, the book might be filled with stories of fruit and travel and the list could be never-ending. Certainly, too, we do take delight in recounting the stories, for they bring back so many memories of our work around the world. At this point, all of our readers have probably joined us with their own reminiscences, their very own stories, their very own personal discoveries. But, of course, that in itself is not a suitable reason for which to do another book, especially one on desserts. Frankly, it transcends our love of fruit. It is time, then, to go past our passion for fruit. It is time to truly write of another reason why this book has come about. For this, we admit, is the skeleton in our closet. It is the fly in our ointment. It is the true story of our weakness, our human frailty, our helplessness, as well as our ability to ignore (at times) the fact that we do occasionally break our own rules about diet, about grains and vegetables and healthful eating, and we treat ourselves to a voluptuous, memorable, opulent dessert.

Oh, we hasten to add that it is not a daily habit. If it were, it wouldn't be a treat! It is a sometime-thing, and keeping it rare gives that treat a special anticipation, an aura, an admired and appreciated coda to the perfect lunch, the memorable dinner.

We also feel that it is utterly ungracious to eliminate dessert when guests are at our table. They also become the excuse for *us* to indulge. And then, when we are dining alone, we revert to the simplest of fruit desserts once again, many of which are included in this book along with their richer relatives.

In dealing with the recipes on the pages that follow, we have attempted to address our concerns about cholesterol by relying more upon spices, herbs, citrus, and liqueurs to provide flavor, while being quite prudent in paring down the amounts of cream, eggs, butter, and

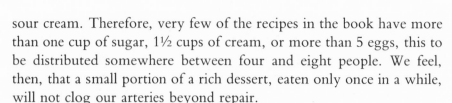

sour cream. Therefore, very few of the recipes in the book have more than one cup of sugar, 1½ cups of cream, or more than 5 eggs, this to be distributed somewhere between four and eight people. We feel, then, that a small portion of a rich dessert, eaten only once in a while, will not clog our arteries beyond repair.

And finally, we would like to add just one more thing about the recipes in the book. We are all part of an increasingly busy generation, with commitments both to our work and to our lives. We are also a visual generation, most of us having been weaned on television and on the popular picture books. Indeed, many of us, especially the younger ones among us, seem to have time for *only* the pictures, and they become our models and our goals when we cook or bake. Too often we look at the elaborate fruit desserts, only to say to ourselves, "I wonder if I could do that!" Indeed you can. We have tried to keep the recipes simple, and we have tried at the same time to present them artfully, since we are quite aware that we eat first with our eyes. The combination should guarantee you success as well as applause.

So, if indeed, you love fruit of all kinds, as we do, and if you agree that there is no reason on earth why you cannot indulge in a gift to yourself once in a while, then we think that this cookbook may well be for you. Whether you feel particularly deprived at the moment—or particularly thin—you might choose a combination of an indulgence and a favorite fruit.

We have taken meticulous and loving care in creating and testing the desserts that follow. And, we have compiled some useful information in An Addendum (Making Life Easier, pages 337–346), covering tips, hints and time-saving pointers. We want the desserts to be worthy of that special treat, that delicious ritual at the end of lunch or dinner—and without guilt. So enjoy! But only once in a while!

Sheryl and Mel London
Fire Island, New York

A well-made dessert communicates with those who are going to eat it long before they take the first bite. What appears on the outside is a promise of what awaits within. The cook should always be aware of this promise. Once you have created anticipation, you either fulfill that anticipation, or you disappoint. After all, part of the pleasure of a great dessert is the admiration and appreciation that comes to the cook.

Anonymous

Light Delights

Mélanges, Compotes, Tumbles, Macédoines, Composées, Gratinées, and Poached

> . . . and the fruits will outdo what the flowers have promised.
> —Francois de Malherbe (1605)

The American fondness for the grand finale is legendary, be it in our musical comedy or in our menus. Even when we eat sensibly or we are trying desperately to diet, we occasionally blow it with a calorie-laden sweet, many of which are to be found on other pages in this book. It is, it seems, an irrevocable part of our tradition.

Even as kids, eating at home, we always thought that the dessert was our deserved reward for eating all that other stuff that we hated so much and which we devoured so quickly in order to get to the best part. Though our dinners at home generally included rich pies and luscious puddings, it was in our school lunch boxes that we found the first and foremost of the fast food desserts—fresh fruit—nestled among the sandwiches in its own biodegradable container. There was always an apple (which, in spite of folklore, we did not give to the teacher) or an orange or a pear or a banana. And, as kids, we loved it for very much the same reasons that we delight in fresh fruit today: for the colors, for the sweetness, the shapes, and the crunch. In addition, possibly having grown up somewhat, we may also realize that in addition to taste, it's *good* for us, a philosophy that might well have turned us off if we had been told that when we were kids!

When we compare ourselves to our European, Asian, or African cousins we are a young country that is still in the process of making our own enduring mark on our culinary culture, and stamping it with our own particular fondness for desserts and fresh fruits. For example, fresh herbs have been companions of fruit for centuries, and only in the past few years have we begun to rediscover the instant magic they can make in enhancing the simplest of foods. Pine scented rosemary, sweet basil of all colors and leaf sizes, crisp cool mint, evasive flavored lemon balm, scented rose geranium leaf, and thyme have begun to appear in more and more American dessert recipes. In turn, our interest has been revived in their ancient folklore as we have begun to learn, too, just how undemanding and satisfying they are to grow in our gardens as well as to use them in our recipes.

The same holds true for flowers. Indeed, what is romance without flowers? We decorate our homes with them more lavishly now than ever. We carry them on our wedding day as we always have, we send them on St. Valentine's Day, and—we eat them. They have become a part of our salads and they have become ingredients for our desserts, just as the Colonials did and just as the Europeans have always done. Violets, candied or plain, bright, round leaf peppery nasturtiums, happy pansy faces—all marvelous when mated with fruit.

But, as we mature in our culinary consciousness, fruits themselves are also a part of the story and we are falling in love these days with the exotics of the species. The tropical fruits, some of which look like they were grown on Mars, have been appearing more frequently in our marketplaces. People now hover over them, picking them up, turning them over, smelling them and asking questions of the greengrocer. What are they? How are they used?

Although these exotica have always been a part of the tropical world's food supply, jet transportation is making them more readily available in areas of colder climes, and since seasons are reversed in the Southern hemisphere, many of them are now appearing in the United States during the winter months. These unfamiliar strangers have now become worth experimenting with, for they are the new raw materials for inspiration and for a whole new range of fruit desserts.

There are the fresh, smooth, honey-brown dates that remind us of *Lawrence of Arabia,* the wrinkled purple passion fruit the size of golf balls, looking for all the world as if they might benefit from a face lift. But, oh, the seduction of their almost dizzying and heady scent! And

their flavor once they've been cut and opened. There are the blood red ruby cactus pears, another reminder of the desert, tiny finger-size bananas, funky sweet tasting papayas, and pineapples in their armadillo coats. Cut them open and they drip juices, announcing that they have always been recognized as the symbols of hospitality.

We now see the crackling crisp Japanese chojuro and tottori pears, round as apples with the surprising taste of pears. Sparkling, sunny citrus of all kinds from tiny, oval mouth-tingling kumquats to giant-size crenelated pomelos, all thirst quenching and refreshing, with their brisk wake-up flavor. Perfumed melons, some so small that they can fit in your hand, the tiny pepino and the expensive charantais. Other melons, larger than your head such as yellow fleshed cranshaws, Persians with their outer tracery and a range of rainbow colored flesh from vivid icy greens to lush peachy oranges and pale sundown yellows.

The lovely displays at the greengrocers now include flat, silken textured saffron colored mangoes from Haiti and Jamaica and Mexico and our own Florida, all with a variety of textures and tastes. The slightly astringent persimmon carries the colors of a bright, sun-drenched orange autumn harvest moon. The ancient ruby jewels of translucent pomegranate seeds crunch between your teeth, releasing their tart sweet liquid in tiny bursts of red pleasure. The brown egg-shaped, hairy kiwi—peel it and you are bathed in emeralds.

We are just discovering them, but since time began, in the myths and tales and legends, these fruits and others like them have been extolled. Hesperides in Greek mythology was the guardian of the fabulous "golden apples," which were probably the more exotic quince, and which held the promise of love and eternal youth. And, in the Elysian fields of Paradise from the Garden of Eden's tree of knowledge, came the ubiquitous apple of today, the same one responsible, supposedly, for man's fall from grace (the fruit was probably the quince, since it has been proven historically that the weather in the Garden of Eden was not suitable for apple crops).

Pomegranates were a symbol of love and fecundity and their praises were lauded in the Song of Solomon. Throughout history, other poets have waxed rapturous over the very same fruit. Elizabeth Barrett Browning described it: "which if cut deep down the middle,

shows a heart within blood-tinctured of a veined humanity." (*Lady Geraldine's Courtship*, 1844.)

You need not make a trip to your local museum to remember that almost every artist of any consequence throughout the history of art has been inspired in some way by the forms and colors of fresh fruit, and some of the most enduring and pleasurable of still lifes are harbored in the important collections of the world. In fact, the association of artists with specific fruits is almost synonymous: Renoir and peaches, Cézanne and apples, Chardin and currants, Gaugin and mangoes, Van de Velde and lemons, Fantin-Latour and oranges, to name but a few.

The kings of Europe were also promoters of a sort. They made frequent journeys abroad and brought back the cuttings of exotics, which were then handed over to their patient gardeners to be grown in environments which would closely mimic their natural habitat. Vast orangeries and glass covered conservatories were built so that they might flourish for the tables and the pleasure of royalty. Even in our own country, we find that Thomas Jefferson had an insatiable curiosity for botany and he, too, experimented with fruits that might grow in our varied climates. And today there is a rebirth of that urge to inquire, to probe and to experiment.

Thus, what we have tried to do in this chapter is to create desserts in which the fruits are not disguised, but are instead the featured players. All of the recipes are light, easy to duplicate, and in keeping with today's daily eating habits. They are designed for the times when we don't want to fuss over a special dessert, yet we need to have the reward that we have become accustomed to since childhood.

Some are compositions—composées. They are the freshest, ripest fruit, those that get the highest marks when served raw. We have enhanced them a bit, but only with respect for combinations of flavor first, then an eye-appealing arrangement that considers the colors, relationship, and contrast, shape, texture, scale, and pattern—all the elements with which an artist works. The composées of fresh fruits all keep in mind that it is the eye which must also be seduced.

Since, as we mentioned, it is no longer an oddity to see summer fruits—plums, apricots, peaches, nectarines—in our winter markets, we must also remember that they are all brought from distances that

prevent their being picked at the peak of their flavor and ripeness. They bruise too easily when they're in their prime. Thus, these fruits must be poached, baked, or gratinéed, then enhanced with spices and sweetened with spirits to bring out their potential.

In years past, fruit was boiled in a lot of liquid, resulting in a shapeless mass, and closely resembling the canned, processed product. But we find that poaching and baking fruit is best done in a heavy ovenproof dish, preferably earthenware. The heaviness of the cooking vessel insures the slow cooking in a minimum of liquid, and the shape and the flavor of the fruit are not destroyed.

So, these are the Light Delights: the mélanges, the macédoines, the tumbles, the composées, the gratinées, and the poached and the baked fruits. They are the desserts without guilt, the ones that you can eat without being reminded of your latest cholesterol test. And, they are as delicious as any you'll find.

Moroccan Oranges with
Fresh Dates and Almonds

Serves 6

Fresh dates, although a bit of an oddity in places where they are not locally grown, are the true desert manna, and are now in demand in all climes. Most likely their popularity has been earned, since they contain half the calories of their more common dried cousins. In addition, the dried dates become increasingly sweet as their natural sugars concentrate in the drying process. The prime season for fresh dates from the deserts of California and Israel is from August to December. However, if fresh dates are not available, you can used dried Medjoul dates as an acceptable substitute, though they will be sweeter.

> *6 navel oranges*
> *12 fresh dates (or dried Medjoul dates)*
> *6 teaspoons orange flower water (see note)*
> *Superfine sugar*
> *Cinnamon*
> *6 teaspoons sliced almonds*

Remove the peel from one orange with a vegetable parer, cut into needle thin julienne strips for garnish and set aside. Cut a thin slice from the tops and bottoms of each orange and score the peel with a sharp knife to remove it easily. Remove any white pith and membrane and slice each orange horizontally with a serrated bread knife (so the juices are not lost) into ¼-inch slices. Arrange the orange slices in an overlapping circle on individual serving plates. Taste an end piece of the orange and if it is tart you may want to sprinkle each slice with a bit of superfine sugar.

Remove the stem ends of the dates, allowing 2 dates for each serving. Split each date vertically and remove the pits. Mince one date per serving and scatter over the orange slices. Arrange the other date,

cut in half, in the center of the orange slices. Spoon a scant teaspoon of orange flower water over the oranges for each serving. Dust lightly with cinnamon and scatter 1 teaspoon sliced almonds and a few shreds of the julienned peel over each serving. Cover with plastic wrap and chill until ready to serve.

Note: Middle Eastern and Indian specialty shops carry orange flower water. However, an exquisite French orange flower water, made in Vallauris and which comes in a bright blue plastic bottle, is obtainable at gourmet food purveyors and is far more flavorful. Be advised, also, that fresh dates have skins that can easily be slipped off if you so desire.

Sliced Papaya with
Ruby Cactus Pear Purée and Mint

Serves 6

The distinctive prickly cactus pear plant yields a thorny fruit (with thorns removed, mercifully, before being sent to market). They are sometimes called *Prickly Pear* or *Sabra* fruit in Israel, named after the early original settlers who were said to be just like the fruit—tough, thorny exteriors but sweet and soft inside. As for the papaya, we remember smiling at a poster at the Produce Academy in New York that read euphoniously "Trya Papaya!" Together, these two fruits make earthy companions.

Cactus Pear Purée
> *2 medium-size cactus pears, plus 1 additional for garnish*
> *4 tablespoons sugar*
> *Pinch of salt*
> *2 tablespoons lemon juice (½ lemon)*
> *1 tablespoon butter*
> *1 tablespoon arrowroot plus 2 tablespoons cold water*
> *2 tablespoons kirsch*

Fruit
> *2 large papayas, peeled, seeds removed, and sliced vertically*
> *into ½-inch thick slices*
> *Sprigs of mint for garnish (optional)*

Cut off the tops and bottoms of 2 of the cactus pears, then slit the skin lengthwise on both sides, allowing the outer and inner skins to be peeled in one operation. Cut the cactus pears into small cubes. There should be about 1½ cups. Combine with the sugar and salt in a medium saucepan and bring slowly to a boil, then lower the heat and simmer for 5 minutes, stirring and crushing the fruit against the sides of the saucepan with the back of a wooden spoon.

Add the butter and stir until melted, then remove from the heat and allow to cool. Strain the fruit through a sieve over a small bowl, pressing and scraping it against the bottom of the sieve. Discard the seeds and return the purée to the saucepan. Dissolve the arrowroot in the water, add to the purée, and heat, stirring, until thickened, about 2 to 3 minutes. Remove from the heat and add the kirsch.

Spoon a layer of purée on the bottom of a large serving dish. Lay slices of papaya on top in an attractive manner. Cut both ends from the remaining cactus pear, stand upright, and make several wedge-shape cuts halfway down the fruit on the top side and peel back like a flower. Place it in the center of the dish and chill before serving.

Marinated Figs with Muscat Raisin Wine Sauce and a Julienne of Fresh Pears and Walnuts

Serves 6

An early autumn still-life composition just when figs are ripe and plentiful and fresh pears begin to appear in the marketplace.

> ¾ cup dry white wine
> ⅓ cup sugar
> ⅓ cup muscat raisins (see note)
> 1 tablespoon lemon juice
> 18 small fresh figs, cut in halves
> 2 small ripe Anjou pears
> 1 small wedge lemon
> 2 tablespoons coarsely broken toasted walnuts

Combine the wine and the sugar in a medium-size saucepan. Bring to a boil and boil for 2 minutes without stirring. Remove from the heat and add the raisins and the lemon juice. Place the figs in a bowl and pour the raisin-wine sauce over them. Let the fruit macerate for at least 3 to 4 hours or overnight until ready to serve.

Remove the figs from the sauce and arrange 6 halves on each plate, cut side down, like spokes of a wheel. Pour the sauce into a small saucepan and boil gently for 4 to 5 minutes to reduce. Cool slightly while preparing the pears.

Peel, core, and cut the pears into thin sticks. Place in the center of the figs and squeeze a few drops of lemon juice over the pears to prevent discoloration. Spoon some sauce over the figs and sprinkle each serving with one teaspoon of walnuts.

Note: Muscat raisins are flavorful and very large (about ¾ inch each), but sometimes they are hard to come by. Monukka or plain black raisins can be substituted.

Mango, Strawberries, and Kiwi in Passion Fruit Sauce with Lemon Balm

Serves 4

A tropical composée—arranged for the most visual response. This is a simple and artistic presentation of fruit with a fruit sauce and only the strawberries are grown in the temperate zone.

2 ripe mangoes (weighing about 1 pound each)
1 kiwi, peeled and thinly sliced into 8 slices
12 large strawberries, hulled
8 sprigs of lemon balm (optional)
8 tablespoons Passion Fruit Sauce (page 318)

Cut the mangoes in half with a serrated grapefruit knife. Slip the knife under the flat pit and remove. The four halves will allow ½ mango per serving. Score each half into one-inch cubes, making sure that you do not cut the skin. Fold each half mango back to fan out the cubes and place slightly off center on a serving plate.

Slice 3 strawberries and place the slices, overlapping them, on two sides of the mango. Then place two slices of kiwi on a third side. Spoon 1 tablespoon of Passion Fruit Sauce on the still empty side of the plate and trickle the remaining tablespoon over the fruits. Add 1 sprig of lemon balm to two sides of the plate. Repeat the arrangement for the other three servings. Cover with plastic wrap until serving time. Serve at room temperature.

Persian Fruit Tumble
(Miveh Makhlout)

Serves 6 to 8

The fragrantly beautiful melons of old Persia (Iran) have been enjoyed for centuries, prepared simply and without embellishment. However, when company comes, melons can take on a festive air with the addition of strawberries, nuts, and complimentary flavorings. This recipe was given to us by our guide, Bábak Sassan, on a film trip to Iran before the Ayatollah came to power.

2½ to 3 pounds ripe honeydew melon
1½ pounds ripe cantaloupe
1 pint small ripe strawberries, hulled
3 tablespoons apricot jam
1 tablespoon rose flower water
2 tablespoons kirsch
½ cup orange juice (juice of one orange)
1 tablespoon shredded orange peel made with a zester tool
3 tablespoons toasted, coarsely chopped pistachio nuts
2 tablespoons toasted slivered almonds

Use a lovely crystal bowl large enough to contain the fruit. Cut the melons in half, remove the seeds and strings, and scoop out the flesh with a melon baller. For contrasting shapes, the canteloupe can be cut into one inch cubes and the strawberries left whole. Place the fruit in the serving bowl. Combine the jam, rose flower water, kirsch, and orange juice together in a small cup, add to the fruit, and toss lightly. Sprinkle the shredded orange peel and toasted nuts over all and chill until serving time. Serve cold.

Fuyu Persimmon and Kiwi Tower
with Blackberry Sauce

An arranged composition of beautiful colors and mellow tastes combined here in a sophisticated presentation.

> 2 ripe Fuyu persimmons
> 1 lime
> 3 to 4 small kiwis
> 4 tablespoons sugar
> 3 tablespoons water
> ¼ cup Grand Marnier or other orange-flavored liqueur
> ½ cup blackberries

Remove the stems from the persimmons and slice very thinly. Place them on a piece of waxed paper and set aside. Using a zester tool, make long shreds of lime peel and set aside. Peel and slice the kiwis thinly and set aside. In a small heavy saucepan, mix the sugar and water together, then bring to a boil and boil for 1 minute without stirring. Remove from the heat and when the bubbles subside add the orange liqueur and the blackberries. Return to the heat and simmer for 1 to 2 minutes more. Let the sauce cool while assembling the fruit.

Place the persimmon slices in a circle on the bottom of a round serving plate. Then place the kiwi slices over the persimmons so they are visible when the next layer of persimmon slices is added. Top with another layer of kiwi. Spoon the blackberry sauce slowly over the "tower" and sprinkle shreds of lime peel over the surface. Cover with plastic wrap and chill for at least 1 hour. Bring to room temperature before serving.

Star Spangled Bananas

Serves 4

An attractive presentation for the diet-conscious dessert lover—indeed, one that we "eat with our eyes." Plebian bananas and the exotic star-shaped carambola fruit rest on a fruit purée of two contrasting colors and flavors. The purées can be made well in advance and the assembly takes only minutes. The result is a spectacular mini work of art.

> *8 tablespoons Mango Sauce (page 321)*
> *8 tablespoons Red Currant Sauce (page 325)*
> *2 to 3 bananas, peeled and sliced diagonally*
> *Lemon juice*
> *2 starfruit (carambola), cut thinly*
> *8 small branches of fresh currants, for garnish*
> *Green leaves for garnish*

Spoon 2 tablespoons of the mango sauce on half of a dinner plate. Spoon 2 tablespoons of the red currant sauce on the other half of the plate. Place 8 to 9 overlapping slices of bananas in rows on one side of the plate where the two sauces meet. Squeeze a few drops of lemon juice over the bananas. Lay 5 slices of starfruit in the currant sauce. Sprinkle a few red currants over the mango sauce. Lay 1 branch of currants and a green leaf (mint, rose geranium, or strawberry) on the plate as a garnish. Repeat procedure for each serving.

Honey Poached Kumquats

Serves 6 to 8
(Makes 2 cups)

Tongue-tingling poached kumquats are spooned over cool soothing vanilla ice cream, a fast exotic treat. Another way to use the honey-poached kumquats is with grapefruit sections and pomegranate seeds (see page 18 for recipe). These tiny, egg-shaped fruits are one of the few fruits that are never eaten raw.

1 pound kumquats
Boiling water
½ cup water
¼ cup sugar
2 tablespoons mild, light honey
1 2-inch stick of cinnamon

Put the kumquats in a bowl and pour boiling water over to cover. Let steep for 30 seconds and drain in a sieve. Put the ½ cup water into a small, heavy, deep saucepan and combine with the sugar and honey. Bring slowly to a boil, then reduce to a very low heat and add the cinnamon and kumquats. Cook for 10 minutes, stirring occasionally. Be sure the heat is not too high or the kumquats will burst. Cool, then refrigerate in a sterile container (see note). The kumquats will keep for several months.

When serving over scoops of vanilla ice cream, allow 3 to 4 kumquats and some syrup for each serving.

Note: To sterilize the jar and lid, cover with boiling water in a saucepan and boil for 15 minutes. Lift out with tongs and drain on paper towels.

Poached Oranges
with Green and Red Grapes and
Grenadine Orange Peel

Serves 6 to 8

The oranges are peeled and sliced, poached, and then marinated with pale green and red seedless grapes. The orange peel is cut into julienne strips and steeped separately in a grenadine syrup. It's a colorful and light dessert that is assembled just before serving.

The Oranges
> 6 large navel oranges
> 1 cup water
> ½ cup sugar
> 2 cups seedless green grapes
> ½ cup seedless red grapes
> 3 tablespoons Grand Marnier liqueur, or other orange-flavored
> > liqueur
> 2 teaspoons vanilla extract

Cut off thin slices from both ends of each orange. With a vegetable parer, remove long strips of orange peel as thinly as possible and set aside. Score the oranges and peel away the thick white pith and then slice across into ½-inch slices using a serrated knife. In a skillet large enough to accommodate the oranges in one layer, bring the water and the sugar to a boil. Add the sliced oranges and allow it to come to a boil again, then lower the heat and poach for 3 minutes. Remove the slices with a slotted spoon and place in a glass serving dish, and add the grapes. Boil the remaining syrup in the skillet, until reduced to ½ cup. Remove the skillet from the heat and add the Grand Marnier and the vanilla extract. Cool the syrup slightly and pour over the oranges and grapes. Cover with plastic wrap and chill in the refrigerator for several hours. During this period, tilt the bowl once or twice and baste with the liquid.

Grenadine Orange Peel
  Reserved orange peel strips
  1 cup cold water
  ⅓ cup grenadine syrup (see note)

To prepare the grenadine orange peel, cut the reserved orange peel into very thin long strips. There should be about 1 cup. Add the cold water to a medium-size saucepan along with the julienned peel and bring to a boil. Remove from the heat and drain in a sieve. Repeat this procedure twice more to remove any bitterness. After the third draining, put the peel in a plastic container and pour ⅓ cup grenadine syrup over it. Mix well, cover and refrigerate overnight.

When ready to serve, remove half of the orange peel with a slotted spoon and drain on paper towels before sprinkling over the sliced oranges and grapes. Save the remaining peel for another time.

Note: Grenadine syrup is available at local supermarkets and specialty food shops.

Honey Poached Kumquats with Ruby Grapefruit and Pomegranate Seeds

Serves 4

A colorful, bracing fruit assembly to delight any modern sybarite. It uses a combination of sunny citrus and a scattering of sensually bursting pomegranate kernels, all balanced by the bittersweet flavor of sprightly kumquats and soothed with honey. The whole recipe was inspired by biblical gardens!

1 cup honey poached kumquats plus ½ cup poaching syrup (see note)
2 ruby (pink) grapefruits (or 1 yellow and 1 pink grapefruit)
½ pomegranate, cut in two pieces
1 tablespoon lime juice
1 tablespoon light honey
Shreds of lime peel, made with a zester tool, for garnish

Peel the grapefruits and pomegranate quarters, then remove and discard the white membranes. Divide the grapefruits into segments, holding the segments up to the light to locate any seeds. Pluck them out with the point of a sharp knife. Arrange around the outside of individual glass serving plates and alternate colors if you are using both kinds of grapefruit.

Place a cluster of kumquats in the center of each plate. Scatter 1 tablespoon pomegranate kernels over each assembly. Mix the poaching syrup with the lime juice and honey and spoon over the grapefruit sections. Top with bright green shreds of lime peel.

Note: Honey Poached Kumquats (page 15) may be made well in advance and kept on hand for several desserts in this book.

Poached Brandied Peaches

Serves 6

By using the pits of the peaches when we make this recipe, we intensify the flavor of the ripe peaches themselves, poached in a brew of white wine, cognac, and orange juice.

1 cup fresh orange juice (about 2 large oranges)
1 cup dry white wine
¼ cup cognac or brandy
1 cup sugar
6 large ripe peaches, peeled, cut, and pitted (reserve the pits)

In a heavy, wide-base saucepan or deep skillet, combine the orange juice, the wine, the cognac, and the sugar. Add the peach pits and bring the liquid to a boil. Lower the heat and simmer, stirring occasionally, for 5 minutes. Bring to a boil again and add the peach halves in one layer. Lower the heat and simmer, uncovered, for 8 minutes, tilting the pot and basting the fruit with the liquid. The peaches should be tender, but still slightly firm. Allow the peaches to cool in the liquid, then transfer them using a slotted spoon to a flat bottomed dish with sides. Remove the peach pits with a slotted spoon and discard. Spoon some of the sauce over the peaches and chill slightly before serving.

Note: There will be extra sauce. We like to use it in white wine with ice cubes to produce a delicious "Bellini" wine cooler, topped with a ripe raspberry. Just add enough sauce to taste.

Macédoine of Mixed Fresh Fruit
with Basil Wine Marinade
(Three Ways)

Makes 2 cups

This is a gently perfumed marinade that keeps well for several months when refrigerated. Fruit desserts for all seasons can be made when this marinade is spooned over the various combinations of fresh fruit that we suggest here.

Basil Wine Marinade
 1½ cups dry white wine
 ⅓ cup fresh basil leaves
 ⅓ cup scented rose geranium leaves
 3 2-inch strips of lemon peel (about ½ lemon)
 Vanilla bean, 2 inches long, split, scraped, and cut into small
  pieces
 3 tablespoons sugar
 2 teaspoons crushed cassia bark or cassia buds or 2 2-inch pieces
  cinnamon sticks (see note)

Combine all the ingredients in a heavy saucepan. Slowly bring to a boil, cook 2 minutes, remove from the heat and let steep for 25 minutes, stirring occasionally. Strain and cool before refrigerating in sterile jars. Always allow the fruit to steep for several hours before serving and use about ⅔ cup of the marinade for each combination of fruits. The fruit mixtures suggested here have all been selected for color and scale as well as flavor and seasonal availability. Certainly, you can also invent some of your own, but if you do, just make sure that there is something tart or acidic in each mixture.

Combination One
　　1 mango, peeled and cubed
　　1 kiwi, peeled and sliced horizontally
　　Raspberries
　　1 pineapple, peeled and cubed
　　Blueberries

Combination Two
　　Peaches or nectarines, peeled, pitted, and sliced
　　1 pineapple, peeled and cubed
　　Strawberries, hulled, left whole or halved, depending upon
　　　　their size
　　1 kiwi, peeled and sliced horizontally
　　Blackberries

Combination Three
　　Whole, peeled clementines
　　1 pineapple, peeled and cubed
　　1 papaya, peeled, seeded, and cut in vertical slices
　　1 starfruit, sliced horizontally, seeds removed
　　Red seedless grapes

Note: Cassia bark, and sometimes the buds (which resemble cloves in appearance), are the Asian equivalent of cinnamon, but they are blessed with an extraordinary, mellow, elusive flavor. Speciality shops that sell spices in depth usually stock one or the other or both.

Clementine Pyramid with Candied Violets

The clementine is the smallest of the mandarin oranges, a family that includes tangerines, temple oranges, tangelos, mineolas, and mandarins. These "babies" are used here since they are totally seedless and thus can be left whole and remain intact as a centerpiece for the dessert.

9 clementines

Peel the clementines with a vegetable parer as thinly as possible, removing only the orange part of the peel. Reserve the peels. With a small, sharp knife, peel away the remaining rind and scrape away as much of the clinging white membrane from the clementines as possible. Use the point of a knife against your thumb to do a thorough scraping job. Put the clementines in a plastic bag and chill while preparing the syrup.

Clementine Peel Syrup *Makes 1½ to 2 cups*
   The peels of 9 clementines
   1 cup water
   1 cup sugar
   ¼ teaspoon cream of tartar
   ⅓ cup Cointreau, or other orange-flavored liqueur
   2 teaspoons grenadine syrup
   9 candied violets for garnish (see note)

Cut the peel into very fine julienne. Add them to a medium-size non-stick saucepan and cover with cold water. Bring to a boil, strain, and return the peel to the saucepan with 1 cup water, the sugar, and the cream of tartar. (The cream of tartar will prevent the syrup from crystallizing.) Stir and bring to a boil. Reduce the heat to simmer and cook uncovered until syrupy, about 20 to 25 minutes. Remove from the heat

and add the Cointreau and grenadine syrup. Cool and chill in the refrigerator for one hour. About an hour before serving, assemble the dessert.

Pile the chilled whole clementines on a footed glass rimmed plate in a pyramid shape. Spoon the chilled syrup over the clementines along with the shredded peel. Insert 1 candied violet in the tops of each clementine. Serve at once, or chill and then add the candied violets just before serving time so that they don't melt.

Note: Candied violets can be purchased at specialty gourmet food shops. If there is extra syrup and peel left over, it can be stored in the refrigerator for several weeks for later use. Or, if you like, you can increase the number of clementines you use in the recipe to accommodate any number of people. Just increase the size of the pyramid—there will be enough syrup for double the amount of clementines.

Baked Chojuro Pears with
Caramel Sauce and Pecans

This fruit is of Asian origin and has many aliases. It is known as *Chojuro Pear, Japanese Pear,* and *Tottori: Twentieth-Century Pear.* It is also known as *Apple Pear.* This giant, fawn-colored beauty has a skin that is marked with a scattering of tiny black dots and it's been making its way from the Orient to our local greengrocers in ever increasing numbers. It's easy to understand its growing popularity, since it has a sweet, crisp flesh and, though it resembles an apple, its flavor is reminiscent of pears, giving it the best of two worlds!

Pears
> *3 Chojuro pears (see note)*
> *1 teaspoon lemon juice*
> *1 tablespoon melted butter*

Preheat the oven to 425 degrees. Peel the pears with a vegetable parer and cut in half from stem to base. Using a small sharp knife, cut out the core. Turn each pear over and slice ¾ of the way through in ⅜-inch-thick slices. Place the halves core side down in a buttered baking dish large enough to accommodate the pears in one layer and bake for 15 to 20 minutes, or until the pears are firm yet tender. Remove from the oven and cool. While the pears are baking, prepare the caramel sauce.

Caramel Sauce
> *½ cup light brown sugar*
> *¼ cup light corn syrup*
> *4 tablespoons butter*
> *¼ cup heavy cream*
> *18 toasted pecan halves*
> *Whipped cream*

Combine the brown sugar, corn syrup, and butter in a nonstick saucepan and cook over medium heat. Bring to a boil, without stirring, until the sauce reaches the soft ball stage (234 to 240 degrees) on a candy thermometer. Remove from the heat and stand back a bit while stirring in the cream (it could splatter).

When the pears and the sauce have cooled, place ½ of a pear on a serving dish. Spoon 2 tablespoons caramel sauce around the base of the pear and trickle only a bit over the top of the pear. Place three pecan halves in a fan shape at the stem end of the pear and pipe a small rosette of whipped cream at the base of the centered pecan.

Note: Firm large Bosc pears or Delicious apples can be substituted for the Chojuro pears in this recipe, but the elusive apple-pear flavor will not be present.

Red Plums Baked in Tea with
Orange Liqueur Meringue

Serves 4 to 6

Italian prune plums and greengage plums are the only freestone plums, which means the fruit easily separates from the pit when it's cut in half. All others are cling stone, including the lovely red ones available in summer and which are supplied to the colder climates in the winter by South American growers. Thus, this dessert, featuring the red plum variety, has now become a year-round dessert.

The Plums
> 1 cup boiling water
> 4 Earl Gray tea bags
> 1¼ pounds red plums
> ½ cup sugar
> 1 2-inch strip of orange peel

Pour the boiling water over the tea bags in a cup and let steep for 10 minutes. Preheat the oven to 300 degrees. Cut the plums in half down to the pit. With a twisting motion of the hands, separate the plums. Cut the pits out with the tip of a sharp knife and place the plums skin-side down in a 9-by-1½-inch baking dish. Discard the tea bags, add the sugar to the tea and stir to dissolve. Add the orange peel and pour over and around the plums. Bake for 15 to 20 minutes, basting every 5 minutes. While the plums are baking, prepare the meringue.

Orange Liqueur Meringue
> 3 egg whites
> Pinch of salt
> Pinch of cream of tartar
> ½ cup sifted confectioners' sugar
> 2 teaspoons finely minced orange peel
> 3 tablespoons Grand Marnier, or other orange-flavored liqueur

Beat the egg whites with a rotary or electric hand beater until frothy, then add the salt and cream of tartar and beat until foamy. Using a small strainer, gradually add the confectioners' sugar to the egg whites as you continue beating. Continue to sift and add sugar gradually until the egg whites are stiff and shiny. Add the orange peel and the Grand Marnier and set aside.

Remove the plums with a slotted spoon, pour off the liquid and orange peel and discard, then return the plums to the baking dish. Spoon the meringue over the plums and return to the oven for 10 minutes at the same temperature and continue to bake until the top is golden. Serve at room temperature.

Baked Glazed Figs with Crème Anglaise

Serves 6

The Crème Anglaise can be prepared well in advance and the figs bake for no more than 10 minutes. It's a good, last minute dessert that looks as if a lot more effort has gone into it when it really is one of the easiest recipes in the book.

6 large fresh figs
1 teaspoon lemon juice
1½ tablespoons sugar
2 tablespoons seedless raspberry jam
1 teaspoon kirsch
1 recipe Crème Anglaise II (page 333)

Preheat the oven to 400 degrees. Butter a shallow 9-by-1½-inch round baking dish, preferably earthenware. Cut the figs in thirds from stem to base. Arrange four of the slices with their stems pointing toward the center of the dish, with the remaining slices placed around this hub. Sprinkle the figs with the lemon juice and sugar and bake for 8 to 10 minutes. While the figs are baking, melt the jam in a small heavy saucepan. Add the kirsch and cook until a thick glaze is formed, then spoon a bit over each fig. To serve, spoon a layer of Crème Anglaise onto each serving plate and arrange 3 sliced figs centered over the sauce.

Baked Maple Walnut Bananas with Cranberries

Serves 6

Surveys show that Americans eat *50 tons of bananas every nine minutes,* so this is our entry in the banana popularity contest. Tart cranberries take the edge off the sometimes cloying sweetness of maple syrup and walnuts add a crisp contrast to the tender-textured bananas.

6 ripe but firm bananas, peeled
⅓ cup maple syrup
1 cup finely ground walnuts
¼ cup coarsely broken walnuts
½ cup cranberries
⅓ cup melted butter
3 tablespoons dark rum

Preheat the oven to 350 degrees. Butter a large ovenproof shallow baking dish large enough to accommodate a single layer of bananas. Pour the maple syrup into a flat pie pan and put the ground walnuts on a piece of waxed paper. Dip and roll each whole banana first in maple syrup and then in the ground walnuts. Arrange in the prepared dish. Scatter the broken walnuts and cranberries around the bananas, or place one walnut half and 2 cranberries on top of each banana, scattering the rest. Mix the melted butter with the rum and spoon around the bananas, but not over them. Bake for 8 to 10 minutes without basting. Serve warm with some of the cranberry walnut mixture spooned on the side of each serving.

Gratin of Poached Apples with
Rosemary, Lemon, and Frangipane

Serves 6

The apples are poached first, then baked beneath a light rosemary and lemon scented frangipane, resulting in a puffy tortelike dessert.

1½ cups sugar
½ cup water
2 pounds Granny Smith apples (or other tart green apples),
  peeled and cored
¾ cup whole blanched almonds
3 eggs
¼ cup lemon juice
1 tablespoon finely minced lemon peel
1 tablespoon rosemary leaves, finely minced
Pinch of salt
½ teaspoon vanilla extract
Lightly whipped cream, if desired

Preheat the oven to 350 degrees and butter a 1½-quart round ovenproof baking dish. In a large saucepan, dissolve 1 cup of the sugar in the water. Bring slowly to a boil and boil for 1 minute without stirring, then remove from the heat. Slice the apples thinly right into the hot syrup, bring slowly to a boil and boil gently for 3 minutes. Drain the apple slices through a sieve and arrange on the bottom of the prepared pan. Discard the syrup or save for poaching other fruit. Grind the almonds very fine in a blender; there will be about two cups.

In the bowl of a food processor beat the eggs with the remaining sugar until very thick and creamy. Add the almonds, lemon peel and juice, rosemary, salt, and vanilla and process until well combined. Pour over the apples and bake for 35 minutes, or until golden. Serve at room temperature with lightly whipped cream, if desired.

Gratinée of Pineapple with Bourbon and Brown Sugar

Serves 6

Since this dessert only takes ten minutes to cook, the most difficult step in its preparation is the peeling of the pineapple. These days, however, even that minor chore can be eliminated as more and more supermarkets now sell whole, peeled, and cored fresh pineapples.

1 small ripe pineapple
4 tablespoons butter
½ cup dark brown sugar
¼ cup bourbon

Peel the pineapple, cutting out the "eyes" (the small, circular, rough indentations). Slice it into eight ⅜-inch-thick slices and cut out the tough core in the center of each slice. Preheat the broiler and butter a large ovenproof dish that will hold six slices of pineapple in one layer. Place the six rings in the pan and set aside. Finely chop the remaining two slices of pineapple.

In a skillet, melt the butter and add the sugar, stirring over medium heat until the sugar is dissolved, about 1 minute. Add the chopped pineapple and sauté, stirring over low heat for 2 to 3 minutes and then spoon equal amounts over each slice of pineapple. Broil for 10 minutes, basting with the brown sugar–butter mixture.

While the pineapple broils, heat the bourbon in a small pot with a lid. Stand back and ignite with a match to burn off some of the alcohol for a few seconds. Then cover with the lid to extinguish the flame. Pour over the pineapple and serve at room temperature.

Apricot Gratin with
Apricot Crème Fraîche

Serves 6 to 8

The best fresh market apricots are the freestone Royals—golden yellow-orange with a bit of blush. However, these are not always available and because of the fragility of these apricots they are often shipped before they can thoroughly ripen on the tree. Unfortunately, it is only the tree-ripened fruit that is ambrosial, and even though it is possible to now get apricots out of normal season from growers in South America, they are also shipped before being tree-ripened. The solution is to either move closer to an orchard while the ripening process takes place, or complete the process yourself by putting the apricots in a brown paper bag with a few holes punched in it until they become more tender. Then, as in this recipe, you can lightly poach them to let them develop extra flavor.

Apricot Crème Fraîche   *Makes 2 cups*
  1 cup heavy cream
  2 heaping tablespoons sour cream
  ¼ cup apricot preserves
  1 tablespoon Cointreau, or other orange-flavored liqueur

Whip the cream with a rotary hand beater just until it holds soft peaks but is not stiff. Mix the preserves with the Cointreau and add to the whipped cream, stirring. Chill in the refrigerator until ready to serve.

Apricots
> ½ cup sugar
> ½ cup water
> Pinch of cream of tartar
> 1 teaspoon lemon juice
> ½ pound large apricots (about 8), halved & pitted
> ¼ teaspoon almond extract
> 2 tablespoons softened butter
> ¼ cup Amaretti cookie crumbs
> Sliced almonds for garnish, if desired
> Muscat raisins for garnish, if desired

In a saucepan off the heat combine the sugar and water and add the cream of tartar, stirring until partially dissolved. Bring to a boil over medium heat and boil for 1 minute without stirring. Remove from the heat and add the lemon juice and the apricot halves. Return to medium high heat and cook for 4 to 5 minutes. Remove the apricots with a slotted spoon and place on a flat dish to cool. When cool enough to handle, slip off the apricot skins. Strain the cooking liquid and add the almond extract to it. Spoon over the cooled apricots and let steep for 30 minutes.

Preheat the broiler and butter a gratin dish large enough to accommodate the apricots in one layer. Remove the apricots with a slotted spoon, reserving the liquid, and transfer them to the gratin dish.

Mix the butter with the cookie crumbs until well combined and distribute equally into the cavities of each apricot half. Broil the apricots 3 to 4 inches away from the heat source for a minute or two. Let cool for 5 minutes, then again using a slotted spoon, place 2 to 3 apricot halves on each serving plate. Spoon the cold Apricot Crème Fraîche on top of each apricot half. Trickle a tiny bit of the remaining poaching liquid over all. If you like, you can add a few sliced almonds and tuck in a muscat raisin for garnish.

Baked Seckel Pears in
Mulled Red Wine

Serves 6

The diminutive, flavorful Seckel pears, the smallest variety marketed, marry well with a wide range of sweet spices such as cloves and cinnamon. Their exteriors are stained burgundy, but when they're sliced, they reveal a pale, creamy white interior.

> *12 Seckel pears (see note)*
> *1½ cups dry red wine*
> *1 cup sugar*
> *5 whole cloves*
> *1 cinnamon stick*
> *2 strips each of orange peel and lemon peel, about 3 inches long*

Peel the pears with a vegetable parer, leaving the stems on. Cut a very thin slice off the bottom of each pear to allow them to stand upright and arrange them as close together as possible in a 1½-quart shallow baking dish. Preheat the oven to 400 degrees.

In a medium-size saucepan, bring the remaining ingredients to a boil, stirring frequently until the sugar is dissolved. Pour the mixture over the pears and bake, basting several times, until the pears are tender, about 10 to 15 minutes. Test for doneness with a skewer or the point of a sharp knife. Remove the pears with a slotted spoon and transfer them to a serving platter. Pour the sauce back into the saucepan. You should have about 1½ cups. Cook over high heat until the sauce becomes thick and syrupy and is reduced to ¾ cup. Strain and spoon over the pears. Baste a few more times before serving warm or chilled.

Note: Bosc pears can also be used if you cannot find the smaller Seckel pears. Allow one Bosc pear per person.

Baked Apple Porcupines

Serves 6

Crusty apple halves are baked in pineapple-orange juice and studded with almond slivers.

> *½ cup slivered almonds*
> *¼ cup flour*
> *½ cup sugar*
> *1 teaspoon cinnamon*
> *3 tablespoons cold butter, cut into small pieces*
> *6 apples, peeled, cored, and halved (see note)*
> *1 egg, lightly beaten*
> *¾ cup pineapple-orange juice, made from frozen concentrate*
> *Heavy cream as an accompaniment, if desired*

Preheat the oven to 350 degrees. Place the almonds in a pie plate and toast until golden, about 4 to 5 minutes. Remove and set aside. Mix the flour, sugar, and cinnamon in a food processor. Add the butter and process only until the mixture is crumbly. Set aside. Brush each apple half with the egg, then dip in the sugar, cinnamon, and butter mixture. Place curved side up, in a 9-by-14-inch baking pan. Pour the pineapple-orange juice into the bottom of the pan, *not* over the apples. Bake, uncovered, for 20 to 25 minutes without basting.

Remove the apples from the oven and stud with the toasted almond slivers. Carefully remove the apples to a serving dish using a spatula. Allow two halves per person. Spoon sauce around the base of the dish. Serve warm, with or without heavy cream.

Note: Slightly tart, firm apples should be used such as Empire, Ida Red, Pippin, or Winesap. Although Cortland and Rome Beauty are generally considered baking apples, they lose their shape when peeled and, if you use them, they may require less baking time. Test for doneness with the tip of a pointed knife after 15 or 20 minutes.

Baked Summer Fruits with Nasturtiums

Serves 6

Peaches, plums, and strawberries, all in their summer glory, rest on a bed of puréed rhubarb and strawberries. Peppery nasturtium blossoms add their color and pique the flavor of the fruit with just the right note in this colorful, festive dessert.

> ¼ *cup water*
> ¼ *cup sugar plus 2 tablespoons*
> ¼ *pound rhubarb, trimmed and cut into ½-inch pieces (about*
>   *1 cup)*
> *1 tablespoon arrowroot*
> *1 cup strawberries, hulled (½ pint) plus 3 whole strawberries*
> *2 large peaches, peeled, pitted, and thinly sliced*
> *1 large red plum, unpeeled, pitted, and sliced*
> *1 small lemon wedge*
> *2 tablespoons butter, cut into small pieces*
> *4 to 5 nasturtium leaves (or fresh black pepper) (see note)*

Butter a 10-inch quiche or round ovenproof baking dish. Preheat the oven to 400 degrees. In a medium size saucepan, combine the water and ¼ cup of the sugar and bring to a boil. Add the rhubarb, stir, and cook over medium heat for 10 to 15 minutes. Mix the arrowroot with 2 tablespoons water and add to the rhubarb. Cook, stirring, for one minute. Remove from the heat and stir in the strawberries. Purée in a blender until very smooth. There should be about 1¼ cups.

Spoon the purée over the bottom of the prepared pan. Lay the sliced peaches in a circle around the outside of the pan over the purée. Then add a circle of plums and place the three strawberries in the center. Squeeze a few drops of lemon juice over the fruit. Sprinkle with

the remaining 2 tablespoons of sugar and dot with the butter. Bake for 15 minutes, then cool to room temperature before serving.

Note: If you do not have access to nasturtiums, sprinkle with black pepper *before* baking. However, if you are using nasturtiums, finely mince 2 to 3 green leaves, and *after cooling,* sprinkle them over the cooled fruit. Place 4 to 5 nasturtium blossoms over the sliced fruit just before serving.

A Mélange of Baked Winter Fruit

Serves 6 to 8

In the dead of winter citrus, pears, apples, and grapes beckon to us to enjoy them at their peak flavor. That is the perfect time to combine them all for a celebration of their compatibility.

8 pitted dried prunes
½ cup apple juice
2 large navel oranges
1 large pink grapefruit
3 large tart green apples
3 medium Anjou pears
15 green seedless grapes
15 red seedless grapes
2 teaspoons finely minced lemon peel
½ teaspoon vanilla extract
⅓ cup light brown sugar
Pinch of salt
2 tablespoons flour
½ teaspoon ground cinnamon
6 tablespoons butter, cut into small pieces

Preheat the oven to 400 degrees and butter a 12-inch ovenproof baking dish 2 inches deep. In a small saucepan, bring the prunes and apple juice to a boil. Remove from the heat and let steep while preparing the fruit.

Using a vegetable parer, remove the peel from half of one orange and mince it finely. You should have about 1 teaspoon. Set aside. Cut off the ends of the oranges with a sharp knife, then remove the peel and the pith. Separate sections and place in the baking dish. Squeeze the juice that is in the membrane part right into the baking dish and discard the membrane. Repeat the same procedure with the grapefruit, then

peel, core, and thickly slice the pears and apples and add to the baking dish. Scatter the grapes over all.

Sprinkle the lemon peel and the reserved orange peel and then drizzle the vanilla over the fruit. Then, in a small cup, mix the brown sugar, salt, flour, and cinnamon together and sprinkle over the fruit. Add the reserved prunes and the apple juice and dot with the pieces of butter over all. Bake for 15 minutes. Baste and continue to bake for 10 to 15 minutes more, basting twice more. Test the apples and pears with the point of a knife to see if they are tender but still holding their shapes. Serve warm.

Gratin of Cantaloupe with
Rose-Flavored Chantilly Cream

Serves 8

The melon is baked just long enough for the heat to let the flavorings permeate, resulting in an ambrosial blend.

2 ripe cantaloupes, about 2½ pounds each
1 tablespoon finely minced lemon peel
2 tablespoons lemon juice
1 tablespoon vanilla
1 tablespoon light, mild honey
1 tablespoon orange-flavored liqueur, such as Cointreau
1 teaspoon rose water
1 cup whipping cream

Preheat the oven to 350 degrees. Cut each melon in half, scoop out, and discard the seeds and strings. Peel off the rind and discard, then cut the melon into slices about 1-by-1-by-2 inches.

Butter a round 9½-by-1½-inch baking dish, and arrange the melon attractively on it. In a small cup mix together the lemon peel, lemon juice, vanilla, honey, and orange-flavored liqueur and sprinkle over the melon. Bake for 20 minutes, basting once during baking, then chill in the refrigerator. Just before serving, whip the cream with the rose water until it holds soft peaks and add a dollop to each plate.

Sweet Indulgences

The Rich, the Luxurious,
and the Lavish

If we were to give the very simplest reason for the existence of desserts, it would be that of announcing that the dinner has ended! However, if we dig more deeply, we would probably find that the real reason is solely to indulge our irrepressible appetites for sweets. The "indulgences" of which we speak come from a long history of marking the special events in our lives. As symbols and as colorful and very rich creations, these edible extravaganzas have come to be expected as we mark the milestones and celebrations in our lives. After all, what would a wedding be like without the glorious and ornate cake to mark the event? Or a birthday? Or, indeed, even a special dinner?

Since the earliest of times, sweets have been synonymous with celebrations: to fête the birth of a new prince, to commemorate an historical or military event, to pay tribute to a beautiful voice of a great diva, to extol a king, or to honor an empress. Many of the eighteenth- and nineteenth-century creations have become a part of our classic dessert repertoire today.

When in the eighteenth century King George III of England married Charlotte Sophia, the *Apple Charlotte* was conceived in her honor. *Riz à L'Impératrice,* an elaborately decorated and molded rice creation was named for Empress Eugénie. Later, *Peach Melba,* the poached peach in a raspberry purée, was inspired by and presented to the famous diva Nelly Melba. The fanciful baked meringue ring, slathered with whipped cream and filled with fruit, *The Pavlova,* was one chef's token gift to the ballerina, Anna Pavlova, when she toured Australia and New Zealand in the early 1920s.

When sugar and spices were rare commodities, they provided an ostentatious way for hosts to show off their great wealth and power, with elaborate confections prepared by their pastry chefs. However, as these two important ingredients became more commonplace, the challenge to create even more ornate, towering sugar constructions was taken up by the other chefs of the European aristocracy.

The nineteenth-century French chef, Antonin Carême, who was called the Cook of Kings and the King of Cooks, was perhaps the most influential and inspirational figure to others who followed him. It was he who created the first and the most impressive of the molded, spun-sugar-encrusted, gold-leafed fantasies. What finally emerged might well have been considered extreme by those of us who cook today, for the Victorian Era began to overflow with offshoots of Carême's imagination, with every dessert elaborately decorated with pastry bows, rosettes of whipped cream, fondant, marzipan fashioned into flowers, crystalized blossoms, and glazed fruits arranged and decorated to become overblown spectacles, accompanied by the gasps of spectators and diners as these desserts were ceremoniously carried to the table of the guest of honor.

And then—poof! They just disappeared and fell out of fashion.

Simplicity, bordering on the pristine took over. Everything that had been invented and devised, tested and built, decorated and ornamented, and bespangled became superfluous. *Flavor* began to reign. Though some desserts were (and still are) artful with some degree of complexity, it was a deliberate and sophisticated attempt to bring out the nuances of flavor rather than to emphasize décor.

What is beginning to happen today is that temptation is once again starting to rear its Gorgon head (as if temptation is really necessary when it comes to desserts!). As we look around us, it becomes quite evident that the imprint of the elaborate dessert extravaganzas of the past are having a revival in this once again prosperous society. Restaurant menus are becoming notorious for seducing us with desserts described as "sinfully rich" or "Satan's Temptation," or if retributions from Heaven are not enough, there's always "Death By Chocolate"!

Granted, some of these irresistible creations are not quite as ornate and sugary as they were at one time in the past, and many are designed on a more modest, tempered scale. But, along with the emphasis of achieving flavor by using unexpected combinations, these offerings still make a gorgeous first impression, for the pastry chefs are once again considering the decorative dimensions of their desserts.

In addition, we now have begun to consider just how these desserts can fit perfectly into the context of the *whole meal,* frequently with respect to the season of the year. After a hearty meal, a rich dessert might not be welcomed whereas a light, refreshing one might be chosen. Who, for example, could stomach a flaming English Plum Pudding in the heat of August at a beach picnic?

And so, dinner has ended, and in this section, we have designed the desserts to tempt even the most abstemious into submission. All of these desserts use fruit as part of the basic framework, and all of them are based on a variety of cream fillings, cream sauces, and rich cream puddings or mousses. Most particularly, all of them are festive. All of them are lavish and luxurious. Any one of them would be well chosen to commemorate an event or a special celebration.

Variations on a Theme of Creams

The word alone—*cream*—and the sound itself conjures up all sorts of connotations. The cream of the crop. The crème de la crème. The best. The choice. The quintessence. Cream. It virtually rolls off your tongue, dissolves unctuously in your mouth and, unfortunately makes its way right down to your hips! In moving on to this chapter, we can merely advise, "never mind." You have already taken the plunge.

With cream or milk as a principal ingredient, often combined with eggs and sugar, we are able to create a repertoire of desserts that reflect the very foundation of the classics about which we've written. By combining the simplest of ingredients, and by incorporating or accompanying them with fruit, we can transform them as if by magic into a wide range of desserts and sauces which can be airy and light or as grandly sumptuous as any special occasion might demand.

For simple starters, there is plain *whipped cream,* to be used as a modest dollop or as a lavish slathering to accompany any number of fresh fruit desserts.

Add sugar and you have just made a classic French *crème chantilly*. Mix cream with a bit of buttermilk and let it stand at room temperature overnight and, Voilà! you have crème fraîche, the thickish cream with a slightly sour edge, perfect with any sweet fruit.

Slowly reduce the cream and you have *English clotted cream.* Add a bit of sugar and you are left with an almost solid cream with a slight hint of caramel: *Kaymak* or *Turkish cream.*

Mix whipped cream with any number of fresh fruit purées and you have created a *Fool. Crème anglaise* is the luxurious basic cream-egg mixture, a light custard, that can be used alone as a sauce or as the base for a whole range of desserts such as *Petits pots de crème,* the little French baked custards. Or, mix crème anglaise with whipped cream, set it with unflavored gelatin along with additional fruit purées and flavorings and you have transformed it into a rich, voluptuous *Bavarois,* a Bavarian cream.

The luscious textured crème anglaise is also one of the layers for the sinful, very English dessert called *Trifle,* which is, indeed, an understatement. This is a layered mélange of cake soaked in sherry, crème

anglaise, jam, or fresh fruit, topped with whipped cream, covered with glacéed cherries, angelica, and almonds and served in a traditional glass bowl so that the layers are visible. It is, as you can see, anything but a trifle. There is also an Italian cousin called *Zuppa Inglese,* or English Soup.

When Mary, the daughter of Henry VIII of Great Britain married Philip II of Spain, she brought back to predominantly Protestant England a sherry-soaked dessert called *Bizcocho Borracho,* literally translated from the Spanish as *Drunken Biscuits.* Mary was not so innocent, we assume, since the dessert became a hidden device for the imbibing of spirits under the guise of eating dessert. Its name became *Tipsy Parson.*

While researching old cookbooks at the New York Academy of Medicine, which strangely has an excellent collection on the subject of the culinary arts, we came across a recipe printed in London in 1770 from *The Court and Country Confectioner:*

TO MAKE A TRIFLE

> *Lay mackroons over the bottom of your dish, and pour upon them a glass of sack; then have ready a custard made pretty stiff, which lay over them. Make a froth of cream, sugar, wine and cover your custard over with it and stick citron in it.*

Yet another extravaganza that relies upon crème anglaise is the molded *Charlotte.* Actually, fruit charlottes are served warm in a buttered, bread-lined mold. The tasty *Charlotte Russe,* created by Carême with a sponge-finger-lined mold containing a vanilla Bavarois, has a parallel in our childhood memories with a bastard version sold in the local neighborhood candy stores, which we called a *Charlie Rooster.* Along with Mello-Rolls and Popsicles, it was a regional street food made in a scalloped white paper cup with a bottom cardboard disc that could be pushed up like an elevator for easy eating without utensils. The concoction was composed of a piece of usually stale sponge cake, topped with a huge mound of sweetened whipped cream and crowned with a red maraschino cherry. Part of the tradition of eating it was that you had to get the whipped cream on your nose.

The Charlie Rooster is pure nostalgic ambrosia, better left undisturbed in our memories, for realistically we know that our tastes have changed and that we could never now swallow a red dye #2 maraschino cherry with the abandon of our youth. So, to grow up once again. . . .

Crème pâtissière is a cooked, thickened crème anglaise, an all-purpose spreadable milk or cream and egg-based custard, and the classic filling for fruit tarts. Lightened with whipped cream and stiffened a bit with gelatin for density, and with a fruit purée of your choice, and you have a perfect *fruit mousse* to serve by itself or to fill a cream puff made of choux paste. Top the puffs with chocolate sauce and you have *Profiteroles.*

Make a ring of choux paste and fill it with crème pâtissière or fruit mousse and present the elaborate, traditional Parisian birthday cake, the *Gâteau St. Honoré* to your favorite birthday boy or girl.

Creams such as *Sabayon, Zabaglione* or *Berliner Luft* may or may not contain cream or milk along with their egg base, but they are still classified as cream desserts. The list seems almost endless, but is a wonderful example of how slight variations in cooking can change the name, the texture, and the country of origin of a dessert.

Crème caramel or *Flan* is composed of milk, eggs, and sugar with a liquid burnt-sugar sauce, yet the base is the same as that in a crème anglaise. One is baked in a water bath, the other cooked on top of the stove. *Crème Brûlée*, the smooth, rich custard, sugar-topped and quickly broiled to make a crackling crisp contrast, is yet another cream dessert put together by using a slightly different technique with the very same ingredients. And let's not forget *ice cream,* the frozen, every day grandaddy of all the cream desserts!

These are all the festive, rich, basic classic creams developed over the years by cooks who had the daring and the confidence to alter and interpret recipes which used basic ingredients and who experimented with different techniques, adding seasonings and flavors almost instinctively.

We suppose that it's all very much like the same eighty-eight keys on the piano. You start as a child playing "Chopsticks" and the most basic of scales, and somehow you might develop into a Rubinstein playing Mozart and Chopin. As they used to tease when they told the story of the tourist asking, "How do you get to Carnegie Hall?" and the wise guy answering, "Practice," it is the first of the four key words in cooking or baking with the desserts we've offered on the following pages: Cream, eggs, experiment, and *practice!*

Nectarine Mousse with Blueberries and Strawberry Rose Geranium Sauce

Serves 6

A peach-colored mousse is garnished and accented with blueberries while it sits in a rosy pool of puréed strawberries. Both parts of the recipe must be prepared the day before serving for flavors to blend properly.

> *2½ pounds of ripe nectarines, about 6 or 7 large*
> *1 envelope unflavored gelatin*
> *¼ cup lime juice (about 1 large lime)*
> *½ cup sugar*
> *½ cup heavy cream*
> *1 tablespoon orange-flavored liqueur*
> *1 recipe Strawberry Rose Geranium Sauce (page 320)*
> *1 cup blueberries for garnish*

Peel and pit the nectarines and cut them in large pieces into a bowl. Set them aside. In a small saucepan, sprinkle the gelatin over the lime juice and let sit for 5 minutes. Purée the nectarines in a food processor with the sugar, cream, and orange liqueur. Heat the lime-gelatin mixture over low heat, stirring until it is dissolved. Let it cool for 5 minutes, then process with the fruit mixture for 1 or 2 pulses to combine.

Spray a 5-cup metal mold with vegetable oil spray (or line the mold with plastic wrap, for easier removal) and pour the mousse into the mold. Cover with plastic wrap and chill for a minimum of six hours or overnight.

Prepare the Strawberry Rose Geranium Sauce the day before serving the dessert, cover, and chill in the refrigerator.

Just before serving, run a sharp knife around the mold. Dip the mold in warm water to loosen and invert it onto the center of a large serving plate with a rim. Spoon the sauce around the base of the mousse. Scatter blueberries over the sauce and a few on top of the mousse.

Note: For a variation and a Mousse Melba, substitute peaches for nectarines in the mousse and Raspberry Sauce with Chambord (page 322) for the Strawberry Sauce.

Orange Chocolate Mousse with Clementines and Chocolate Orange Sauce

Serves 6

Chocolate and orange. These two distinctive flavors and colors complement each other in a winsome manner, such as in this two-toned mousse surrounded by a bed of tiny clementine sections. Then a Jackson Pollock trickle of chocolate over all creates a modern work of art.

Orange Mousse
    3 tablespoons frozen orange juice concentrate
    1 teaspoon fine sugar
    1 teaspoon finely minced orange peel
    1 large egg, separated
    1½ teaspoons unflavored gelatin
    1 tablespoon Cointreau
    ½ cup heavy cream, whipped

In a small heavy nonstick saucepan, heat the orange juice, sugar, and orange peel, stirring a few seconds until the sugar is dissolved. Add the egg yolk to the orange-juice mixture and whisk over low heat for 2 minutes until thickened. Remove from the heat and cool. Sprinkle the gelatin over the Cointreau in a small saucepan and after it stands for 5 minutes, warm it over low heat, stirring only until the gelatin dissolves. Add to the orange-egg-yolk mixture and cool completely, stirring from time to time while it cools, until it is the consistency of raw egg white. Beat the egg white with a few grains of salt until stiff. Fold into the orange mixture and then fold into the whipped cream.

Spray the insides of six ½-cup molds (such as tall Dariole molds) with vegetable oil spray. Spoon about 2 heaping tablespoons of the mousse into each mold and refrigerate, covered with plastic wrap, for 2 hours before preparing the Chocolate Mousse.

Chocolate Mousse
   3 ounces good quality bittersweet chocolate
   1 tablespoon water
   1 large egg, separated
   1½ teaspoons sugar
   1½ teaspoons unflavored gelatin
   2 tablespoons Kahlua, or other coffee liqueur
   ½ cup heavy cream, whipped

In the top of a double boiler, melt the chocolate with the water, stirring constantly with a whisk over simmering water, about 1 to 2 minutes. Whisk in the egg yolk and sugar and continue to beat vigorously for 1 to 2 minutes more. Remove from the heat and cool.

Sprinkle the gelatin over the Kahlua in a small saucepan. Let stand for 5 minutes, then warm over low heat, stirring constantly until the gelatin dissolves. Whisk into the chocolate mixture and cool completely, stirring occasionally until slightly thickened. Beat the egg white with a bit of salt until stiff. Fold it into the chocolate mixture, then into the whipped cream.

Remove the molds from the refrigerator and spoon the chocolate mousse over the orange mousse. Cover with plastic wrap and refrigerate again for at least 4 hours or more. Prepare the sauce and fruit.

Sauce and Fruit
   4 to 5 clementines, peeled and sectioned, white pith removed
   1 Recipe Chocolate Orange Sauce (page 334)
   Whipped cream
   Shredded orange or clementine peel

Loosen the mousse by running a knife around the insides of the molds and dipping the bottoms of the molds in warm water for a few seconds. Invert each onto the center of an individual serving plate. Surround each two-tone mousse with clementine segments. Dip the tip of a small paring knife into the Chocolate-Orange Sauce. (Dilute with 1 or 2 tablespoons of Cointreau if too thick.) Trickle the chocolate sauce slowly over the fruit and the mousse. Top each mousse with a small rosette of whipped cream and a few shreds of orange or clementine peel.

Strawberry Mousse with
Three Berry Sauce

Serves 6 to 8

A mousse is merely a lighter version of a bavarois with the custard eliminated. This lovely pink mousse is made in a decorative mold and it relies upon the ripest, most flavorful strawberries you can find. They are left uncooked so they don't discolor or change flavor.

*2 pints of hulled, washed, and dried strawberries, plus one
extra large one for garnish with stem intact (see note)*
⅔ cup fine sugar
1 teaspoon lemon juice
*1 tablespoon Chambord (Black Raspberry liqueur), or an
orange-flavored liqueur*
2 packages unflavored gelatin
¼ cup cold water
1½ cups heavy cream
1 recipe Three Berry Sauce (page 326)
Whipped cream for garnish

In a medium-size bowl, add the strawberries, sugar, lemon juice and liqueur, stir and let steep for 30 minutes. Purée in a food processor and transfer to a stainless steel bowl and set aside. Sprinkle the gelatin over cold water in a small saucepan and let stand for 5 minutes. Then warm over low heat, stirring constantly to liquify. It will take a few seconds. Stir into the purée and transfer to a larger bowl of ice and water to chill rapidly. Every few minutes for the next 8 to 10 minutes, stir the purée from the outside of the bowl toward the inside until the purée begins to thicken.

Whip the cream until stiff and gently fold it into the purée until completely combined. Spray a 6-cup decorative mold with vegetable oil spray and spoon the mixture into the mold. Cover with plastic wrap

and chill for at least 3 hours. If you like, the mousse can be made a day ahead of time.

Prepare the Three Berry Sauce and either refrigerate until ready to use or set aside. Bring the mousse to room temperature before unmolding. Run a knife around the inside of the mold and invert onto a large serving platter with a rim. Spoon or pipe a small rosette of whipped cream on top of the mold and place one whole unstemmed fresh berry on top. Warm the Three Berry Sauce slightly and spoon around the base of the mold. Pass the remainder of the sauce in a bowl.

Note: Defrosted frozen strawberries can be used when flavorful fresh ones are not available. However, make sure that the purée is not cold or the gelatin will set too quickly and become stringy.

Raspberry Bavarois Hearts with Blueberry Sauce and Star Fruit

Serves 8

The starfruit, properly called *carambola,* is a 5-spined waxy, pale yellow oval. When sliced crosswise, it is one of the most charming and decorative tropical additions to American cuisine. Here, the golden stars sit in a dark blueberry sauce, wreathing pale pink hearts of classic raspberry bavarois. The classic bavarois is a molded dessert with a soft custard base, whipped cream to lighten it, and gelatin to give it body.

> *2 cups raspberries (fresh or frozen and thawed)*
> *¾ cup fine sugar*
> *2 eggs, separated*
> *1 cup milk*
> *½ teaspoon vanilla extract*
> *1 envelope unflavored gelatin*
> *2 tablespoons kirsch*
> *1 cup heavy cream*
> *Blueberry Sauce (page 327)*
> *1 starfruit, thinly sliced and seeded*
> *Whipped cream for garnish, if desired*

Purée the raspberries in a blender and then force through a sieve with a wooden spoon, pressing the fruit against the sides of the sieve and scraping the bottom occasionally. You will have 1 cup of seedless purée. Stir in ½ cup of the sugar and set aside.

Off the heat, in the top of a double boiler, beat the egg yolks and remaining ¼ cup sugar with a whisk until thick. Slowly whisk in the milk and place over the bottom of the double boiler containing simmering water. Stir constantly with a wooden spoon until the custard thickens and coats the spoon. Do not overcook or the eggs will curdle. Add the vanilla and set aside.

Sprinkle the gelatin over the kirsch in a small saucepan and let sit for 5 minutes. Stir the mixture over low heat just until it liquifies. Add to the custard mixture, strain into a bowl, and cool to room temperature. When cool, stir in the reserved raspberry purée. Beat the egg whites with a pinch of salt, using a rotary hand beater, until stiff but not dry. Fold into the raspberry custard mixture. With the cleaned beater whip the cream until it stands in soft peaks. Gently fold into the raspberry custard mixture. Spray ½-cup individual heart-shaped molds (or a decorative 4 cup mold) with vegetable oil spray and spoon the bavarois into them. Wrap with plastic wrap and refrigerate for a minimum of 4 hours.

Prepare the Blueberry Sauce, but rewarm it before serving.

Run a thin knife around the inside of the molds and dip the bottoms into warm water to loosen. Unmold on individual serving plates. Spoon some blueberry sauce around the raspberry heart and arrange slices of star fruit over the blueberry sauce. If you wish, you may garnish the heart with a tiny rosette of whipped cream and a raspberry.

Kiwi and Strawberry Trifle with
Kirsch and Vanilla Crème Anglaise

Elegant, festive, and rich, as all trifles are, this one is colorful as well with the addition of bright red strawberries and lime green kiwis.

1 recipe Crème Anglaise I (page 332)
12 lady fingers, split open into halves
⅓ cup kirsch
2 tablespoons fine sugar
2 kiwis, peeled and sliced thinly
4 large strawberries, hulled and sliced vertically
¾ cup heavy cream
2 tablespoons sliced almonds, lightly toasted

Prepare the crème anglaise and set aside to cool. Line the bottom of a 1½-quart deep glass bowl with the lady fingers and place those remaining on a dinner plate in one layer. Stir the kirsch and sugar together until the sugar is dissolved and spoon some over all the lady fingers. The reserved lady fingers will be used later on as a top layer.

Place a layer of kiwi slices over the lady fingers and then alternate slices of kiwi and strawberries standing on edge against the sides of the bowl. Carefully pour the cooled custard into the bowl. The sliced fruit should remain upright. Gently press a piece of plastic wrap directly onto the surface of the custard and chill for 2 hours or until the custard has thickened. Remove the plastic wrap and place the reserved moistened lady fingers over the custard layer. Cover and chill again until serving time.

Just before serving, whip the cream until stiff, place large mounds of it over the top, and garnish with the sliced almonds.

Fresh Fig Trifle with
Marsala and Orange Crème Anglaise

Serves 6 to 8

This trifle, based upon the very British dessert, has a decidedly Italian accent. It is reminiscent of zabaglione, although not quite as eggy.

> *1 recipe Crème Anglaise I flavored with orange liqueur (page 332)*
> *⅓ cup plus 2 tablespoons sweet Marsala wine*
> *½ pound fresh figs, stemmed and cut in half lengthwise*
> *12 lady fingers, split open into halves*
> *1 cup heavy cream*
> *1 teaspoon fine sugar*
> *1 teaspoon vanilla*
> *Long shreds of orange peel made with a zester tool, for garnish*

Prepare the Crème Anglaise and set aside. Pour the Marsala into a glass dish or any nonmetal baking dish with sides. Place the figs, cut side down, in the Marsala and cover with plastic wrap. Let macerate at room temperature for several hours.

Remove the figs to a piece of waxed paper. Dip the inside of the lady fingers into the Marsala remaining in the dish and line the bottom of a 2-quart glass soufflé dish or a deep, round glass bowl (about 8-by-3 inches), with half of them. Cover with the Crème Anglaise, press a piece of plastic wrap directly onto the surface, and chill for one hour.

When cool, remove the plastic wrap and arrange the figs evenly over the custard, reserving a few for the top of the trifle. Distribute the remaining lady fingers over the fig layer. Wrap and chill until serving time.

When ready to serve, whip the cream with a rotary hand beater until frothy. Add the sugar, whip until fairly stiff then whip in the vanilla and spoon over the trifle. Arrange the reserved figs in a circle over the cream and scatter shreds of orange peel over all.

Persimmon Flan with
Burnt Sugar Sauce

Serves 6

Molded, sweet, and silky baked fruit custard contrasts with a richly dark bittersweet sauce. This is a classic with Spanish overtones and it's particularly welcome and soothing after a spicy Southwestern dinner.

1 large ripe persimmon (about ½ pound) stemmed
1 teaspoon lemon juice
1½ cups sugar
1½ cups milk
1 stick cinnamon
Several long strips orange peel (from 1 orange)
4 eggs
1 teaspoon cornstarch dissolved in 1 tablespoon cold milk
1 teaspoon vanilla extract

Purée the persimmon in a food processor or blender, add the lemon juice, and set aside.

In a medium-size nonstick saucepan, caramelize 1 cup of sugar over low heat, stirring constantly with a wooden spoon until the sugar is melted and turns dark amber in color. Pour quickly into a rectangular metal 6-cup mold (or charlotte mold). Tilt the mold slowly in a swirling circular motion to coat the bottom and sides of the mold. Set aside.

In another medium-size nonstick saucepan, slowly bring the milk, remaining sugar, cinnamon stick, and orange peel to a boil, stirring occasionally. Remove immediately and cool until lukewarm. While the milk is cooling, preheat the oven to 375 degrees and bring a kettle of water to a boil.

Beat the eggs in a food processor or blender. Remove the cinnamon stick and orange peel from the milk and add the dissolved corn-

starch. Add the vanilla and stir. Pour the milk mixture slowly into the egg mixture with the food processor on. Add the persimmon purée and combine. Pour into the caramel-lined mold and place the mold in a larger pan. Fill the pan with the boiling water to make a water bath. The water should come halfway up the sides of the mold.

Bake for 40 to 45 minutes then test the center with a knife; it should slip out cleanly. Remove from the water bath. Cool the mold, cover with plastic wrap, and chill in the refrigerator for several hours before unmolding. When ready to serve, loosen the flan by running a sharp knife all around the inside edges of the mold. Invert onto a large serving plate with a rim to hold the burnt sugar sauce. Decorate if you wish with an additional small persimmon centered on the top of the flan.

Two-Tone Terrine of Citrus and
Cranberries with
Lime and Campari

Serves 10 to 12

This two-tone terrine is a challenge that takes two days to prepare, but we think it's well worth it for the end result. When the terrine is unmolded, the bottom layer is a creamy, opaque, luscious custard studded with jewel-like cranberries and tiny sections of clementines. The top layer is transparent, bittersweet, bright orange-red with bits of ruby and yellow grapefruit floating alongside emerald green shreds of lime and punctuated by dots of garnet cranberries. It is a true sensual spectacle!

Transparent Layer
> 3 envelopes unflavored gelatin
> 2 cups white grape juice
> ½ cup Campari (see note)
> 1 teaspoon grenadine syrup
> 2 teaspoons lime juice, strained (juice of ½ lime)
> 1 tablespoon Cointreau, or other orange-flavored liqueur
> ½ cup fresh cranberries
> 6 tablespoons sugar
> 1 tablespoon shredded lime peel, made with a zester tool (use
>   2 very dark green limes)
> 3 or 4 Ruby grapefruit sections, white membranes removed
> 3 or 4 white grapefruit sections, white membranes removed

Line an 8-cup bread loaf pan (9-by-5-by-3) with a piece of lightly oiled plastic wrap large enough to overlap the sides of the pan by 5 inches. This will facilitate easy removal of the terrine. Set aside and prepare the transparent layer.

Sprinkle the gelatin over ½ cup of the grape juice in a nonstick saucepan and let stand for 5 minutes. Heat slowly, stirring to dissolve the gelatin, about 2 to 3 minutes. When the gelatin is dissolved, add the remaining grape juice and the Campari. Heat and stir occasionally for 3 to 4 minutes. Transfer to a small bowl, add the grenadine, lime juice, and Cointreau. Chill in the refrigerator for 45 to 60 minutes. Stir after 30 minutes to see if the consistency is that of raw egg white; if it is not, check again after 10 to 15 minutes more.

Meanwhile, in a small pot, cook the cranberries slowly along with the sugar for 3 to 4 minutes, just until the berries begin to pop but still keep their shape. Strain, then drain on paper towels. Put ¼ cup of the cooked cranberries in a container and reserve in the refrigerator. Transfer the remaining cranberries to a piece of waxed paper and set aside. When the gelatin mixture is the proper consistency, stir in the lime shreds and spoon 1 cup into the prepared mold. Arrange the grapefruit sections and the cranberries over this layer in an artistic fashion. Then spoon the remaining cup of gelatin over the fruit layer. Cover the loaf pan with plastic wrap and refrigerate for at least 4 hours or more. When the gelatin is firm, prepare the next layer.

Opaque Layer
> *2 envelopes unflavored gelatin*
> *1 cup milk*
> *2-inch piece of vanilla bean, split*
> *5 tablespoons sugar*
> *3 egg yolks*
> *½ cup cold heavy cream*
> *1 clementine, peeled, sectioned, white membrane removed*
>   *(about ½ cup)*
> *¼ cup cooked, reserved cranberries*
> *Large bunch of mint for garnish*

Sprinkle the gelatin over ¼ cup of the milk in a small saucepan and set aside. Combine the remaining milk with the vanilla bean (scrape the seeds into the milk as well). Stir in 3 tablespoons of the sugar and

(continued on next page)

Two-Tone Terrine (*cont.*)

transfer the mixture to the top of a double boiler over gently simmering water (don't allow the bottom of the pot to touch the water). Simmer, stirring occasionally, until bubbles begin to form around the edges of the pan, then remove from the simmering water and set aside.

Beat the egg yolks with a whisk or hand beater in a medium-size bowl. Add the remaining 2 tablespoons of sugar and continue to beat until thick and pale yellow, about 2 to 3 minutes. Whisk ¼ cup of the hot milk slowly into the egg mixture, then pour back into the hot milk in the top of the double boiler. Set over simmering water once again and stir constantly with a wooden spoon for about 5 minutes or until the custard has thickened and coats the spoon. Remove from the simmering water and stir for 1 minute more to cool. Then set aside.

Warm the gelatin mixture, stirring until dissolved for 1 minute, then add to the custard. Strain into a bowl. Cover with plastic wrap and refrigerate for 30 minutes, stirring twice until it is the consistency of raw egg white. Beat the cold cream with a hand beater until stiff, then fold it gently into the completely cooled custard. Fold in the clementine sections and the ¼ cup reserved cranberries. Spoon carefully over the transparent fruit layer in the mold, press a piece of plastic wrap onto the surface and chill overnight.

When ready to serve, grasp the ends of the plastic wrap, place a platter over the mold, invert the terrine onto the platter and peel off the wrap. Garnish with sprigs of mint around the base of the entire terrine.

Dip a sharp knife in hot water before cutting each slice and wipe the knife dry with a paper towel after cutting each slice. Place a sprig of mint alongside each slice on the serving place.

Note: Campari is an Italian bittersweet aperitif with just a hint of orange. It includes 69 herbs, fruit tree barks, and spices in its secret recipe.

Gâteau St. Honoré with
Passion Fruit Mousse

Serves 8

Named for the patron saint of Parisian pastry chefs, this traditional French birthday cake has the spectacular grandeur and triumph worthy of the ultimate in the art of the pastry cook. Although the French confer the title of *gâteau* on the most elaborate of their pâtisseries, the paté à choux (cream puff pastry) used in this recipe is not complicated or time consuming to make. In addition, it has the extraordinary ability to expand into a crisp, puffy delight. This Gâteau St. Honoré is a stream-lined version, made without the traditional baked pastry base.

Passion Fruit Mousse
    4 to 5 purple passion fruit (about ½ pound)
    1 cup heavy cream
    3 eggs
    ⅓ cup sugar
    2 teaspoons unflavored gelatin
    4 tablespoons cold water

Cut the fruit in half over a small bowl to catch any juice. Scoop out the liquid and edible seeds. There will be ½ cup. Strain out the seeds, pressing the pulp against the strainer and discard. You will now have ⅓ cup strained passion fruit juice. Set this aside.

With a rotary hand beater, whip the cream in a deep bowl until stiff, then chill in the refrigerator. Place a saucepan over barely simmering water and add the eggs and sugar. Don't let the bottom of the saucepan touch the water. Using an electric hand beater, beat the eggs and sugar together for 10 minutes until thickened and tripled in volume. Remove from the heat and continue to beat for 1 minute more.

(continued on next page)

Gâteau St. Honoré (*cont.*)

In a small saucepan, sprinkle the gelatin over the cold water and let stand for 5 minutes. Then place over very low heat to dissolve the gelatin, stirring constantly, about 1 to 2 minutes. Remove from the heat and stir for a few minutes to cool the mixture. Dip a finger in to test it, making sure that it is *warm,* not *hot* or the mousse will be stringy when it is added. Fold the egg mixture into the whipped cream, then add the gelatin and then the passion fruit juice. Chill in the refrigerator, whisking once or twice to prevent separation. Then chill for 2 hours before assembling. Whisk again just before assembling. While the mousse is chilling, prepare the Paté à Choux, wreath, and puffs, all of which may be prepared well in advance.

Paté à Choux
   1 cup flour
   ¼ teaspoon salt
   2 tablespoons fine sugar
   1 cup water
   ½ cup butter (1 stick) cut into pieces
   ½ teaspoon finely minced lemon peel
   4 eggs

Line two baking sheets with parchment paper. Using a 9-inch round pan as a guide, draw a circle on one piece of the parchment paper with a marking pen and turn the paper over (so the ink won't touch the pastry). Set the pans aside and preheat oven to 375 degrees.

Sift the flour, salt, and sugar together in a bowl until well combined. Set aside. In a medium-size saucepan, add the water, butter, and lemon peel. Heat slowly until it begins to boil. Add the sifted dry ingredients all at once and beat with a wooden spoon until the batter leaves the sides of the pan. Continue to beat over low heat for 2 minutes or more, put into a food processor and let the batter cool for 10 minutes. Add the eggs one at a time, processing each egg until it is well incorporated and the batter is very thick, smooth, and shiny.

Scrape all of the batter into a medium-size bowl for easier handling. Using a large serving spoon (one that holds about 3 tablespoons), carefully drop ⅔ of the batter onto the parchment paper along the ring you drew to make the wreath. Smooth the batter with your fingers as you place it on the paper. On the other prepared baking sheet, drop 1 teaspoon of the batter at a time, leaving a space of about 2 inches between each one. These will be your individual puffs. There should be six puffs.

Bake for 15 minutes, then lower the heat to 350 degrees and bake 10 minutes more. Remove the small puffs and place on a wire rack to cool. Continue to bake the wreath for 15 minutes more or until puffed, crisp, and lightly golden. Then remove to a wire rack and cool completely. Assemble the Gâteau no more than one hour before serving.

Using a serrated knife, cut the wreath and puffs in half horizontally. Lift off the top of the wreath carefully, spoon the passion fruit mousse onto the bottom (reserving about 6 teaspoons to fill each puff), and replace the top. Repeat the procedure with the puffs.

Caramel
 2 tablespoons sugar
 1 tablespoon water

To make the caramel, stir the sugar and water together in a small saucepan until the sugar is dissolved. Cook over medium high heat until golden and thick. Remove from the heat, dip the tip of a knife into the caramel and drop six dabs of the caramel, one at a time and spacing evenly, on top of the gâteau so that you can attach the small cream puffs. Gently place each small filled puff on the caramel spots. As it hardens, the caramel will hold the puffs in place. Using the tip of a knife, lightly trickle some caramel only on top of each puff. (If the caramel has hardened, warm over low heat again for a few seconds until it is workable.) Sift a bit of confectioners' sugar on the wreath part only.

To serve, cut only with a serrated knife to prevent the filling from oozing out.

Glazed Warm Apple Charlotte with Calvados

Serves 6

Charlotte, the wife of George II of England, has given her name to this gorgeous warm apple dessert, worthy of the most festive winter dinner party. The apple filling can be prepared the day before. Early in the day, you can assemble the charlotte and then bake it right before dinner. While the guests dine, it will come to the perfect temperature for serving at the end of the meal.

*3½ pounds Granny Smith apples (about 8 large apples),
    peeled, cored, and sliced thinly*
2 teaspoons finely minced lemon peel
⅓ to ½ cup sugar, or to taste
1 teaspoon vanilla extract
2 tablespoons butter
¼ teaspoon cinnamon
¼ teaspoon nutmeg
4 tablespoons Calvados, or applejack or rum
1 cup apricot preserves, forced through a sieve
½ pound clarified butter (see note)
12 to 14 slices of orange-raisin bread or cinnamon-raisin bread

Place the apples in a 12-inch-wide Dutch oven or deep skillet (preferably nonstick), add the lemon peel, cover, and cook over very low heat, stirring occasionally, for 20 to 25 minutes or until the apples are tender. Add the sugar, vanilla, butter, cinnamon, and nutmeg to the apples. Stir the Calvados into the apricot purée and add only ½ cup to the apples, reserving the remainder for a final glaze. Cook the apple mixture, uncovered, over high heat for 10 minutes, stirring constantly for the last 5 minutes or more, until all the liquid has evaporated and a very thick purée remains. There will be about 3½ cups of purée. Set aside. This recipe can be prepared up to this point well in advance.

Pour the clarified butter into a metal pie pan. If it has begun to solidify, heat it over low heat until it liquifies. This should take only a few seconds. Use a 5-cup charlotte mold or any other cylindrical mold that is 3¼ inches high and 4½ inches in diameter. Trim the crusts off the bread. Cut 1 square and 4 semicircles of bread to fit the bottom of the mold exactly. Dip these pieces of bread quickly into the clarified butter and sauté in a pan until lightly golden. Fit into the bottom of the mold. Cut the remaining bread into 1¼-inch strips. Dip each strip into the clarified butter and arrange, overlapping slightly around the inside of the mold. Trim any protruding ends.

Heap the apple purée inside the bread, making a dome shape, about ¾ inches higher in the center (since it will collapse when it cools). Cover with the strips of bread dipped in the butter and pour any remaining butter around the edges of the mold.

Preheat the oven to 425 degrees. Set the mold on a foil-lined jelly-roll pan to catch any drippings, and bake for 30 minutes. (If the top browns too quickly, cover with foil while continuing to bake.) Let cool on a wire rack for 40 minutes before inverting onto a serving plate. While the charlotte is cooling, add 1 tablespoon sugar to the remaining puréed apricot preserve mixture and boil over high heat until thick. Spread the glaze over the warm charlotte. Serve by cutting with a serrated knife.

If you wish, the lighter Crème Anglaise II (page 333) or softly whipped cream can be passed at the table.

Note: Clarified butter is used to prevent the bread from browning too quickly. To clarify butter, melt slowly in a small, heavy pot. Skim the surface and let stand until a milky residue settles on the bottom. Pour off the clear melted butter to use in the recipe, leaving the residue on the bottom to be discarded.

Brandy Pear Charlotte

Serves 6 to 8

This recipe uses Comice or Anjou pears, which are by far the most succulent. They are gently poached, then layered with a cognac-flavored custard enveloped by lady fingers. The juices of the pears are then boiled down to intensify the flavors and used to form a light crowning glaze.

> *12 lady fingers*
> *3 to 4 Comice or Anjou pears, peeled and sliced thinly*
> *1 tablespoon lemon juice*
> *Pinch of salt*
> *¼ cup sugar*
> *1½ cups milk*
> *2 inch piece of vanilla bean, split*
> *4 egg yolks*
> *½ cup sugar*
> *1 tablespoon cognac or other brandy*
> *1 envelope unflavored gelatin*
> *¼ cup cold water*

Using parchment paper, cut a circle to fit the bottom of a 5-cup charlotte mold (see note). Cut and trim the lady fingers into triangles and arrange them, tightly together, first on the bottom, then the sides of the mold. Alternate the triangles so that they fit snugly and set the mold aside.

Put the pears, lemon juice, salt, and sugar in a medium-size saucepan. Simmer over low heat for 5 minutes stirring constantly with a wooden spoon. Set aside to cool. In the top of a double boiler, add the vanilla bean to the milk, scraping the seeds into the milk, and simmer over medium heat. When bubbles form around the edge, remove from the heat.

In a small bowl, whisk the egg yolks and sugar together until pale in color and fairly thick. Add ¼ cup of the hot milk to the egg mixture, whisking constantly, then whisk this mixture slowly into the rest of the milk. Return to the stove and, over slightly simmering water, stirring constantly with a wooden spoon, cook for about 5 minutes, or until the custard coats the spoon. Remove the vanilla bean and stir in the cognac.

Sprinkle the gelatin over the cold water in a small saucepan and let sit for 5 minutes. Then heat, stirring until dissolved. Add to the custard and chill for 20 minutes in the refrigerator, stirring occasionally. Drain the pears of their accumulated liquid and reserve the liquid. Spoon ⅓ of the pear slices into the prepared mold, then cover with ⅓ of the custard, alternating layers until the fruit and custard are used up. Cover with plastic wrap, pressing it directly onto the surface and refrigerate for at least 4 hours or overnight.

When ready to serve, boil down the accumulated pear liquid until it is reduced to 2 tablespoons. Set aside to cool. Remove the plastic wrap and invert the mold onto a serving plate. Peel off the parchment paper. Trickle the reduced pear liquid over the top. Add a small puff of whipped cream and a sprig of mint for garnish if you desire.

Note: A brioche mold can also be used instead of a charlotte mold. Just shape the lady fingers into tear-drop shapes instead of triangles and fit them closely together.

Raspberry Charlotte with Orange Liqueur

Serves 6 to 8

Part charlotte and part bread pudding, this raspberry flan bakes inside a bread and butter casing. To make it even more festive, top it with a puff of whipped cream, a single fresh raspberry sitting on top, and a sprig of fresh mint or a rose geranium leaf.

> *10 to 14 slices of orange raisin bread*
> *¼ pound clarified butter (page 67)*
> *2 cups fresh raspberries*
> *⅓ cup sugar*
> *1 teaspoon finely minced orange peel*
> *1 tablespoon Cointreau, or other orange-flavored liqueur*
> *3 eggs*
> *1 egg yolk*
> *⅔ cup milk*
> *1 tablespoon cornstarch*
> *½ teaspoon vanilla extract*

Trim the crusts from the bread and cut all but one of the slices diagonally into triangles. Cut the remaining slice in a circle to fit the bottom of a 5-cup charlotte mold. Pour the clarified butter into a flat pie pan and quickly dip the bread into the butter before fitting it into the sides of the mold. Start with the bottom circle and then slightly overlap the triangular pieces on the sides, pressing lightly so no gaps show. Preheat the oven to 400 degrees.

Combine the berries, sugar, orange peel, and Cointreau and set aside. In a medium-size bowl, beat the eggs and egg yolk with a whisk until foamy. Stir the cornstarch into ¼ cup of the milk. When dissolved, combine with the remaining milk and add to the eggs, along with the vanilla and any remaining melted butter. Spoon the berries

into the bread casing and slowly pour the egg-milk mixture over the berries. Cover the top with the remaining butter dipped bread fitted tightly together and bake for 45 to 55 minutes. Cool on a wire rack and then refrigerate for 2 hours in the mold. Loosen the sides of the mold with a thin knife and invert onto a serving plate to serve. If you like, top the charlotte with the whipped cream puff, fresh raspberry, and a sprig of mint or rose geranium.

Mixed Berry English Summer Pudding
with Chambord

Serves 6 to 8

We have always been both dazzled by the color of summer pudding and disappointed by the standard flavors and textures of unbaked, soggy commercial white bread and overly sweetened fruit. Our version is enhanced with raspberry liqueur, sparked with citrus for flavor, and red berries mixed with a purée of other darker berries. In this recipe, the bread is nothing more than a thin wall between the berries and the cream, all of it enriched by a delicious fruit purée. We think you'll find it a welcome change from the summer puddings that you've seen before. For best results, prepare 24 hours or more before serving.

> *3 cups small ripe strawberries, hulled*
> *2 cups ripe raspberries*
> *8 tablespoons fine sugar*
> *3 tablespoons Chambord (raspberry liqueur)*
> *2 teaspoons finely minced orange peel*
> *Pinch of salt*
> *1 cup red currants*
> *1 cup blueberries*
> *1 cup blackberries*
> *1 loaf dense white bread, unsliced*
> *1 cup heavy cream*

Set aside a few of each kind of berry and chill them covered with plastic wrap, until serving time.

In a medium-size bowl, mix the strawberries and raspberries together. Add 4 tablespoons of the sugar, the Chambord liqueur, orange peel, and pinch of salt. Mix well and let stand for 1 hour to accumulate liquid, stirring occasionally. Combine the currants, blueberries, and

blackberries with the remaining sugar in a large saucepan and bring slowly to a boil. Lower the heat and simmer for 5 minutes, then strain the cooked berries into a bowl. Force the berries against the strainer, scraping the bottom of the strainer with a clean spatula and adding this to the bowl. Discard the seeds and skins from the strainer and wash and dry the strainer. Strain the liquid that has accumulated from the raspberry-strawberry mixture into the cooked purée, reserving the whole berries.

Spray a 2-quart mixing bowl or a souffle dish at least 3 inches deep with vegetable oil spray. Trim the crusts off the bread and cut into thin slices. Flatten them by rolling the slices with a rolling pin. Fit the bread into the bowl overlapping the slices by ¼ inch and pressing lightly together so there are no gaps. Reserve a few slices of bread for the top.

Fill the bread casing with the whole berries and pour only ½ cup of the cooked purée over them. Top with the remaining bread slices, trimmed to fit the bowl. Brush the bread with some of the purée. Cover with plastic wrap and place a plate that will fit inside the bowl on top of the pudding, weighing down the plate with a can that weighs about 3 pounds. (A large can of Italian plum tomatoes is a good size and a perfect weight.) Place in the refrigerator for 24 hours.

When ready to serve, loosen the pudding by running a knife around the inside of the mold and invert onto a serving plate with a rim. Whip the cream with a rotary hand beater until almost stiff. Combine half the whipped cream with the remaining purée. Continue to whip the remaining cream until it is stiff. Pour the purée and the cream sauce slowly over the pudding. Spoon a few dollops of whipped cream around the sauce that has accumulated around the pudding. Then sprinkle the reserved berries over all.

Fuyu Persimmon Fool with Lime, Almonds, and Blueberries

Serves 4 to 5

The Fuyu persimmon has been cultivated and eaten for hundreds of years throughout the Orient. Unlike the lobed variety of persimmon, the Fuyu has the shape of a flattish tomato and it can be eaten when fully colored but still firm. This sensually textured, sweet-fleshed fruit makes a luxurious yet simple dessert when mixed with whipped cream, almonds, and blueberries.

> 2 large Fuyu persimmons (about ¾ pound)
> 2 tablespoons lime juice
> 3 tablespoons finely ground almonds
> ¼ cup sugar
> ½ teaspoon almond extract
> 1 cup heavy cream, whipped until it holds stiff peaks
> Sliced almonds
> Shreds of lime peel
> Blueberries

Stem the persimmons and cut into quarters. If the persimmon is a female fruit, it will have 2 flat seeds in each quarter. Remove and discard them (or plant them!). The male fruit is seedless. Put the persimmons and lime juice in a blender and purée. Add the sugar and almond extract and continue to blend well.

Using a rubber spatula, scrape the purée out of the blender into the whipped cream. Fold the mixture carefully but do not blend it completely, leaving streaks. Spoon the mixture into individual wine glasses or into a decorative glass serving bowl. Sprinkle the surface with sliced almonds, shredded lime peel, and sprinkle a few blueberries on top.

Fresh Fig Fool with
Dark Rum and Toasted Walnuts

Serves 4

This fresh fig fool has an evanescent flavor. It is an ambrosial concoction contrasting with crisp, toasted walnuts.

12 ripe, fresh figs, stemmed and cut into quarters
4 tablespoons dark rum
4 tablespoons sugar
2 tablespoons buttermilk
½ pint heavy cream
2 tablespoons coarsely broken walnuts, toasted
4 walnut halves for garnish
Sprigs of mint for garnish

Purée the figs in a blender then add the rum, sugar, and buttermilk. Transfer the purée into a measuring cup with a rubber spatula. There should be about 1 cup.

In a small, chilled bowl, beat the cream with a rotary hand beater until it holds stiff peaks. Fold the purée into the cream with a rubber spatula. Stir in the broken walnuts and spoon the mixture into individual chilled glass dessert or champagne flutes. Garnish with a walnut half and a sprig of mint.

Quince Fool with
Pumpkin Pie Spices and Toasted Pecans

Serves 6

A no-cholesterol version of a classic fruit fool. Here, the fruit is the pungent autumn quince, sweetened with honey and mixed with no-fat yogurt instead of whipped cream.

> *1 pound quince (about 3 small), peeled, quartered, pitted,*
> *   cored, and thinly sliced (about 4 cups)*
> *1 cup water*
> *⅓ cup sugar*
> *¼ teaspoon pumpkin pie spice*
> *1 small wedge of lemon*
> *1 cup no-fat yogurt*
> *1 teaspoon vanilla extract*
> *2 tablespoons mild honey*
> *10 to 12 pecan halves*

In a large nonstick saucepan, mix the quince with the water, sugar, and spice. Squeeze the lemon over the mixture and add the lemon wedge to the pot. Cover and bring to a boil, then lower the heat and simmer, stirring occasionally for 15 minutes. Let cool, remove lemon wedge and discard, and purée the mixture in a food processor. You should have 1½ cups of thick purée. Add the yogurt, vanilla, and the honey to the processor with the quince purée and process until the mixture is well combined.

Serve in a small glass bowl garnished with a circle of pecan halves.

Peach and Raspberry Pavé à l'Été

Serves 8 to 10

The pavé, like a cold charlotte, is encased in lady fingers and is traditionally made with a stiff butter cream filling and always in a square
mold. Here, we've used *two* squares of different sizes which we've
layered and towered like a small skyscraper. It's filled with peaches and
butter cream, then slathered with whipped cream and studded with
bright red raspberries. You can prepare it in stages, assemble it for your
party guests, and then lean back and bask in the "oohs" and "aahs" of
a spectacular presentation.

Hazelnut Bourbon Butter Cream   *Makes 2¼ cups*
    2½ ounces hazelnuts
    12 tablespoons (1½ sticks) butter, softened to room temperature
    1 egg
    4 egg yolks
    2 tablespoons bourbon
    ¾ cup sugar
    ⅓ cup water

Toast and grind the hazelnuts (page 338). There should be about ¾ cup.
Set aside. In a food processor, cream the butter until light and fluffy,
transfer it to a small bowl, and set aside. Wash and dry the bowl of the
food processor and add the egg, the egg yolks, and the bourbon. Process until pale and very frothy.

In a medium-size nonstick saucepan, combine the sugar and the water, stirring over low heat until dissolved. Bring the syrup to a boil without stirring, and boil until it reaches the "soft ball" stage, about 4 minutes.
Remove from the heat and transfer the syrup to a glass measuring cup for
easy handling. Let the syrup cool for one minute, but no longer or it will
harden. Start the food processor and pour the hot sugar syrup slowly
down the sides of the bowl into the egg mixture. Process for five minutes,

(continued on next page)

Peach and Raspberry Pavé a l'Été (*cont.*)

or until it has cooled. Add ¾ of the butter through the feed tube, a bit at a time, processing all the while. The mixture should begin to thicken. Add all the ground nuts and then the remaining butter. Transfer to a bowl and chill for a minimum of one hour.

The Fruit
 2 cups peaches, peeled and pitted (about 1¼ pounds)
 1 teaspoon lemon juice
 2 tablespoons fine sugar
 1 tablespoon bourbon
 ½ cup raspberries for garnish

Mix together the peaches, lemon juice, sugar, and bourbon and let steep for 30 minutes. Drain in a sieve and set aside.

The Molds
 36 lady fingers (3 packages, 3 ounces each)

Use one 5-cup square mold (6-by-6-by-2 inches) and one 3-cup square mold (4½-by-4½-by-2 inches). Spray the insides lightly with vegetable oil spray. Cut pieces of plastic wrap large enough to fit the insides of molds leaving a slight overhang and fit into each mold. Spray the wrap. Trim both ends of the split lady fingers and fit the trimmed pieces into the bottom and around the sides of both molds and set aside.

Beat the butter cream lightly for a minute, spoon a layer on the bottom of each mold and add a layer of peaches. Alternate the layers until all of the peaches and the butter cream have been used. Cover with plastic wrap and chill at least 3 to 4 hours.

Whipped Cream
 1 cup heavy cream
 1 tablespoon fine sugar
 2 to 3 drops vanilla extract

When ready to serve, prepare the whipped cream. Beat the cream until it is almost stiff, then add the sugar and vanilla. Continue to beat the cream until it holds stiff peaks and set aside.

Invert the larger mold onto a serving plate and remove the plastic wrap. Invert the smaller mold onto a wide spatula, peel off the plastic wrap and place in the center on top of the larger mold. Gently slide the spatula out. Spread whipped cream over the top and sides, stud with fresh raspberries, and garnish with a green leaf or sprig of mint on top. Serve immediately.

Gooseberry Fool with Orange Flower Water

Serves 4

In England, the most commonly used fruit for fools is the gooseberry. Its extremely acidic properties make it a most welcome contrast to rich English clotted cream. Since the rich creams are most difficult to come by in the United States, our substitute is a heavy cream reduction, cooked down, chilled, and softly whipped. It's best to prepare the fruit purée a day or two in advance, since it thickens when well chilled and is just perfect to swirl lightly into the cream.

The Fruit (prepare a day or two in advance)
   4 cups gooseberries (see note)
   ¾ cup fine sugar, or to taste
   ¾ teaspoon orange flower water

Put the berries in the top of a double boiler and cook, covered, over gently boiling water for 10 to 15 minutes or until soft. Strain the berries through a nylon or other nonreactive sieve, stirring and pressing them with a wooden spoon against the sieve and scraping the bottom of the sieve often. Discard the skin and seeds. There should be about 1½ cups of purée. Stir in the sugar and orange flower water, chill slightly, then taste to adjust the sweetness. Cover and chill until serving time.

The Cream
   1 cup heavy cream (not ultrapasteurized)

Pour the cream into a small, heavy nonstick saucepan and cook gently over medium heat, stirring constantly for about 10 minutes. Keep stirring so that a skin does not form on the surface, and reduce to ⅔ cup. Pour into a small bowl and chill. When ready to serve, bring the cream to room temperature. It will be quite thick (see note). Mix the cream with the cold gooseberry purée, but stir in only enough to combine the

two evenly. Don't blend them completely since both tastes and colors should remain distinct. Spoon the mixture into tall parfait or champagne flutes to show the swirls of pale green and cream colors. Cover and chill until serving time.

Note: It is unnecessary to cut off the blossom and stem ends of the gooseberries in this recipe since the fruit will be sieved.

If the cream is very thick, dilute it with 1 tablespoon of the purée before swirling it into the remaining purée.

Cold Rhubarb and Strawberry Sabayon

Serves 6

Rhubarb and strawberries have an affinity for each other, just as they do in this cold sabayon, lightened with whipped cream. Sabayon—or zabaglione—when it is served warm, is a classic cream dessert blending wine with eggs. Instead of the wine, we have used a fruit purée. The dessert is chilled until serving time, eliminating any last minute fuss.

> *6 ounces rhubarb, trimmed and cut into 1 inch pieces (about ½ cup)*
> *1 cup sliced ripe strawberries plus 18 whole, firm berries for decoration*
> *8 tablespoons sugar*
> *Pinch of salt*
> *3 egg yolks*
> *1 cup heavy cream, chilled*
> *1 teaspoon cognac*
> *Mint, rose geranium, or lemon balm leaf for garnish*

In a medium-size saucepan, mix the rhubarb, sliced strawberries, salt, and 3 tablespoons of sugar together. Bring slowly to a boil, stirring occasionally. Reduce the heat and simmer for 8 to 10 minutes, or until the rhubarb is tender. Strain through a nonmetallic sieve, pushing the fruit through with the back of a wooden spoon and scraping the bottom of the sieve to get as much purée as possible. There should be ⅔ cup. Set aside.

Off the heat in the top of a double boiler, whisk the egg yolks and remaining 5 tablespoons sugar together until combined, then place the top of the double boiler over gently simmering water. Make sure the top does not touch the water. Whisk for about 2 minutes, then add 2 tablespoons of the rhubarb-strawberry purée. Continue to whisk until

thick, about 4 to 5 minutes. Remove the top of the double boiler from the heat and continue to whisk for a few minutes to cool slightly. Place the top of the double boiler over a bowl of ice water or chill it in the refrigerator for 10 minutes, whisking occasionally.

Whip the chilled cream until stiff and fold into the remaining purée. Then fold in the egg yolk mixture and the cognac. Spoon into 6 shallow wide-rim glasses or serving dishes and chill for at least 1 hour. Just before serving, slice the strawberries thinly and place on top in a rose pattern. Top with green leaf of choice.

Japanese Plum Wine Cream with
Melon Balls and Mint

Serves 8

This airy, light dessert is a classic, but depending upon *where* you are when you savor it, the name changes. In Austria it's called *Wien Schaum*, in Germany *Berliner Luft*. This interpretation has an oriental touch. The wine used is Japanese plum wine, so perhaps we might call it *Tokyo Cream*. It relies strictly on muscle power to achieve its lofty, airy quality.

> 4 eggs (at room temperature), separated
> ½ cup sugar plus 2 tablespoons fine sugar
> Pinch of salt
> 2 tablespoons lemon juice (about ½ lemon)
> ½ cup Japanese plum wine
> 1 envelope unflavored gelatin
> 3 tablespoons cold water
> 1 cup heavy cream
> ½ medium-size honeydew and 1 small cantaloupe, seeded and
>   cut into balls with a melon baller
> Sprigs of fresh mint for garnish

In the top of a double boiler over barely simmering water, combine the egg yolks, ½ cup of the sugar and a pinch of salt. Do not allow the bottom of the pan to touch the water. Use an electric hand beater or a whisk so that the texture will be very light, and beat the mixture constantly until it has thickened, about 4 to 5 minutes. Add the lemon juice and the plum wine and continue to whisk or beat for another minute or two. Let the mixture cool to room temperature. Sprinkle the gelatin over the cold water in a small saucepan and let it stand for 5 minutes. Then stir over low heat for 1 minute and whisk into the egg yolk mixture. Chill in the refrigerator for 10 minutes. Meanwhile, beat

the egg whites until stiff, gradually adding a pinch of salt and the remaining fine sugar. (Use a hand beater, not an electric beater, to get additional volume.)

Whip the cream with cleaned beaters until it holds stiff peaks. Stir the egg mixture first then fold it into the beaten egg white, and then into the whipped cream. Distribute the melon balls among the bottoms of 8 wine glasses, reserving 8 melon balls in the refrigerator to use as a garnish. Spoon the wine-cream mixture over the melon balls and chill the dessert at least 3 hours. Before serving, top each with a melon ball and a sprig of mint.

Turkish Kaymak with
Black Plums and Ekmek Kadayif

Serves 8

Kaymak is Turkish clotted cream and Ekmek Kadayif is known as *Palace bread*. As in most Middle-Eastern desserts, this one is sweet enough to placate even the most depraved sweet tooth! A slow reduction of heavy cream thickens dramatically into a rich, ivory-colored confection with a faint caramel flavor. Tiny scoops of this cream accompany a syrup-soaked translucent amber disc topped with a wheel of fresh, tart, black plums and a light shower of green pistachio nuts.

Kaymak
> *2 cups heavy cream (do not use ultrapasteurized)*
> *2 tablespoons fine sugar*

Prepare this the day before serving

Pour the cream into a 10-inch nonstick skillet and slowly bring to the boiling point, just when bubbles begin to appear on the surface; but do not allow to boil or scald. Cook the mixture over very low heat for 30 to 35 minutes, stirring occasionally, until the cream is reduced to 1 cup and is very thick. (A skin might form on the surface, but will be strained out later.) Stir in the sugar and cook for 1 minute, stirring, until the sugar is completely dissolved. Strain into a small, flat glass bowl, such as an 8-inch Pyrex pie pan. Let the cream cool at room temperature for 2 hours. The cream will thicken further as it cools and should be malleable at this point. After an additional 1 hour of chilling in the refrigerator, the cream will stiffen. Chill the cream overnight until ready to serve.

Ekmek Kadayif
   1 round loaf (preferably day old) Italian peasant bread (see
       note)
   1½ cups sugar plus 2 tablespoons
   ½ cup water
   A small wedge of lemon
   ½ cup light mild honey

Prepare a few hours in advance.

Slice the bread 1½ inches thick, trim the crusts, and cut out 8 circles, each 2½ inches in diameter. (A cookie or biscuit cutter or an ordinary glass is useful.) Set aside.

In a medium-size nonstick saucepan, stir 1½ cups of the sugar and the water together and warm over medium-low heat until the sugar dissolves. Squeeze the lemon juice into the syrup and add the lemon wedge into the saucepan. Simmer without stirring for 10 to 15 minutes or until the syrup thickens. Remove the lemon wedge and stir in the honey. Continue to simmer for 2 minutes longer.

In a small saucepan, add the remaining sugar and cook it until it has caramelized and is dark amber in color. If it begins to bubble, remove from the heat and let the bubbles subside, then stir into the syrup. Transfer the syrup to a large skillet or to an ovenproof gratin dish. Bring to a simmer and add the bread circles in 1 layer. Turn the bread over and press down with the back of a wooden spoon to help it absorb the syrup. Turn again until no white shows. The bread should look soft and heavy with the syrup. Remove the pan from the heat. Turn the discs several times more while cooling for 10 minutes. The syrup will get very thick and the bread will be a translucent amber color. Cover with plastic wrap and keep at room temperature until ready to serve.

The Fruit
   8 small black Eldorado plums, halved, pitted, and sliced thinly
       (8 slices per plum)
   Ground cinnamon
   3 to 4 tablespoons finely ground toasted pistachio nuts

(continued on next page)

Turkish Kaymak (*cont.*)

For each portion, place an Ekmek Kadayif bread disc on a serving plate. Arrange 4 slices of plum close together in a spiral design on one half of the disc. Arrange 4 more slices of plum on the plate. Sprinkle the plums with a dash of cinnamon. Using a melon baller dipped in warm water, scrape up 4 small balls of Kaymak. Remove the balls of cream by loosening them with the tip of a knife. Place one ball on top of the plums and 3 balls around the plums at the base of the plate. Sprinkle lightly with ground pistachios.

Serve with a knife and fork. Each forkful should contain some of each element in the dessert to blend the flavors properly: the Ekmek, the plums, and the Kaymak.

Note: Use bread that has an even texture. Some peasant breads have large holes inside, which will affect the texture of the Ekmek.

Sweet Nostalgias

The Everyday Desserts from Our Past

The desserts in this section are about the tastes of the past. They are humble and extremely simple to make. Their rough country appearance and their simplicity are truly a part of their charm. Even more than that, they are soothing, totally satisfying, and, since they are generally served warm, they are indeed comfort food.

These desserts also reflect our heritage and the traditions of the early settlers, who arrived here to find an abundance of wonderful wild fruits and berries, to be picked at the peak of their flavor, color, and ripeness. These fresh fruits then became the hallmark of American desserts and the inspiration of our regional American cooks. They were the creations of our great-, great-, great-grandmothers, who tried to duplicate the beloved dishes from their own countries of origin, perhaps to quell the pain of homesickness.

Many of the desserts had no written recipes, and changes were constantly made right on the spot, depending upon what was available at the time, combined with memory of the old country, intuition, and good judgment. Then, still unwritten, these treasures were passed on by word of mouth to succeeding generations, who continued to enjoy making and serving these traditional favorites. It is in this same spirit of continuity that we also wish to pass on our humble efforts to you.

Of course, along the way, since very little was recorded and each cook added her (mostly her, seldom his) personal touch, these favorites have accumulated both a charming history as well as a number of raging controversies. Regional definitions vary for the very same dessert. Even the names change. But this delightful confusion merely adds to the mystique when we begin to search for their origins, their "correct" spelling, or the specific ingredients.

They have also acquired their own euphonious names: buckles, grunts, cobblers, crisps, slumps, crumbles, crunches, brambles, roly-polies, brown bettys, and pandowdies.

On the other hand, they all have several things in common: They are *all* some combination of fresh, perfumed, succulent, sun-ripened fruits and berries, contrasting with a hurriedly prepared batter or crisp crust. Even the names that we've listed above give you a good idea of the final results. Read them aloud for an even better impression!

For us, there is also a special magic that comes to mind. These desserts become a celebration of each harvest. We have the fondest recollections of blueberry picking expeditions. We have memories of swinging our empty pails, finding the tiny purple-blue berries, eating our fill out of hand as we picked them, then delivering the bounty to our mothers for the soon-to-be-made fruit desserts, the balance to be divided into little containers and sold for pennies to our neighbors. It has not changed to this day, as we watch the berry bushes blossom and ripen on the path near our beach house.

There are the other fruits of summer's generosity: wild plums, raspberries, blackberries, strawberries, and currants, to name but a few. And there are the cranberries of autumn, hidden in the dunes near the sea or in the small bogs that dot our island, and we pick them crawling in the dampness, unmindful of the tiny thorns of the surrounding weeds.

In general, we are thankful for America's bounty and the incredible range of climates that are capable of producing such a vast variety of fruits and berries, all of them inspirations for the making of these old-fashioned desserts. And we openly admit the existence of a very deep nostalgia that evokes the dessert cravings and the elusive flavors of our early childhood, for they are truly a trip back to grandmother's kitchen. They are a voyage that the passing of time can never erase.

Each time you bake one, it will conjure up the perfume of your own memories, a time when one of these very same desserts may have scented your kitchen or graced your table. They are time tested and they are uncomplicated. They are the nostalgic sweets that are truly the stuff of the continuity of generations, a sweet and easy link to the past.

Brown Betty

Brown Betty is a baked fruit dessert made with either coarse toasted and buttered bread crumbs or bread cubes, alternating with layers of fruit. Unlike their close relatives, bread puddings, brown bettys do not have milk and eggs in them.

Original bettys were completely simple and almost primitive in their concept with just butter, sugar, bread, and fruit as their prime ingredients. Our recipes, however, are reflective of contemporary tastes and therefore we have included the use of more spices as well as some spirits for additional flavor in these almost effortless, earthy desserts.

Pear Brown Betty with
Poire William and Pecans

Serves 6 to 8

Rough-textured, russet-skinned Bosc pears are blended with toasted cinnamon bread cubes and toasted pecans and spiked with *eau-de-vie* in a classic dessert gone modern.

> *3 cups small bread cubes, made with orange or cinnamon raisin*
>   *bread*
> *6 tablespoons butter, melted*
> *6 Bosc pears, peeled, quartered, and cut into ⅛-inch-thick slices*
> *¾ cup light brown sugar*
> *¼ teaspoon freshly grated nutmeg*
> *½ teaspoon cinnamon (see note)*
> *1 teaspoon finely minced lemon peel*
> *1 tablespoon lemon juice*
> *⅓ cup Poire William*
> *½ cup toasted pecans, broken coarsely*

Preheat the oven to 375 degrees. Butter an 8-cup soufflé dish. Put the bread cubes on a cookie sheet and toast them in the oven for 8 to 10 minutes. Transfer to a bowl and toss with the melted butter. Set aside.

In another large bowl, mix the sliced pears thoroughly with the remaining ingredients. Spread ⅓ of the bread cubes on the bottom of the prepared dish, top with a layer of pears, another layer of bread cubes, and then another fruit layer. Top with the remaining bread cubes. Cover with foil and pierce the foil with the point of a knife in several places to allow the steam to escape. Bake for 45 minutes, then

remove the foil. Return to the oven and continue to bake 10 to 15 minutes more, or until the top is golden. Serve the brown betty warm with a pitcher of cream.

Note: If cinnamon raisin bread is not used, add an additional ½ teaspoon of cinnamon and ½ cup of raisins when combining the sliced pears with the spices.

Apple Brown Betty with Walnuts, Calvados, and Monukka Raisins

Serves 6

Whole grain bread crumbs, plus the oat bran, walnuts, apples, and raisins in this recipe, all help to add the extra necessary fiber and nutrition to your daily diet—and in a very painless way. This brown betty can become a healthful addiction.

> ½ cup coarsely chopped walnuts
> 2 cups coarse whole-wheat bread crumbs
> ¼ cup oat bran
> 6 tablespoons butter, melted
> 6 to 8 medium Granny Smith apples, peeled and thinly sliced
>   (about 7 cups)
> The juice of 1 lemon
> 2 teaspoons grated lemon peel
> 1 cup light brown sugar
> 1 tablespoon cornstarch
> 1 teaspoon cinnamon
> ¼ teaspoon nutmeg
> 2 tablespoons Calvados or apple jack or rum
> ½ cup Monukka raisins (see note)
> 1 tablespoon butter, cut in small pieces

Preheat the oven to 350 degrees. Butter a 2-quart casserole or soufflé dish. Combine the walnuts, bread crumbs, oat bran, and 5 tablespoons of the melted butter and set aside. In a large bowl, mix the apples with ½ of the lemon juice and all of the remaining ingredients, reserving the remaining lemon juice and the remaining 1 tablespoon of butter. Spread

⅓ of the bread crumb mixture on the bottom of the prepared casserole. Add ½ of the apple mixture. Repeat the layers, ending with the remaining bread crumb mixture. Sprinkle the rest of the lemon juice over the top and dot with butter. Cover with aluminum foil and bake for 20 minutes. Remove the foil and bake 30 minutes longer. Serve warm with a pitcher of cream if desired.

Note: Monukka raisins are preferable because of their smokey, winey flavor. However, black raisins can also be used.

Autumn Quince Brown Betty with Rum Raisins

Serves 8

The quince has been the victim of food fashions, but it is gaining popularity once again, and happily so. This aromatic fruit possesses a distinctive, delicate flavor. Here, instead of traditionally layered fruit and bread crumbs, this brown betty has bread cubes, tossed with quince and enhanced with rum-soaked raisins and wine.

½ cup dark raisins
2 tablespoons dark rum
4 large quince (about 2 pounds), peeled, quartered, cored, pitted, and thinly sliced (about 8 cups)
3 thick slices of bread, such as challah or Italian peasant bread, cut into ¾-inch cubes (3 cups)
¼ pound (1 stick) butter
1 cup light brown sugar
1 teaspoon ground cinnamon
1 tablespoon finely minced orange peel
½ cup dry white wine

Steep the raisins in the rum for 1 hour before preparing the rest of the recipe. While the raisins are soaking, toss the slices of quince with the cubes of bread in a large bowl and set aside. Preheat the oven to 325 degrees and butter a 2½-quart soufflé or other deep baking dish.

In a nonstick skillet, melt the butter over low heat. When the butter has melted, add the brown sugar, the cinnamon, the orange peel, and the wine. Stir until well combined, then add the rum-raisin mixture.

Pour the rum-raisin mixture over the fruit and bread mixture, stirring to combine them well. Spoon the mixture into the prepared baking dish, cover with foil, and bake, covered, for 1 hour. Remove the foil, turn up the heat to 400 degrees, and continue to bake for 15 minutes. Serve warm, plain, with a pitcher of cream, or a bowl of whipped cream passed at the table, if desired.

Ginger Peach Brown Betty

Serves 6

"Ginger-peachy" as you may well know, is American slang for *great!* And that's exactly what this easy, double-ginger dessert is.

2 cups fresh, dry bread crumbs (preferably made from whole-wheat bread)
¼ cup oat bran
⅓ cup butter, melted
¼ teaspoon ground ginger
6 cups peeled and pitted, thickly sliced peaches (7 to 8 peaches)
⅓ cup light brown sugar
1 teaspoon peeled and freshly grated ginger root, about a ¾-inch piece
¼ teaspoon pumpkin pie spice
½ teaspoon finely minced lemon peel
2 tablespoons lemon juice
1 tablespoon cold butter, cut into tiny pieces

Preheat the oven to 350 degrees. Butter a 2-quart soufflé dish, or other deep baking dish. Combine the bread crumbs, oat bran, and melted butter, add the ground ginger, and set aside. In a large bowl, mix the sliced peaches with the sugar, ginger root, pumpkin pie spice, lemon peel, and 1 tablespoon of the lemon juice. Spread ⅓ of the bread crumb mixture on the bottom of the prepared baking dish. Top the bread crumbs with ½ of the peach mixture, then ⅓ of the bread crumbs and the rest of the peaches. Top the peaches with the remaining bread crumbs. Dot with the pieces of butter and sprinkle the remaining tablespoon of lemon juice over the top. Cover with aluminum foil and bake for 20 minutes, then uncover and bake for 25 minutes longer. Serve warm with a pitcher of cream to pour over each serving.

Slumps, Brambles, and Grunts

In most of Massachusetts, a *slump* or a *bramble* is a sweet dumpling mixture dropped onto a simmering fruit and sugar base, covered, and then steamed. However, when we questioned home cooks about the differences, they added yet another bit of New England magic and, depending upon the region, all agreed to disagree.

A friend in Boston told us that slump dumplings are steamed on top of the stove, while the bramble or *grunt* dumplings are baked in the oven after the fruit is cooked. However, in Cape Cod, the steamed dumplings are called grunts, while in most other parts of New England, a grunt is a steamed pudding with berries!

There is also another thin line. We were told that when the basic biscuit dough is rolled out without being cut into pieces, then that dessert becomes a *cobbler!* Slumps—grunts—brambles—obviously a matter of geography!

Mixed Berry Bramble with
Scented Rose Geranium Leaf

Serves 4 to 6

The early colonists were partial to the scent and flavor of rose geranium leaf and they used it lavishly, particularly with berries. A teaspoon of French rose flower water can be substituted for the leaf. However, if you'd like a generous supply of these fragrant leaves, you might try growing a pot of rose geranium on your windowsill or in your garden.

Fruit
> 3 cups mixed blackberries, blueberries, and raspberries (fresh or
>   frozen)
> ½ cup sugar
> Pinch of salt
> 1 cup water
> 2 tablespoons cornstarch
> 1 large rose geranium leaf

Combine all the ingredients in a large bowl and then spoon into a saucepan. Bring to a boil, then turn down the heat and simmer for 5 minutes. Transfer the fruit to a large, flat, buttered, 1½-quart gratin dish. (Use a gratin dish rather than a deep baking dish so that the dumplings don't touch each other.) Preheat the oven to 400 degrees and prepare the biscuit dough.

Biscuit Dough
> 1 cup flour
> 2 teaspoons baking powder
> ½ teaspoon ground cinnamon
> ¼ teaspoon salt
> 3 tablespoons cold butter, cut into small pieces
> ⅓ cup milk
> 1 egg white, lightly beaten

Sift all the dry ingredients together on waxed paper, then transfer to a bowl. Distribute the pieces of cold butter over the dry ingredients and, using a pastry blender, blend the mixture until crumbly.

Add the milk and combine the mixture with a wooden spoon, just until a soft dough is formed. Drop heaping tablespoons of dough evenly onto the berry mixture, making sure that there is space between each dumpling.

Brush the tops of the dumplings with the egg white and bake 20 to 25 minutes or until the top is light golden and the fruit is bubbly. Serve warm with cream.

Note: If you wish to make a slump, cover the baking dish tightly and cook on top of the stove for 15 to 20 minutes, or until the dumplings are steamed.

Raspberry Slump with Orange Dumplings

Serves 6

These puffy, orange-scented dumplings are steamed over a bed of raspberries.

Fruit
> 2 cups fresh or frozen raspberries (see note)
> 1/3 to 1/2 cup sugar, to taste
> 2/3 cup water
> 1 teaspoon finely minced orange peel

Put the raspberries, sugar, water, and orange peel into a 10-inch skillet, cover, and simmer for 8 minutes. While the fruit is cooking, prepare the dumplings.

Orange Dumplings
> 1 cup flour
> 3 tablespoons sugar
> 2 teaspoons baking powder
> 1/2 teaspoon baking soda
> 1/4 teaspoon freshly grated nutmeg
> 1/4 teaspoon salt
> 1 tablespoon finely minced orange peel
> 2 tablespoons melted butter, cooled
> 1/2 cup buttermilk, at room temperature

Sift all the dry ingredients together on a piece of waxed paper, then transfer to a medium-size bowl. Add the orange peel and stir to distribute, then add the melted butter and the buttermilk. Stir the mixture with a wooden spoon, but do not overmix or the dumplings will not be light. Drop the batter by heaping teaspoons over the simmering

fruit. Cover the skillet tightly and steam the dumplings over low heat for about 30 minutes without lifting the lid.

To serve, place one dumpling in a dessert dish and spoon some of the poaching sauce over it. Serve warm with cream or vanilla yogurt.

Note: You may substitute 4 cups of whole cranberries for the raspberries. If you do so, increase the sugar to 1 cup.

Peach and Ginger Grunt

These ginger and lemon-flavored dumplings bake over a bed of luscious peaches in a simple brown-sugar sauce.

Fruit
> 5 large, ripe peaches, peeled, pitted, and thickly sliced (about
>   5 cups)
> 1 tablespoon lemon juice
> ⅔ cup light brown sugar
> ½ teaspoon ground cinnamon
> 1 tablespoon cornstarch
> ¼ cup cold water

Preheat the oven to 400 degrees and butter a 6-by-10-inch baking dish, preferably earthenware. In a large bowl, mix the peaches with the lemon juice, brown sugar, and cinnamon. Dissolve the cornstarch in the water and add it to the peaches. Mix carefully, then transfer to the baking dish and prepare the dumplings.

Dumplings
> 1 cup flour
> 4 tablespoons sugar
> 1½ teaspoons baking powder
> ½ teaspoon baking soda
> ¼ teaspoon salt
> ½ teaspoon ground ginger
> 1 teaspoon finely minced lemon peel
> 1 egg yolk
> 3 tablespoons cold butter, cut into small pieces
> ⅓ cup buttermilk, at room temperature (more or less may be
>   necessary)

In a medium-size bowl, sift the flour with 3 tablespoons of the sugar, baking powder, baking soda, salt, and ground ginger. Stir in the lemon peel. Add the butter and, using a pastry blender, blend it until the mixture has a crumbly texture. Do not overmix.

Beat the egg yolk in a measuring cup and add enough buttermilk to measure a generous ⅓ cup. Pour the mixture into the dry ingredients and, using a fork, stir gently until a very soft dough forms. Knead the dough once or twice on a lightly floured surface to combine, then pat it out gently to a thickness of ½ inch.

Cut the dough with a knife into 1½-inch squares. Arrange the squares of dough over the fruit, spacing them evenly. Sprinkle the dough with the remaining tablespoon of sugar and bake until the top is lightly golden and the fruit is bubbling, about 20 to 25 minutes. Cool slightly before serving. Serve warm with Crème Anglaise II (page 333), whipped cream, or vanilla ice cream.

Crisps, Crumbles, and Crunches

Crisps are the homey American version of the British *crumbles*. The fruit is always on the bottom and the top is usually a shortbread mixture of butter, sugar, flour, oats, and sometimes nuts, which forms a crisp, crumbly crust as it bakes. Hence, the descriptive names from both continents are very appropriate.

A *crunch* is related to the American crisp and the British crumble. However, the fruit in a crunch is layered *between* a shortbread mixture, rather than being topped by it.

Nectarine and Blackberry Crisp with Crème de Cassis and Almonds

Serves 6

Called a crisp or a crumble (if you want to give it an authentic British accent), this dessert is sometimes made with oats and nuts—at other times, the oats are omitted, as we have presented it here.

Fruit

> 6 ripe nectarines, peeled and thickly sliced
> ½ pint blackberries
> 2 tablespoons lemon juice
> 2 tablespoons crème de cassis
> ¾ teaspoon peeled, finely minced, fresh ginger root
> Sugar to taste

Preheat the oven to 375 degrees and butter an 8-by-11-by-2-inch deep baking dish, preferably earthenware. Set aside.

In a large bowl combine the sliced nectarines and blackberries and gently stir in the lemon juice, crème de cassis, and ginger root. Add sugar to taste, if necessary. Set aside while preparing the topping.

Topping

> ⅓ cup flour
> 3 tablespoons sugar
> 3 tablespoons light brown sugar
> ⅓ cup coarsely chopped toasted almonds
> 4 tablespoons cold butter, cut into very small pieces

In a bowl, combine the dry ingredients and cut in the butter with a pastry blender until the texture is crumbly. Spoon the fruit into the prepared baking pan, then top with the nut mixture. Bake for 35 to 40 minutes, or until golden. Let cool for 5 to 10 minutes before serving warm, by itself or with Crème Anglaise II (page 333), vanilla ice cream, or cream.

Blueberry Crisp with Rose Flower Water

Serves 4 to 6

This is a blueberry picker's delight, whether you pick them from a favorite bush or buy them from your own local market. Rose flower water was lavishly used by the Shaker community, who grew prized herb gardens and made their own rosewater from scented damask roses.

Fruit
>   4½ cups blueberries
>   1 teaspoon lemon juice
>   ¼ cup sugar
>   2 teaspoons rose flower water
>   2 tablespoons quick-cooking tapioca, pulverized in a blender

Preheat the oven to 400 degrees. Butter a 1½-quart ovenproof baking dish. Mix all the fruit ingredients together in a large bowl and spoon into the prepared dish.

Topping
>   ½ cup brown sugar
>   ½ cup flour
>   ¾ cup quick-cooking oats
>   ¼ cup coarsely chopped walnuts
>   1 teaspoon ground cinnamon
>   ½ teaspoon ground ginger
>   4 tablespoons cold butter, cut into small pieces

In a bowl, mix all the dry topping ingredients, then, with two knives or in a food processor, cut in the butter until mixture has a crumbly texture. Stir in walnuts. Spoon over the fruit and bake for 20 to 25 minutes. Let cool on a wire rack for 10 minutes, allowing the top to become crisp.

Serve warm with a scoop of vanilla ice cream or vanilla yogurt.

Peach Crisp with Almonds and Amaretto

Serves 6

The golden-fleshed succulent peach is only at its best when it is tree-ripened, since it stops developing sweetness once it is picked, unlike fruit such as pears, which continue to ripen even after being plucked from the tree. If fresh peaches are not at their ripest, use frozen peaches, since they have usually been tree-ripened before freezing.

Fruit

> 5 ripe peaches, peeled and cut into thick slices (about 3 cups)
> 1 teaspoon lemon juice
> 3 tablespoons brown sugar
> 1 tablespoon quick-cooking tapioca, ground in a blender
> 1 tablespoon Amaretto liqueur
> ⅛ teaspoon freshly ground nutmeg

Preheat oven to 375 degrees and butter a 9-by-1½-inch round baking dish. In a bowl, combine the fruit ingredients. Set aside for 10 to 15 minutes and prepare the topping.

Topping

> ¾ cup quick-cooking oats
> ½ cup flour
> 3 tablespoons light brown sugar
> 2 tablespoons granulated sugar
> ¼ teaspoon ground ginger
> 4 tablespoons cold butter, cut into small pieces
> ⅓ cup slivered almonds

In a bowl, combine the oats, flour, both sugars, and ginger. Add the butter and, using a pastry blender, blend the butter into the dry ingredients until the mixture is crumbly. Stir in the nuts. Spoon the fruit into the prepared baking dish, top with the oat-nut mixture, and bake for 35 to 40 minutes, or until golden brown. Serve warm.

Pear and Hazelnut Crumble

Serves 6 to 8

The Greek poet, Homer, referred to the pear as the gift of the gods. We, too, praise the pear, the wide-base Bosc with its long tapered neck and mottled russet skin, combined here with crisp hazelnuts—an elegant offering of a homey dessert.

Fruit

    4 large Bosc pears
    1 tablespoon lemon juice
    1 tablespoon Poire William
    Pinch of salt
    1 cup hazelnuts, toasted and coarsely chopped (see page 338)
    ¼ cup sugar
    ¼ teaspoon ground mace
    ¼ teaspoon cinnamon
    2 tablespoons butter

Preheat oven to 375 degrees and butter a 1½-quart soufflé dish. Peel, core, and slice the pears vertically into thin slices. Toss in a large bowl with the lemon juice, Poire William, and salt. In a small bowl, mix ¾ cup of the chopped hazelnuts, the sugar, mace, and cinnamon. Arrange some of the pears in the bottom of the prepared dish, just covering the bottom. Sprinkle with the 2 tablespoons of the sugar-nut mixture and dot with 1 tablespoon of the butter. Add another layer of pears, more of the nut mixture, and the remaining butter. Continue layering in this manner until all of the pears have been used. Reserve about ⅓ cup sugar-nut mixture; set it aside and prepare the topping.

Topping
>*½ cup light brown sugar*
>*⅔ cup flour*
>*½ cup quick-cooking oats*
>*Pinch of salt*
>*¼ teaspoon mace*
>*¼ teaspoon cinnamon*
>*4 tablespoons soft butter, cut into small pieces*
>*Whipped cream for garnish, if desired*

In a medium-size bowl, mix the sugar, flour, oats, salt, mace and cinnamon. Add the reserved sugar-nut mixture. Working with your fingers or a pastry blender, add the butter, mixing only until a crumbly mixture forms. Spread the mixture over the pears and bake 45 minutes, or until the top is golden.

Serve slightly warm with dollops of whipped cream and an additional sprinkle of chopped hazelnuts.

Rhubarb and Strawberry Crisp with Amaretti Cookies

Serves 6 to 8

In this more elaborate presentation of a simple crisp, most of the sweetness comes from the raisins and strawberries, both of which modify the tartness of the rhubarb. Crushed Italian Amaretti cookies replace the oats for the shortbread topping.

Fruit
> *2 pounds rhubarb, washed, trimmed and cut into ½ inch pieces (7½ cups)*
> *1 pint strawberries (if large, cut in half; reserve one strawberry for garnish)*
> *1 cup golden raisins*
> *¼ cup Grand Marnier, or other orange-flavored liqueur*
> *⅓ to ½ cup sugar, or to taste*
> *2 tablespoons quick-cooking tapioca, ground in a blender*
> *1 tablespoon finely minced orange peel*
> *Pinch of salt*

Generously butter a 3-quart shallow, oval baking dish and set aside. In a large bowl, combine the rhubarb, raisins, liqueur, sugar, tapioca, orange peel, and salt. Stir well with a wooden spoon and let steep for 20 minutes. While the flavors are blending, preheat the oven to 350 degrees. Stir the mixture and spoon it into the prepared baking dish and set it aside.

Topping
> *2 cups coarsely crushed Amaretti cookies*
> *1 cup quick-cooking oats*
> *¼ cup dark brown sugar*
> *1 heaping teaspoon cinnamon*

½ cup coarsely chopped almonds
¼ pound (1 stick) cold butter, cut into small pieces
1 egg, lightly beaten

In a bowl, combine the cookies, oats, sugar, cinnamon, and almonds. Work in the cold butter with fingertips until combined. Add the egg and stir the mixture with a wooden spoon until it is just combined. Sprinkle the mixture over the fruit and bake 40 to 50 minutes, or until the top is golden and the fruit is bubbling. Let cool for at least 10 minutes on a wire rack, or until the top is crisp.

Serve the crisp slightly warm with a large dollop of whipped cream and a whole Amaretto cookie placed on top in the center surrounded by slices of strawberries in a flowerlike design.

Plum Crisp with
Lemon Peel and Cardamom

Serves 6

In this easy-to-prepare dessert, only four tablespoons of butter are used, to be distributed among six servings. For cholesterol-watchers, that's minimal—plus there are oats, which also are said to help lower cholesterol. They're used in abundance here which makes for a well-balanced finale, indeed.

Fruit
>   *4 cups (about 2 pounds) Italian purple plums, cut into halves*
>   *and pitted*
>   *1 teaspoon lemon juice*
>   *1 teaspoon finely minced lemon peel*
>   *⅓ cup sugar*
>   *2 tablespoons quick-cooking tapioca, ground in a blender*

Preheat the oven to 400 degrees. Butter a 2-quart soufflé dish. Mix the plums with the lemon juice, lemon peel, sugar, and tapioca. Put in the prepared baking dish and let stand for 20 minutes. Stir after 10 minutes to distribute the ingredients.

Topping
>   *1½ cups quick-cooking oats*
>   *½ cup flour*
>   *½ cup light brown sugar*
>   *¼ teaspoon ground cardamom*
>   *Pinch of salt*
>   *4 tablespoons butter, cut into small pieces*

In a bowl, blend all the dry ingredients together with a pastry blender or in a food processor, working the butter into the dry ingredients until

crumbly. Spoon evenly over the fruit mixture and bake for 25 to 30 minutes, or until the top is golden and the fruit bubbles around the edges.

Cool on a wire rack for 10 minutes to allow the top to get crisp and serve warm.

Cranberry and Mango Crunch

Serves 8

One of the advantages of living in a large country with a variety of climates is that the tropical mango from Florida can be used with the New England cranberry at exactly the right time of the year—just as they are in this dessert.

Fruit

    4 cups cranberries (one 12-ounce package), fresh or frozen
    ⅔ cup sugar
    Pinch of salt
    1 teaspoon each finely minced orange peel and finely minced
        lemon peel
    ¼ teaspoon ground cloves
    1 large, or 2 small, mangoes (about ½ pound total)

Preheat the oven to 350 degrees. Butter a 10-by-2½-inch baking dish and set aside. In a large, nonstick saucepan, mix the cranberries with the sugar, salt, citrus peel, and ground cloves. Cook over low heat for 5 to 8 minutes until the berries begin to pop. While the berries are cooking, cut the mango in half lengthwise and, with a small sharp knife, cut out the pit and discard. Peel the mango and cut it into ¾-inch cubes, add to the cranberries, and stir. Remove the saucepan from the heat and set aside while preparing the shortbread.

Oat Shortbread

    1 cup quick-cooking oats
    ½ cup flour
    ¾ cup dark brown sugar
    1 scant teaspoon ground cinnamon
    4 tablespoons butter, cut into small pieces

In the bowl of a food processor, combine all the dry ingredients together with a few pulses. Add the butter and process just until the butter is incorporated and the texture is crumbly. Put half of this mixture on the bottom of the prepared dish. Spoon the cranberry-mango mixture over this layer and then top with the remaining shortbread mixture.

Bake for 40 to 45 minutes, until the top is golden. Serve warm with either Crème Anglaise II, (page 333), whipped cream, or heavy cream.

Almond Apple Crunch with
Apple Cider

The pale green, waxy-skinned, tart Granny Smith apple is a variety that originated in New Zealand. It is now grown commercially in America and available the year round. We think it is a most superior apple, not only for cooking, but for eating raw as well. In this baked dessert, the tartness of the apple is tempered with sweet cider and crisped with crunchy almonds.

Fruit
> 4 large, tart green apples (such as Granny Smith), peeled,
>   cored, and thinly sliced (about 10 cups)
> 2 teaspoons lemon juice
> 2 teaspoons finely minced lemon peel
> 2 tablespoons dark brown sugar
> 2 tablespoons cornstarch
> Pinch of salt
> ½ cup apple cider
> ½ cup sliced almonds

Preheat the oven to 375 degrees. Butter a 2½-quart ovenproof baking dish and set aside. In a large bowl, toss the apples with the lemon juice, lemon peel, and sugar. Dissolve the cornstarch and salt in the apple cider, and pour over the apples. Add the almonds and stir the mixture to combine it. Set aside and prepare the almond shortbread.

Almond Shortbread
 ½ cup flour
 ⅔ cup dark brown sugar
 1 teaspoon ground cinnamon
 ¾ teaspoon ground nutmeg
 4 tablespoons chilled butter, cut into small pieces
 1 cup sliced almonds

In the bowl of a food processor, process the flour, sugar, cinnamon, and nutmeg together until combined. Add the butter and process for a few pulses until the butter is incorporated and the mixture is crumbly. Transfer the mixture to a bowl and stir in the almonds. Spread half of the almond mixture on the bottom of the prepared pan, spoon the apple mixture over the almond mixture, and top with the remaining almond mixture. Bake 35 to 40 minutes, or until the top is golden and the apples are tender (test them with the point of a knife).

Serve warm with vanilla ice cream or vanilla yogurt.

Pandowdy

The pandowdy is somewhat like a deep-dish fruit pie with the fruit on the bottom and a cake or pastry crust on top. It is reminiscent of a cobbler. However the crust, when served, is traditionally pushed into the fruit. In New England, this process is called *dowdying,* which is how the dessert, obviously, got its name. *The Yankee Cookbook* by Imogene Walcott says that when a pandowdy is prepared with apples, some New England cooks call it an *Apple Jonathan* or an *Apple Pot Pie.* As with many of these desserts, there is also an English relative, called *Tewksbury Pie.*

Pear Pandowdy with Bourbon

Serves 6

A buttery, rich, crisp golden top covers bourbon-spiked pears in this quick-to-assemble modern version of an old favorite. The dessert shows perfectly just how a classic can evolve into a brand new creation.

Fruit
> 4 medium-size ripe Bartlett or Comice pears, peeled, halved,
>   cored, and cut into thick slices
> 1 tablespoon lemon juice
> Pinch of salt
> 2 tablespoons bourbon
> 4 tablespoons sugar
> 1 teaspoon cinnamon
> ½ teaspoon vanilla extract

Preheat the oven to 350 degrees. Butter a 10-inch Pyrex tart or quiche pan (do not use metal). Arrange the pears on the bottom and sprinkle with the lemon juice, salt, bourbon, 3 tablespoons of the sugar, the cinnamon, and vanilla. Set aside and prepare the pastry dough.

Pastry
> 1 egg
> 1½ sticks (12 tablespoons) butter, melted and cooled
> ½ cup sugar
> 1 cup flour
> Pinch of salt

In the bowl of a food processor process the egg for a few pulses, and slowly add the melted butter through the feed tube with the processor on. Add the sugar and flour and process until just combined. Spoon over the pears, smoothing the surface lightly with a rubber spatula. Sprinkle the remaining sugar over the batter and bake 40 to 45 minutes, or until the top is crusty and pale golden in color. Cool on a wire rack and serve with whipped cream or Burnt Caramel Cream Sauce (page 335).

Nectarine Pandowdy

Serves 5 to 6

Spices are used minimally in this pandowdy, which gets most of its flavor from the ripest nectarines that are available.

Filling
> 6 large nectarines (about 2 pounds)
> 1 teaspoon lemon juice
> ½ cup light brown sugar, or to taste
> ½ teaspoon cinnamon

Peel and cut the nectarines into thick slices into a large bowl. Combine them gently with the lemon juice, sugar, and cinnamon. Let stand for 10 to 15 minutes. Preheat the oven to 425 degrees and butter a 1½-quart shallow baking dish. Set aside.

Pastry
> ¾ cup flour
> 1½ teaspoons baking powder
> 2 tablespoons sugar plus 1 tablespoon for sprinkling over pastry
> Pinch of salt
> 4 tablespoons butter, cut into small pieces
> ⅓ cup milk
> ½ teaspoon vanilla extract

In a medium-size bowl, combine all the dry ingredients well. Cut in the butter with a pastry blender until the mixture has a crumbly texture. Add the milk and vanilla and combine. Do not overmix or the pastry will toughen. Roll out on a lightly floured surface in a circle about ½ inch larger than your baking dish. Put the fruit into the bottom of the prepared dish and cover with the pastry crust. Roll up the edges to form

a thick crust, and crimp with your fingers or the tines of a fork. Slash the top with a knife in 2 or 3 places, sprinkle the surface with the remaining sugar, and add a few extra shakes of cinnamon if you wish. Bake for 25 minutes or until the pastry is golden. Let cool slightly.

To serve, spoon the crust, fruit, and sauce onto individual serving plates.

Papaya and Blackberry Pandowdy
with Lime and Cassia

This is an upside-down "pie," another homey relative of the cobbler. The fruit on the bottom is the mellow and sweet tropical Papaya, and our native blackberry. Cassia, or Chinese Cinnamon, is the unusual spice that brings it all together. The top crust is a rich one and is made with heavy cream.

Cream Dough
> 2 cups flour
> ¼ teaspoon salt
> 1 tablespoon baking powder
> 2 tablespoons sugar
> 4 tablespoons cold butter, cut into ½-inch pieces
> 7 ounces heavy cream (1 scant cup)

In the bowl of a food processor, combine the flour, salt, baking powder, and sugar with a few pulses until blended. Add the pieces of butter and process until crumbly. Pour the cream through the feed tube and process just until a dough starts to form. Gather the dough together and slam it down on the counter to get the air out. Form into a thick round, wrap in plastic wrap, and chill for at least 1 hour or overnight. Bring the dough to room temperature before rolling it out.

Roll the dough out on a floured surface into a large, roughly oval shape about ¼ inch thick. Invert a 2-quart oval ovenproof baking dish upside-down onto the dough and press down. Lift the dish off and, using the indentation left on the dough as a guide, cut the dough. Crimp the edges of the dough with your fingers and slash the center into a herringbone pattern. Place the dough on a piece of waxed paper

and chill for 15 minutes while preparing the fruit. Gather up the remaining dough, wrap it, and freeze it for future use.

Fruit
> *4 1-pound papayas*
> *½ cup blackberries*
> *1 lime*
> *½ cup dark brown sugar*
> *½ teaspoon ground, sifted, cassia bark (see note)*
> *3 tablespoons cold butter, cut into small pieces*

Cut off the ends of both papayas, then peel them with a vegetable parer. Cut in halves, scoop out the seeds and any stringy material with a spoon, and discard. With the fruit cut-side down, slice into ¼-inch slices. Arrange the slices in the baking dish and scatter the blackberries over the papaya slices.

Shred the peel of the lime with a zester tool onto a piece of waxed paper and set aside. Cut the lime in half and squeeze the juice (you should have a scant tablespoon of peel and 2 tablespoons of juice.) Pour the lime juice over the fruit. Combine the brown sugar with the cassia and spoon it over the fruit. Dot with pieces of butter. Sprinkle the shredded peel onto the top.

Preheat the oven to 400 degrees. Place the chilled dough over the fruit, centering it so that there is a visible border of fruit. Bake for 30 to 35 minutes, or until the top is crusty and golden. Let rest for 15 minutes. Sift confectioners' sugar over the top before serving.

Note: Cassia comes in two forms: buds, and the coarse bark that needs to be ground in a spice grinder or blender until it is a fine powder.

Roly-Poly

This old-fashioned farm-style dessert is basically fruit rolled up in dough, very much like a jelly-roll. It is then wrapped in cheesecloth, tied, and steamed in a covered steamer. The roly-poly is closely related to the sailor's version of a *duff,* which is a stiff dough and fruit mixture that is also boiled in a cheesecloth bag. In Britain, it was a traditional nursery pudding, and it was prepared with a suet crust, filled with fruit or jam, and then boiled or baked.

Italian Plum Roly-Poly with Kirsch

Serves 6

Although the traditional roly-poly was tied in a dampened cheesecloth and steamed for as much as 2½ hours, this time-saving version is baked instead. It is also not quite as sticky as the old-fashioned version, catering to our contemporary tastes.

Dough

    2 cups flour
    2 teaspoons baking powder
    Pinch of salt
    2 tablespoons sugar
    1 teaspoon finely grated orange peel
    6 tablespoons butter, cut into small pieces
    ⅔ cup milk

Process all the dry ingredients in a food processor. Add the butter and process until the texture is crumbly. Trickle the milk into the mixture through the feed tube and process just until a ball of dough is formed. Turn the dough out onto a floured board and knead for 1 minute. Cover with plastic wrap and let rest for 20 minutes while preparing the fruit filling.

Filling

    14 to 15 Italian plums (depending upon size), pitted and
        thinly sliced
    1 tablespoon kirsch
    4 tablespoons sugar
    Pinch of salt
    2 tablespoons quick-cooking tapioca, ground in a blender
    2 tablespoons cold butter, cut into small pieces

(continued on next page)

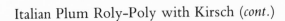

Italian Plum Roly-Poly with Kirsch (*cont.*)

Combine the plums, kirsch, sugar, salt, and tapioca and let stand for 20 minutes. Stir, then strain the liquid and discard. Set the fruit aside in a bowl.

Preheat the oven to 375 degrees. Line a cookie sheet or jelly-roll pan with buttered parchment paper. Roll the dough out onto a floured board into a rectangular shape ⅛-inch thick. Trim to an 11-by-15-inch rectangle and place on a large piece of waxed paper. Spoon the drained, reserved fruit into the center of the dough, dot the fruit with the butter and fold the long sides of the pastry over to enclose the fruit. Brush cold water on the ends of the shorter side of the pastry. Use the waxed paper to help roll the pastry over to enclose the filling. Press and seal the seam. Pick up the waxed paper, forming a kind of hammock, and roll the enclosed pastry over onto the prepared pan, seam side down. Slash the top three times with a sharp knife and bake for 40 minutes.

Glaze
> *1 tablespoon sugar*
> *1 tablespoon water*

Mix the sugar and water together to make a glaze while the roly-poly is baking. Remove the roly-poly from the oven and brush with the glaze. Return to the oven and bake for 20 minutes more or until brown. Cool completely in the pan, then loosen with a spatula and slide off onto a serving platter. Pass a bowl of softly whipped cream with freshly grated nutmeg at the table.

Pear Roly-Poly with Pear Sauce

A sumptuous treatment of a homey dessert. This pastry roll is filled with vanilla-flavored pears, walnuts, and raisins and is decorated with leaves and covered with a sauce of puréed caramel-flavored pears and just a touch of cream.

Fruit Filling
> 2 pounds Anjou pears (about 8 small pears), peeled, cored, and
> > cut into small pieces
> 1 tablespoon lemon juice
> 2 teaspoons vanilla extract
> 3 tablespoons dark muscat or Monukka raisins
> Pinch of salt
> 1/3 cup light brown sugar
> 5 tablespoons finely ground toasted walnuts
> 1 tablespoon flour
> 3 tablespoons butter, melted and cooled

In a large bowl, toss the pears with the lemon juice, vanilla, raisins, and salt and let sit for 25 minutes. Mix the brown sugar, ground walnuts, and flour together in a cup and set aside.

Crust
> 1 recipe Basic Cream Cheese Pie Pastry (page 165)
> Milk or cream

Preheat the oven to 350 degrees and butter and flour a shallow oven-proof baking dish at least 14 inches long. Roll the pastry out on floured waxed paper and trim it to a 1/4-inch thick rectangle 12-by-15 inches.

(continued on next page)

Pear Roly-Poly with Pear Sauce (*cont.*)

Cut leaf shapes out of the scraps of dough and score a vein pattern on the leaves with the back of a paring knife. Set aside.

Drain the pears and reserve the liquid for the sauce. Sprinkle half the walnut-sugar mixture over the bottom of the pastry, leaving a 1½-inch border all around the mixture. Mound the drained pears onto the walnut-sugar mixture, pushing the pears toward the center. Sprinkle the remaining walnut-sugar mixture over the pears and trickle the melted butter over this. Brush cold water around the border of the pastry and fold over both of the shorter sides of the pastry. Use the waxed paper to help roll the pastry over to enclose the filling rather than stretching the dough to join at the seam. Press and seal the seam. Using the waxed paper, roll the pastry over onto the prepared baking pan, seam side down.

Brush the surface with water and gently press the leaves into the surface at angles. Make 3 small slashes on top between the leaves. Brush the leaves with a bit of milk or cream to glaze the roll and bake it for 40 to 45 minutes, or until golden. (If any liquid runs out, just scrape it away with a spoon while the roly-poly is warm.) While the roly-poly is baking, prepare the sauce.

Pear Sauce   *Makes 1½ cups*
    1 pound Anjou pears (about 4 small pears)
    Reserved pear liquid
    ⅓ cup liquid brown sugar
    1 tablespoon water
    2 tablespoons butter
    1 tablespoon Poire William
    3 tablespoons heavy cream

Peel and core the pears. Cut one pear into tiny cubes and set aside in a small bowl. Purée the rest in a food processor and add the reserved liquid. In a small saucepan, mix the sugar and water, add the butter, and cook over low heat, stirring until the butter is melted and the

mixture is thick. With the food processor on, pour the mixture through the feed tube into the pear purée and process for a few seconds. Add the Poire William and the cream and process for another few seconds. Scrape the purée out with a rubber spatula into the bowl of cubed pears. Stir the mixture and keep at room temperature.

Let the roly-poly cool in its pan. Slice and arrange on plates with some of the sauce spooned around it.

Dumplings

The ethnic patchwork quilt that is America has left its mark on a vast array of pastry-enveloped fruit desserts: *Holaches,* the fruit-filled Bohemian potato-based pastry from the Midwesterners of Slavic background; Southwestern fruit-filled *empañadas,* a gift from Americans of Hispanic heritage; the *Germknödel* or yeast dumplings of Austria; and the German *Klösse* or *Nöckerln.*

According to the *Dictionary of Gastronomy,* the word, *dumpling* is said to be derived from the word, *dumpf*—a southern German colloquialism which roughly translates into a "damp, unformed piece." This word was used disparagingly to describe a person who is rough around the edges, so to speak.

Dumplings are a classic example of desserts that carry different names for different cooks. One type of dumpling is made by dropping the dough onto boiling fruit, such as Slumps and Brambles. The dumplings that are included in this section are those that *enclose* fruit. Some are baked; others, like the slumps and brambles, are steamed. Either way, a dumpling is a dumpling is a dumpling, whatever its origin and however it's prepared.

Italian Plum and Raspberry Dumplings

Serves 6 to 8

In this recipe a rich cream cheese pastry encloses a whole plum. And, within each plum, a raspberry is nestled. The pastry is baked to perfection and served warm with a small dollop of whipped cream.

> *14 Italian plums*
> *14 whole raspberries*
> *Sugar*
> *Cinnamon*
> *Whipped cream, optional*
> *1 recipe Basic Cream Cheese Pie Pastry (page 165)*

Make a small incision on the sides of each plum and dig out the pit with the tip of a small paring knife. Replace the pit with a whole raspberry. Repeat with all the plums and raspberries and set aside.

Preheat the oven to 425 degrees. Butter a 10-by-15-inch jelly-roll pan (or spray it with vegetable oil spray) and set it aside. Roll out the pastry on a lightly floured surface and cut out fourteen 4-by-4-inch squares. Place one stuffed plum in the center of each square and sprinkle with ¼ teaspoon of sugar. Brush the edges of the pastry with water and fold two of the opposite corners over the plum, pinching to seal the pastry. Fold over the third corner, pinching the seams together, then the last corner, pinching all the seams together to seal and enclose the plum.

Sprinkle the top of each dumpling with another ¼ teaspoon sugar and dust it with cinnamon. Place on the prepared pan and freeze the dumplings for 10 minutes before baking. Bake for 10 minutes, then reduce the heat to 350 degrees and bake for 35 to 40 minutes. Let the dumplings cool for 5 minutes, and transfer them with a spatula to warm, individual serving plates.

Äpfel im Schlafröcke
Whole Apple Dumplings Wrapped in Orange Pastry

Serves 6

The Pennsylvania Dutch, of German background, have given us this dessert—literally "apples in sleeping gowns"—or more simply, apple dumplings.

Orange Pastry
    1 cup flour
    1 teaspoon baking powder
    3 tablespoons sugar
    Pinch of salt
    2 teaspoons finely minced orange peel
    5 tablespoons cold butter, cut into small pieces
    ¼ cup milk

Sift dry ingredients onto a piece of waxed paper and combine with the orange peel in the bowl of a food processor. Add the pieces of butter and process only until a dough begins to form. Gather the dough and slam it down onto a waxed-paper-covered work surface to release air bubbles. Press the dough into a thick flat round and wrap in the waxed paper. Chill for 30 minutes in the refrigerator. While the pastry chills, prepare the filling.

Filling
    3 Amaretti cookies
    1 tablespoon raisins
    1 tablespoon Grand Marnier, or other orange-flavored liqueur
    2 tablespoons dark brown sugar
    ¼ teaspoon cinnamon
    2 tablespoons soft butter

Put the cookies in the bowl of a food processor and process until fine.

Add all the remaining ingredients and process to a paste. Scrape into a bowl and set aside to prepare the apples.

Apples
> *6 very small apples (the variety used depends upon the region*
> > *of the country)*
> *Water*
> *Wedge of lemon*

Peel and core the apples and put them into a bowl of water into which you have squeezed a wedge of lemon. This will keep them from discoloring. Set the bowl aside.

Preheat the oven to 400 degrees. Butter a sheet of aluminum foil or parchment paper and place it on a cookie sheet. Bring the pastry to a workable temperature and divide into 6 even pieces. Flatten each piece and roll each one out into a thin 6-inch round on a lightly floured surface.

Dry the apples well with paper towels and spoon 1 scant teaspoon of filling into the cavity of each apple. Drape a circle of pastry over the top of the apple. Pick up the apple and the dough and gently press the dough between the palms of your hand to seal the bottom. Repeat with each apple, and place each one on the prepared baking sheet, filling side up.

Egg Wash Glaze
> *1 egg, beaten*
> *1 tablespoon milk or cream*

Combine the egg and the milk or cream. Pierce the surface of the pastry with the tines of a fork and, using a pastry brush, brush the tops of each dumpling with the egg-milk glaze. Then sprinkle the top of each dumpling with sugar and bake for 10 to 12 minutes. Lower the heat to 325 degrees and bake for 20 to 25 minutes until golden brown. Let cool 5 to 10 minutes on the pan before removing the dumplings carefully with a spatula to a serving plate. Serve them warm with softly whipped cream or unadorned if you wish.

Nectarine and Candied Ginger Dumplings

Serves 4 to 6

The nectarines in this dumpling recipe are cut in half, then flavored with candied ginger root and enclosed in a biscuit dough before they are baked. Ginger Cream Chantilly (page 323) would be the perfect accompaniment to this dumpling.

Filling
    4 nectarines, peeled, cut into halves, and pitted
    4 teaspoons dark brown sugar
    8 small cubes of candied ginger
    8 small pieces of cold butter
    1 teaspoon lemon juice

Line up the halved nectarines on a counter and in each half add ½ teaspoon brown sugar, a small cube of the ginger and a piece of the butter. Sprinkle a few drops of lemon juice over each half. Preheat the oven to 400 degrees and butter a 12-by-18-inch jelly-roll pan (or spray it with vegetable oil spray) and set it aside.

Biscuit Dough
    2 cups flour
    ¼ cup sugar plus 2 teaspoons sugar for the tops
    2 teaspoons baking powder
    ½ teaspoon cinnamon
    ¼ teaspoon salt
    6 tablespoons cold butter, cut into small pieces
    ⅓ cup milk, or additional if necessary
    1 egg white, lightly beaten

Put all dry ingredients into a mixing bowl and, using a pastry blender, cut in the butter until the texture is crumbly. Add the milk and stir just until a dough is formed. Gather up the dough and roll it out onto a lightly floured surface. Make eight 5-inch circles about ⅜-inch thick reserving the scraps. Brush the surface of each circle with egg white to prevent the dough from getting soggy. Place a nectarine half on each circle, gather the dough to enclose the fruit, and dampen the top with water so it will seal.

Cut a small 1-inch square from the pastry scraps with a serrated pastry wheel, and attach it to the top of the dumpling with a dampened finger. (The function of the square is both decorative and a means of hiding the seam at the top of the dumpling.) Brush the top of each dumpling with milk and bake for 30 minutes until golden. Cool for 10 minutes and dust with confectioners' sugar before serving.

Whole Cherry Dumplings with Cherry Kirsch Sauce

Serves 6 to 8

This is a Central European classic, but it's steamed in the ancient Chinese manner. Dumplings were usually put into boiling water, rendering them gluey in texture and requiring that they be drained on tea towels—to which they invariably adhered. Chinese steaming techniques avoid all these mishaps, making the recipe easier to handle

Cherry Kirsch Sauce *Makes 1½ cups*

    3 12-ounce packages of frozen, pitted cherries (see note)

    ½ cup sugar

    Pinch of salt

    ¾ cup water

    1 tablespoon arrowroot

    ⅓ cup kirsch

Remove 24 cherries from the package and put them back in the freezer while preparing the sauce. Put the remaining cherries in a nonstick medium-size saucepan, and add the sugar, salt, and water. Bring to a boil, lower the heat and simmer for 5 minutes. Strain the cherry liquid into a bowl, reserving the whole cherries in the strainer. Return the liquid to the saucepan. Dissolve the arrowroot in 2 tablespoons of cold water and add to the liquid in the saucepan. Stir and cook over low heat for 5 minutes until thickened and add the kirsch. Return the whole cherries to the saucepan. Just before serving, reheat the sauce for 2 to 3 minutes.

Cherry Dumplings *Makes 24*

    1 cup flour

    1 teaspoon baking powder

    1 tablespoon superfine sugar

    ¼ teaspoon salt

2 teaspoons finely minced orange peel
1 teaspoon finely minced lemon peel
⅓ cup milk, plus 1 to 2 tablespoons more
2 teaspoons butter, melted and cooled
24 pitted frozen cherries, thawed

Sift the flour, baking powder, sugar, and salt together in a mixing bowl. Add the orange and lemon peels and stir. Trickle the milk and butter over the dry ingredients and mix until the mixture is moistened and blended. You may need 1 to 2 tablespoons more milk. Do not overmix dough.

Divide the dough into 24 even pieces, then roll each piece of dough out on a floured board to a 3-inch circle. Place one cherry in the center of each circle, wet the outside edges of the circle, and fold the dough to enclose the cherry. Place each one in the palms of your hands and roll into a ball. If the dough does not seem to be sticking, lightly dampen your palms with water and press the dough together. Repeat until all the dumplings have been made. Place finished dumplings on a plate covered with waxed paper and chill while preparing the remaining dumplings.

Add one inch of boiling water to a 10-inch skillet with a tight fitting lid. Spray or brush a vegetable steamer or wire rack lightly with oil, put it in the skillet, and place half the dumplings on the steamer, leaving space between each one (see note). Cover and steam for 10 minutes. Pour the cherry sauce in the bottom of a large ovenproof serving dish and keep warm in a low oven. When the first batch of dumplings is cooked, place them in the sauce and repeat the procedure with the remaining 12 dumplings. Serve hot with a sprinkling of granulated sugar on top of each dumpling.

Note: Frozen cherries are available in supermarkets the year round, and are far less labor intensive than fresh cherries, since they are already pitted.

A Chinese bamboo steamer also works well. Use it if you have one, but oil the base for easy removal of the dumplings.

Cobblers

The term *cobbler* comes from the phrase "cobble up," or to "put together in a hurry," according to Maida Heatter. However, in a country such as ours, one filled with people of such diverse ethnic backgrounds, it is easy to understand how definitions for the very same dessert can be misunderstood, misinterpreted, and subject to a vast variety of names. There are as many different names for the cobbler, as there are for countries of origin in our prodigious melting pot.

Not only is there little agreement about the accurate nomenclature of cobblers but there are also countless opinions on just how they should be prepared in order to be "authentic." Basically, the cobbler has a lot of fruit on the bottom, baked along with some kind of thickish one-piece crust of either biscuit or bread dough, or a rough pastry crust.

If we accept that as a basic premise, then the rest should be easy. However, in parts of New England, a cobbler is called a *Bird's Nest* or a *Crow's Nest* for reasons that seemed to evade everyone we questioned. Connecticut Yankees serve it only with soft custard rather than with cream, whereas in other parts of New England the choice seems to be maple sugar or sour cream sauce.

To add to the confusion, some Americans of British descent call it a *Tumble Over* or an *Upside-Down,* since these desserts were sometimes inverted on a platter after being baked in an iron skillet, similar to the country-French *Tarte Tatin*.

To make matters even more complex, if we look carefully, the cobbler is quite similar to the crust-topped fruit concoction that we call a *pandowdy*. Or, maybe we can simplify the whole controversy. Isn't a cobbler just what our native Southerners and Westerners call a *deep-dish pie?*

Strawberry Rhubarb Cobbler

Serves 6

There is only a bit of rhubarb in this mostly strawberry cobbler—but just enough so that you'll taste the added tang that rhubarb seems to lend to the sweet strawberry.

Pastry
> 1 cup flour
> 1½ teaspoons baking powder
> Pinch of salt
> 1 tablespoon sugar
> 4 tablespoons cold butter, cut into small pieces
> ½ cup heavy cream

Put all the dry ingredients into the bowl of a food processor and process for a few pulses until well combined. Add the butter and process for a few more pulses until the texture is crumbly. Add the cream and process until a dough just forms. Slam the dough down on a work surface covered with waxed paper and form a round. Wrap in the waxed paper, chill for 20 minutes, then prepare the filling.

Filling
> 2 pints strawberries, hulled
> ½ pound rhubarb trimmed and cut into 1-inch pieces (about 2 cups)
> ¾ cup light brown sugar
> Pinch of salt
> 3 tablespoons quick-cooking tapioca, ground in a blender
> 1 teaspoon orange flower water or 1 tablespoon orange-flavored liqueur
> ¼ teaspoon cinnamon
> 2 tablespoons butter, melted

(continued on next page)

Strawberry Rhubarb Cobbler (*cont.*)

Preheat the oven to 400 degrees and butter a 1½-quart round ovenproof baking dish (8-by-2 inches). Mix all the filling ingredients together until combined and spoon into the bottom of the prepared dish. Roll the pastry into an elongated rectangular shape ⅜-inch thick. With a scalloped pastry wheel, cut strips one inch wide and lay them over the filling, interweaving them to make a lattice design. Trim and tuck under the edges slightly.

Bake for 30 to 35 minutes or until the top is golden and the filling is bubbly. Cool on a wire rack and sprinkle with confectioners' sugar before serving. Serve warm.

Blackberry Cobbler with Cinnamon

Serves 4 to 6

This dessert is a simple, traditional cobbler that has been associated with American cookery since our earliest Colonial period—when a walk in the country meant finding a profusion of wild blackberries ripe for the picking.

Filling

> ¾ cup sugar
> 1 tablespoon quick-cooking tapioca ground in a blender
> ⅔ cup water
> 3 cups blackberries
> 1 teaspoon lemon juice
> 1 rose geranium leaf (optional)

Preheat the oven to 400 degrees and butter a 9-inch round baking pan or, preferably, a nonmetal quiche dish with a scalloped edge. In a saucepan, combine the sugar and tapioca until well combined. Gradually add the water and cook, stirring, until the mixture comes to a boil. Add the blackberries, lemon juice, and rose geranium leaf and cook for one minute. Remove the rose geranium leaf and spoon the berry mixture into the prepared pan.

Dough

> 1 cup flour
> 1 tablespoon sugar
> 1½ teaspoons baking powder
> ¼ teaspoon salt
> ½ teaspoon ground cinnamon
> 4 tablespoons cold butter, cut into small pieces
> ⅓ cup milk
> 1 egg yolk

(continued on next page)

Blackberry Cobbler with Cinnamon (*cont.*)

Glaze
   1 egg yolk
   1 tablespoon milk

Sift all the dry ingredients onto a piece of waxed paper and then transfer to a mixing bowl. Add the butter and cut it in with a pastry blender until the mixture has a crumbly texture. Beat the milk and egg yolk together and add all at once. Stir only until combined.

Gather the dough and pat into a circle on a floured work surface. With the rim of a water glass, cut circles of dough and gently lay them over the berry mixture in overlapping circles. Make the glaze by combining the egg yolk and milk and brush the dough with the glaze. Bake for 30 minutes or until the top is golden and the fruit is bubbly around the edges of the crust. Serve warm.

Peach Cobbler with Fresh Ginger Root

Serves 6

Pungent ground ginger was a treasured spice that was brought from Europe to the colonies. More recently, with a surging interest in Oriental food and with travel expanding to all parts of the globe, fresh ginger root with its clean, peppery taste is being used more frequently than ground ginger, as it is used in this Colonial-inspired classic.

Filling
>   6 medium ripe peaches, peeled, pitted, and cut into thick slices
>   (about 4 cups)
>   1 teaspoon lemon juice
>   2/3 to 3/4 cup sugar, or to taste
>   1 tablespoon cornstarch
>   1/2 cup boiling water
>   1 1/2-inch piece of fresh ginger root, peeled and finely minced
>   (2 teaspoons)
>   1/2 teaspoon cinnamon
>   1 tablespoon cold butter, cut into small pieces

Preheat the oven to 400 degrees and butter a round 9-by-3-inch ovenproof baking dish, preferably earthenware. Put the peaches in a large bowl, sprinkle lemon juice over them, toss, and set aside. In a small saucepan, mix the sugar and cornstarch. Add the boiling water and ginger. Cook for 1 minute, stirring constantly. Pour over the peaches and combine. Transfer to the prepared baking dish. Sprinkle with cinnamon and dot with butter, then set aside to prepare the dough.

(continued on next page)

Peach Cobbler (*cont.*)

Dough
    1 cup flour
    1 tablespoon sugar
    ¼ teaspoon salt
    1½ teaspoons baking powder
    3 tablespoons softened butter, cut into small pieces
    ½ cup milk

In a medium-size bowl, mix together the flour, sugar, salt, and baking powder. Add the butter and stir with a wooden spoon, pressing the butter into the flour. Add the milk all at once, and stir only until a dough forms. Do not overmix. Drop generous tablespoonfuls of the soft dough on top of the peaches.

Bake 30 to 35 minutes or until the top is slightly golden. Serve warm, topped with vanilla-flavored whipped cream or a scoop of vanilla ice cream.

Individual Chocolate Cobblers with Raspberries

Serves 6

This is a dessert for Marilyn Abraham of Prentice Hall Press, who wistfully said one day, "Are you going to do a dessert with chocolate and raspberries? That's my favorite combination!" So, this is our version of an updated cobbler—dark chocolate–flavored biscuit dough, crème chantilly and fresh, whole raspberries—a cross between simple old-fashioned shortcake and heaven!

Chocolate Biscuit Dough
  1 tablespoon clarified butter (page 67)
  1½ cups flour
  ½ cup sugar
  1 tablespoon baking powder
  ¼ teaspoon salt
  ½ cup unsweetened cocoa powder
  4 tablespoons cold butter, cut into small pieces
  1 teaspoon vanilla extract
  1 tablespoon sour cream
  ⅔ cup half-and-half or light cream

Preheat the oven to 400 degrees. Brush a baking sheet lightly with clarified butter (this will prevent it from burning). In the bowl of a food processor, process all the dry ingredients together until well blended. Add the butter and process for a few pulses until the texture is crumbly. Combine the vanilla with the sour cream and the half-and-half and pour through the feed tube with the processor running. Process only until a dough begins to form; it will be somewhat sticky. Flour a piece of waxed paper. With floured hands, knead the dough 4 or 5 times and shape it into a thick cylinder, about 15 inches long and 1½ inches in diameter, folding the waxed paper over the dough to help shape it.

(continued on next page)

Individual Chocolate Cobblers (*cont.*)

Flour a large, sharp knife and cut the cylinder into six 2½-inch discs. Place on the prepared baking sheet, flat side down, leaving space between each one to allow them to expand while baking. Bake 12 to 15 minutes, then remove and cool on a wire rack.

Crème Chantilly Filling
> 1 cup heavy cream
> 1 tablespoon fine sugar
> ½ teaspoon vanilla extract
> ½ pint fresh raspberries

To make the Crème Chantilly, beat the cream with a rotary hand beater until almost stiff. Add the sugar and vanilla and continue beating until it holds stiff peaks.

Cut the cooled biscuits in half. Put a dollop of crème chantilly on the bottom half. Arrange some of the raspberries around the outer edge of the cream and place a few raspberries in the center of the cream. Top with the remaining half biscuit and a small dollop of cream. Top it with one perfect raspberry and 1 or 2 chocolate leaves.

Chocolate Leaves
> ½ ounce dark chocolate

Heat the dark chocolate in a cup over warm water. Choose 6 small *shiny* leaves from a houseplant (unsprayed, of course) or get them from your florist or greenmarket. Using an artist's sable brush, coat the leaves generously with chocolate by painting directly onto the leaf. Place on waxed paper and put into the refrigerator until hardened, about 10 minutes. Carefully peel away the green leaf and discard, using the chocolate leaf.

Buckles and Crumples

The point of these desserts is to have more fruit than cake. The cake is a sort of dense coffee-cake base, usually made with only enough liquid to hold it all together. It is studded with a lot of fruit and topped with an Austrian streusel mixture made with sugar, flour, butter, and cinnamon.

At first, the batter looks alarmingly thick, but it is only to be used for a very thin bottom layer. It will all puff up, however—"crumple" up or "buckle" up—which, of course, is how it got its descriptive name.

A *buckle* is a lot like a European *torte* in concept and it lends itself admirably to a change in fresh fruits as they make their seasonal debuts.

Blueberry Buckle

Serves 6 to 8

Wild Maine blueberries, Northwestern huckleberries—sometimes called whortleberries—or high bush blueberries are interchangeable in this American coast-to-coast favorite.

> *2 cups sifted flour*
> *2½ teaspoons baking powder*
> *¼ teaspoon salt*
> *4 tablespoons soft butter*
> *½ cup sugar*
> *1 egg, lightly beaten*
> *1 teaspoon finely minced lemon peel*
> *1 teaspoon vanilla extract*
> *⅔ cup milk*
> *2 cups blueberries (if frozen, do not defrost)*

Preheat the oven to 350 degrees and butter an 8-by-8-inch ovenproof baking dish. Sift the flour, baking powder, and salt together on a piece of waxed paper. In the bowl of a food processor, process the butter and sugar until light and fluffy, then add the egg and lemon peel. Combine the vanilla and milk in a small cup and, alternating with the dry ingredients, add through the feed tube to make a very thick batter. Stir in ½ cup of the berries and scrape the mixture into the prepared pan, using a rubber spatula. Distribute the remaining berries over the surface.

Streusel Topping
> *¼ cup light brown sugar*
> *3 tablespoons flour*
> *½ teaspoon cinnamon*
> *¼ teaspoon ground ginger*
> *¼ teaspoon freshly grated nutmeg*
> *3 tablespoons soft butter, cut into small pieces*

Combine all the dry ingredients in a small bowl. Add the butter and combine with a wooden spoon or your fingertips until the butter is absorbed.

Top the blueberries with the streusel topping and bake 1 hour or until the center is cooked through. A tester should come out clean when inserted into the center of the buckle. Cool on a wire rack and dust the buckle with confectioners' sugar. Serve warm from the pan.

Cranberry Apple Orange Buckle

Serves 6

Similar to a crunch, which sandwiches the fruit between two layers of shortbread, this orange-scented buckle has a cake-batter base and a streusel topping.

Batter
>   1 cup flour
>   ¾ cup sugar
>   ½ teaspoon baking powder
>   ½ teaspoon baking soda
>   ¼ teaspoon salt
>   1 egg
>   ½ cup buttermilk
>   1 teaspoon vanilla extract
>   ⅓ cup butter, melted and cooled

Mix all the dry ingredients together in a large bowl and set aside. In a small bowl, beat the egg, buttermilk, vanilla, and melted butter together with a whisk and combine with the flour mixture. Beat until almost smooth and set aside. Prepare the streusel topping.

Streusel Topping
>   ½ cup sugar
>   ⅓ cup flour
>   ¾ teaspoon cinnamon
>   ¼ teaspoon ground ginger
>   ¼ teaspoon freshly grated nutmeg
>   ¼ cup butter (½ stick), cut into small pieces

Mix all the dry ingredients together, then, with 2 knives or a pastry blender, cut in the butter. Set aside.

Fruit Layer
>   2 *cups cranberries*
>   ½ *cup sugar*
>   1 *tablespoon grated orange rind*
>   1 *tablespoon Cointreau, or other orange-flavored liqueur*
>   ½ *cup dried apples, cut into small pieces*

Combine all the ingredients and set aside. Preheat the oven to 375 degrees and butter a round 9-inch baking dish 3-inches deep, preferably earthenware. When ready to bake, pour the batter into the pan, spoon the fruit mixture over the batter, and top with the streusel mixture. Bake 50 to 60 minutes, or until the top is browned and the cake begins to pull away from the sides of the pan. Let the cake cool slightly in the pan on a wire rack. Serve warm with either vanilla ice cream or vanilla yogurt.

Note: The dried apples absorb the liquid that the berries give off as they bake. They are used instead of a thickening agent such as cornstarch.

Italian Plum Buckle with
Lemon and Almonds

Serves 6 to 8

The plums sink or "buckle" into the center of this tortelike dessert. Here, tart plums, buttermilk, and lemon balance the sweetness, while the almonds add flavor and contrasting texture to the top layer.

> 6 tablespoons soft butter
> ¾ cup sugar
> 1 egg
> 1 teaspoon finely minced lemon peel
> ½ teaspoon almond extract
> 1 teaspoon vanilla extract
> ½ cup buttermilk
> 2 cups flour
> 4 teaspoons baking powder
> ¼ teaspoon salt
> ½ teaspoon baking soda
> 14 whole Italian plums, cut in half and pitted

Preheat the oven to 375 degrees and butter a 9-inch springform cake pan. In a food processor, cream the butter and sugar together until light and fluffy. Add the egg, lemon peel, almond extract, vanilla, and buttermilk and process until well combined.

On a piece of waxed paper, sift together the flour, baking powder, salt and baking soda. Gradually add to the mixture in the food processor. The batter will be thick. Scrape into the prepared baking pan and place the plum halves, skin side up, in one layer over the batter. Prepare the streusel topping.

Streusel Topping
> *3 tablespoons cold butter, cut into small pieces*
> *2 tablespoons flour*
> *3 tablespoons dark brown sugar*
> *1 teaspoon cinnamon*
> *3 tablespoons slivered almonds*
> *1 small wedge of lemon*
> *Confectioners' sugar, for dusting the top*

Blend the butter, flour, sugar, and cinnamon together in a bowl using a pastry blender until the butter is absorbed, then add the almonds. Sprinkle the streusel over the plums and squeeze the lemon wedge on top. Bake for about 1 hour, or until a cake tester comes out clean. Cool on a wire rack.

Remove the rim of the springform pan and serve warm with a dusting of confectioners' sugar.

Pear Buckle with Grand Marnier

Serves 8

The Anjou pear, greenish-yellow in color with a bit of a pink blush, is a sweet, white-fleshed, juicy, all-purpose pear. It's presented here in an old-fashioned homey buckle with touches of a contemporary torte.

Filling
>3 large Anjou pears, peeled and thinly sliced
>1 teaspoon lemon juice
>1 tablespoon Grand Marnier, or other orange-flavored liqueur

Preheat the oven to 375 degrees and butter a 9-by-3-inch springform pan and set aside. In a medium-size bowl, toss the sliced pears with the lemon juice and Grand Marnier and set aside.

Cake Batter
>1 cup flour
>¾ cup sugar
>½ teaspoon baking powder
>½ teaspoon baking soda
>¼ teaspoon salt
>1 egg, beaten
>⅓ cup buttermilk
>5 tablespoons butter, melted and cooled
>¾ teaspoon vanilla extract

In a food processor, mix together the flour, sugar, baking powder, baking soda, and salt. In a small bowl, whisk together the beaten egg, buttermilk, melted butter, and vanilla and add the mixture slowly to the food processor; process until smooth. Spoon the batter evenly into the prepared pan. Spoon the fruit evenly over the batter and prepare the Streusel Topping.

Streusel Topping
    ⅓ cup flour
    ½ cup sugar
    ¾ teaspoon cinnamon
    ¼ teaspoon freshly grated nutmeg
    ¼ teaspoon powdered ginger
    4 tablespoons soft butter, cut into pieces

In a small bowl, mix together the flour, sugar, cinnamon, nutmeg, and ginger. Cut in the butter with a pastry blender until the mixture has a crumbly texture. Sprinkle the topping over the fruit and bake for about 1 hour or until the cake is lightly browned and begins to pull away from the sides of the pan. Cool in the pan on a wire rack. Remove the sides of the springform pan. Serve warm with a dusting of confectioners' sugar.

A Penchant for Pies

Pies and Tarts: Vive la Différence!

Although there are many national cuisines that have their own adaptations of the French fruit tart, the domestic, home-spun pie, our own inventive variation on the Gallic tart, is as American as any dessert can be. Indeed, the cliché "as American as apple pie" evokes memories of hearth, home, family gatherings, and special holidays. Even though the indexes of many of our own cookbooks list: "Pies: See also Tarts and Tartlets," there is a difference between the two desserts.

The French tarte aux fruits is always the same—a single crust pastry featuring the fruit itself. In addition the fruit in a tart is either lightly poached or left uncooked, and the pastry is usually prebaked. The fruit is then added at the very last moment for the best texture and most subtle flavor.

Tart pans have straight, crimped rims, that are often removable. Some, called "flan rings" are just that—a ring that is meant to be used on a baking sheet. However, these are generally used by professional chefs rather than the home baker. Pies, on the other hand, use pie pans that have sloping sides and a lip on the edge. The French tarte aux fruits is a dessert that is not served in the tart pan, whereas the pie is always served in its baking pan.

There are, of course, other differences. The pie, in contrast to the tart, usually has a filling that is baked in a raw pastry, sometimes covered with a lid, sometimes latticed, sometimes covered with a streusel crumb top, and sometimes left open-face exactly like a tart. The top crusts make pies juicier and seal in any moisture that accumulates during the baking process. When the color of the fruit is not bright, such as apple or pear, the pie is usually covered completely. However, with the brighter colors of cherry, rhubarb, or plum, a lattice top is used or the pie is left open to expose the glow of the fruit. The most important rule for the home baker is that there are no hard and fast rules for pies. Choose your top crust according to your own whim and individuality.

Pies are generally more heavily sweetened than tarts and they also seem to hold up much better when they are made well in advance because they can be reheated without losing too much flavor.

Although we adore both pies and tarts, as Americans there is no doubt that we are naturally partial to the pie. Unfortunately, in much of the country the commercially mass-produced supermarket pie has done much to sour our warm memories of hearth and home-baked pies, and more and more home bakers have decided once again to make their own.

By following a few simple rules and tips, your home-baked pies will be a far cry from the store-bought variety—crisp, delicious crusts, juicy, succulent fruit, and applause at the table. Here are some of our suggestions.

Some Tips for Pie Bakers

ABOUT PIE PANS

We prefer the heavy, black metal pans, both for pies and for tarts. We find that they absorb the heat well and thus they bake evenly.

The trick to never having pastry stick to the bottom of the pan is to prime new pans when you purchase them. Wash the pan and dry it thoroughly. Rub lightly with a bland oil such as corn oil. Preheat the oven to 400 degrees and bake the empty pan for 10 minutes. Remove and cool completely and then repeat the light oiling and baking process.

THE PASTRY

Our Basic Cream Cheese Pie Pastry (page 165) makes 16 ounces, enough for a 10-inch double-crust pie, a lattice top pie or two 9-inch-open or streusel-top pies.

Remember to chill the pastry at least one hour before rolling it out—this allows the gluten in the flour to relax. If the dough is too hard to roll, let it stand for 10 to 15 minutes until it's workable.

ROLLING THE PASTRY

The easiest way to roll out pastry dough is to lightly wet the surface of the counter and then place a piece of waxed paper down. The paper will adhere to the surface and it's much easier to clean up.

Before rolling, flatten the dough by pounding it with quick, short blows of the rolling pin. Roll the dough from the center out into all directions until the proper thickness is achieved. Place the pie pan upside-down over the center of the dough to use as a cutting guide. With a floured knife, cut a circle 2 inches larger than the pan.

To patch holes or repair an uneven crust, use your fingertips to wet the edges of the area with cold water. Roll out a small scrap of dough and just press it in. It will never show.

TRANSFERRING THE PASTRY

The trick to transferring the pastry from the work surface to the pie pan without stretching the dough is really very simple and there is a method that will help you achieve it. Roll the pastry loosely on to the rolling pin and then slowly unroll it over the pie pan. Press it gently into the pan without pulling the dough.

CHILLING AND BAKING

To get the best results, after rolling out the pastry, it should be chilled again before baking.

For a two crust pie, chill the rolled dough in the pan while preparing the filling. Fill the bottom crust with the filling, add the top crust, and seal and flute the edges of the pie. Slash or prick the top to allow steam to escape and then freeze for 5 minutes or chill for 20 minutes in the refrigerator before baking.

Bottom crusts can be soggy if they are not baked enough or pre-baked, since they are hidden under the filling. The top crust, usually thinner, bakes and browns more quickly. Often a pie is taken out of the oven before the bottom is sufficiently baked. If the top looks as if it is getting too brown before the time given in the baking instructions, make a double ring of aluminum foil, slip it over the edges of the pie rim, and continue to bake for the allotted recipe time.

If you're baking blind (unfilled), before adding the filling, prick the bottom and sides of the pastry with the tines of a fork. Cut a piece of aluminum foil and double it. It should be large enough to cover the entire pan and overlap by two or three inches. Lightly butter one side of the foil and place it, buttered side down, over the pie crust. Fill the foil with aluminum pie weights so that they press down directly on the crust itself. Bake on the bottom rack of a preheated 350 degree oven for 10 minutes. Lift out the foil and pie weights carefully. At this point, a lightly beaten egg should be brushed on the crust to seal it and to prevent the filling from leaking through. Return to the oven and bake about 5 minutes more or until the crust is dry and golden brown. Cool on a wire rack.

Baking temperatures vary from recipe to recipe, depending upon the kind of pie you are baking. However, a general rule is that the oven is usually set at a hot temperature to begin with, to set the crust, and then is lowered to thoroughly bake the pie.

THICKENING AGENTS

We find ground tapioca to be the most unobtrusive thickening agent for fruit pies, since it does not have a starchy, floury taste. We generally buy a box of quick-cooking tapioca, grind the contents in a blender and then keep it on hand to use as "tapioca flour."

Simple Embellishments

The edge of your pie acts as a frame does to a picture. Here are some easy suggestions to make a picture-perfect pie. They're a lot more original and attractive than simply pressing the edges of the crust with the tines of a fork. All of them are done *before* the crust or pie is baked.

THE PASTRY "COLLAR" STANDING UP

Fluted Edge: Holding your left thumb and forefinger on the outside rim to provide support, place your right forefinger on the inside rim and push toward the two outside fingers to form a rounded wedge. Continue around the crust about every inch or so until you've gone completely around.

Ruffled Edge: Put your thumb and forefinger about a half inch apart on the inside rim of the crust. Using your right forefinger on the outside rim, pull the pastry toward the inside to form a ruffle. Continue doing this around the entire pastry.

Rope Edge: For this one, use a single chopstick or a clean, long pencil or any other thin, long object to help you make the edge. Press it, twisting as you do so, diagonally into the pastry, so that you make evenly spaced ridges.

THE TOP EDGE OF THE PASTRY FLATTENED

Double Scallop: This one is very simple and it uses an ordinary teaspoon. Press the tip of the spoon into the pastry rim to make an indentation. Then, make a smaller indentation within the first one. Continue around the pastry crust.

Button Designs: Using your pastry scraps, take an ordinary thimble and cut out tiny pastry rounds. Place them, just touching one another,

around the entire rim, moistening the dough first so that they stick during baking. Then, using a sharp utensil, such as a skewer, poke holes in each one to make them look just like buttons.

Braid: Using the scraps, cut three thin pastry strips and braid them long enough to go completely around the pastry. Brush rim with water and press the braid onto the top.

Basic Cream Cheese Pie Pastry

Makes one 10-inch double crust
or lattice top pie.

Over the years we've tried many pastry crusts and we find that we always go back to this family recipe. It handles well and the delicate cheese flavor marries well with the fruit fillings. We also find that of all the crusts we've tried, our guests seem to comment most often on this one.

1½ cups flour
Pinch of salt
2 tablespoons sugar
4 ounces chilled cream cheese, cut into ¼-inch pieces
¼ pound cold butter (1 stick), cut into ¼-inch pieces
2 tablespoons heavy cream

In the bowl of a food processor, process the flour, salt, and sugar for a few pulses to combine. Add the cream cheese and butter and process until the texture is crumbly. Trickle the cream over all, and process just until a dough begins to form. Gather the dough together and slam down on a work surface to release any air bubbles. Wrap the pastry in aluminum foil and chill for 1 hour or freeze if storing for longer.

Apple Sour Cream Pie with Rum Raisins

Makes one 9-inch pie
Serves 6

Golden Delicious apples are baked in a creamy raisin-studded filling. In this version, the pastry is only partially overlapped, leaving the center of the fruit filling exposed in an appealing pleated frame.

Crust
> *1 recipe Basic Cream Cheese Pie Pastry (page 165)*

Roll the pastry out in a 13-inch circle, ⅛-inch thick and set aside.

Filling
> *2 cups dark raisins, preferably Muscat*
> *2 tablespoons dark rum*
> *½ teaspoon cinnamon*
> *2 tablespoons flour*
> *Pinch of salt*
> *⅓ cup light brown sugar*
> *1 tablespoon butter, cut into small pieces*
> *2 pounds Golden Delicious apples (about 6 or 7)*
> *1 teaspoon lemon juice*
> *1 egg, beaten lightly*
> *1 cup sour cream*
> *1 teaspoon vanilla extract*

Pastry Glaze
> *1 egg yolk combined with 1 tablespoon milk*

In a small bowl, combine the raisins and rum and set aside. Combine the cinnamon, flour, salt, sugar, and butter in the bowl of a food processor and process for a few pulses and set aside.

Peel and core the apples and slice them thinly. Toss them with the lemon juice, add the reserved raisins and rum and the butter-flour mixture.

In another small bowl, combine the egg, sour cream, and vanilla and add to the apple mixture, mixing well. Carefully fit the pastry into a 9-inch pie pan and fill with the apple mixture. Fold the overhanging pastry to partially enclose the fruit, pleating it softly as you fold it.

Chill in the refrigerator for 20 minutes. When ready to bake, preheat the oven to 400 degrees and bake for 15 minutes. Then reduce the oven temperature to 350 degrees and bake for 20 minutes more. Remove and brush the top of the pastry with the glaze. Return to the oven and continue baking for 30 minutes more.

Double Crust Little Old-Fashioned Apple Pies with Cheddar Cheese

Serves 6

Warm, fresh apple pie . . . the most traditional of American pies that has remained number one in our hearts and on our tables. We have designed this all-time favorite to make individual pies so that they may be served for dessert for two, four, or six people. The leftover pies can be frozen and then freshly baked for another time.

> *1½ recipes for Basic Cream Cheese Pie Pastry (page 165)*
> *2 ounces sharp cheddar cheese, shredded (⅓ cup)*
> *8 large green tart apples such as Granny Smith (3½ to 4*
> *   pounds)*
> *3 tablespoons lemon juice*
> *⅔ cup sugar*
> *⅓ cup light brown sugar*
> *1 teaspoon ground cinnamon*
> *¼ teaspoon freshly ground nutmeg*
> *2 tablespoons flour*
> *6 tablespoons fine, dry bread crumbs*
> *2 tablespoons butter, cut into small pieces*
> *1 tablespoon heavy cream*

Divide 1 recipe of the pie pastry into six equal pieces for the bottom crust and the ½ recipe into 6 equal pieces for the top crust. Butter six individual 5-by-1½-inches deep pans (this size holds a generous 1½-cup portion). Roll out the dough for the bottom crusts and fit loosely into each pan. Press a small scrap of dough into a ball and use to press the pastry into the bottom and sides of the pans. Trim the edges evenly, reserving the scraps, then chill. Sprinkle a scant tablespoon of cheddar cheese on each of the six remaining pieces of pastry and press in the cheese as you roll them out. Cover with plastic wrap so the pastry doesn't dry out while preparing the filling.

In a large bowl, peel, core, and slice the apples thinly. Toss with the lemon juice. In a small bowl, mix both sugars, the cinnamon, nutmeg, and flour together so they are well combined. Sprinkle over the apples and coat them well. Sprinkle 1 tablespoon of the bread crumbs onto the bottom of each pan to absorb some of the liquid. Distribute the apples between the six pans, piling them up towards the middle. Dot each with the butter, distributed evenly, and brush the rims with water. Place the top crusts, cheese side down, over the apples. Press the edges together, then fold under and crimp. Cut leaves out of the pastry scraps and score a vein pattern on each leaf with the back of a knife. Brush the tops with a bit of water and press the leaves on to the surface. Chill again for 30 to 45 minutes, or freeze to bake another time.

Preheat the oven to 400 degrees and before baking, brush the leaves lightly with the cream and make 2 or 3 slashes around the tops of the pies for steam to escape. Bake on the bottom shelf of the oven for 15 minutes, then lower the heat to 350 degrees and continue baking for 30 to 35 minutes more, or until the crust is golden. Remove to wire racks to cool slightly. Serve warm.

Note: If you wish to make one large pie instead of the six individual pies, use a 9-inch pan and only *one* recipe of the Basic Pie Pastry. You will need the same amount of apples, 3 tablespoons of bread crumbs and 2 tablespoons of cheddar cheese for the top pastry crust. Increase the baking time by 5 to 10 minutes.

Springtime Strawberry Rhubarb Pie

Makes one 9-inch pie
Serves 6 to 8

The young, thin stalks of rosy rhubarb are the first to show in the garden. Rhubarb also begins to appear in the marketplace around Easter time and it seems to be most flavorful just then. The appearance of the tangy rhubarb is as welcome as the flowering of our springtime bulbs. They are both a joy and a delight.

1 recipe Basic Cream Cheese Pie Pastry (page 165)
1½ pounds trimmed rhubarb, sliced into ½-inch-thick pieces (6 cups)
2 cups strawberries, hulled and sliced
1¼ cups sugar
¼ teaspoon salt
1 tablespoon finely minced orange or tangerine peel
1 tablespoon orange-flavored liqueur
3 tablespoons finely ground quick-cooking tapioca
2 tablespoons fine dry bread crumbs
2 tablespoons butter, cut into small pieces
1 to 2 tablespoons heavy cream

Roll out half the pastry and fit it into a 9-inch pie pan. Flute the edges and place in the freezer until needed. Roll out the remaining pastry and, using a fluted pastry wheel and a ruler as a guide, cut ½-inch-wide strips. Place the strips on a cookie sheet to chill in the refrigerator until needed.

In a large bowl, stir together the rhubarb, strawberries, ¼ cup of the sugar, salt, orange peel, and liqueur. Let the mixture stand for 25 minutes, then drain the fruit through a sieve, reserving the liquid to use as an addition to sauces for other mixed fresh fruits.

Preheat the oven to 425 degrees. In a small bowl, mix the remaining sugar with the ground tapioca and stir gently into the drained fruit.

Sprinkle the bottom of the frozen pie pastry with the bread crumbs. Spoon the fruit over and dot with the butter. Brush the fluted edge and pastry strips with the cream. Arrange the lattice strips over the fruit, twisting them as you weave them, and attach to the fluted rim with a dot of water. Bake for 15 minutes on the bottom shelf of the oven. Lower the heat to 350 degrees and continue to bake for 40 to 45 minutes more, or until the pastry is golden and the fruit bubbly. If the edge of the crust begins to brown before the end of the baking time, cover it with aluminum foil and continue to bake. Cool completely on a wire rack before serving at room temperature. This allows the thickening agent to solidify the juices so they don't run out when the pie is cut.

Note: As with all fruit pies, the fillings bubble up and sometimes leak their juices. A sheet of aluminum foil, placed shiny side down on the floor of the oven will catch any spills and make for an easier clean-up job.

Italian Plum and Blackberry Pie

Makes one 9-inch pie
Serves 6 to 8

Although this pie is a two crust pie, the top crust is cut into leaf shapes to cover the fruit in a more festive and decorative way. The leaves are glazed and then sprinkled with sugar to catch the light.

1 recipe Basic Cream Cheese Pie Pastry (page 165)
2½ pounds prune plums, pitted and quartered (about 6 cups)
1 cup blackberries
⅔ cup sugar
3 tablespoons finely ground quick cooking tapioca
1 teaspoon finely minced lemon peel
2 tablespoons gin
1 tablespoon butter, cut into small pieces
2 tablespoons fine, dry bread crumbs
2 tablespoons finely ground almonds
1 egg yolk
1 tablespoon cream
1 teaspoon sugar

Roll out a bit more than half the pastry to fit into a 9-inch pie pan. Press the edges with the tines of a fork and place in the freezer until needed. Roll out the remaining pastry to a ⅛-inch thickness and cut into leaf shapes with a small sharp knife. Score a vein pattern on each leaf and place them on a cookie sheet. Chill in the refrigerator until ready to assemble the pie.

Preheat the oven to 425 degrees. In a large bowl, toss the plums, blackberries, sugar, tapioca, lemon peel, gin, and butter to combine. Mix the bread crumbs and almonds together and sprinkle onto the bottom of the frozen pastry. Spoon the fruit into the pie shell, mounding it slightly toward the center.

In a small cup, whisk the egg yolk and cream together to make a glaze. Using a pastry brush, glaze the rim of the pastry and attach the leaves all around. Brush the glaze over the leaves and attach another row, working toward the center. Overlap some of the leaves, leaving some spaces for steam to escape while baking. Brush the surface of all the leaves with the egg wash and sprinkle the surface with the sugar.

Bake on the bottom shelf of the oven for 10 minutes, then lower the heat to 350 degrees and bake for one hour more or until the pastry is golden and the fruit is bubbly. Let cool completely on a wire rack. Serve at room temperature.

Blueberry Pie with Oat Crust

Serves 6 to 8

For those who prefer not to make the Cream Cheese Pie Pastry, or who are intimidated by rolling out pie pastry, there is another solution, and a still easier method of making a delicious fresh fruit pie. If we take the unwritten rule for crisps—fruit on bottom and oat shortbread on top and reverse the assembled components with the shortbread on the bottom and fruit on top, it becomes a pie! That's exactly what we've done here.

Oat Crust
>   2 cups quick-cooking oats
>   1 cup flour
>   ¾ cup dark brown sugar
>   1 teaspoon cinnamon
>   1½ sticks butter (12 tablespoons), melted and cooled slightly

Preheat the oven to 325 degrees. Butter a 10-inch pie pan and set aside. In the bowl of a food processor, process the oats, flour, sugar, and cinnamon. Add the melted butter and process a few more times until combined. Press into the bottom and up the sides of the prepared pan. Bake for 15 minutes.

Filling
>   4 cups blueberries (thawed and drained if frozen), plus ¼ cup
>   blueberries for garnish
>   2 tablespoons sugar
>   1 tablespoon finely minced orange peel
>   2 tablespoons flour
>   Yogurt or sour cream for garnish
>   Long shreds of orange peel made with a zester

In a medium-size bowl, combine the blueberries, sugar, minced orange peel, and flour. Spoon into the prebaked crust and return to the oven for 25 minutes. Cool completely on a wire rack. Before serving, top with dollops of yogurt or sour cream. Sprinkle a few reserved berries and a few shreds of orange peel on top.

Baked Summer Fruits with Nasturtiums.

Papaya and Blackberry Pandowdy with Lime and Cassia.

Strawberry Rhubarb Cobbler.

Japanese Plum Wine Cream with Melon Balls and Mint and Star Spangled Bananas.

Dutch Baby Filled with Mixed Fruit.

Apple Sour Cream Pie with Rum Raisins.

Stilton Cheese Tartlet with Ruby Port Glazed Pear and Roasted Walnuts.

BOTTOM LEFT: *Peach Tart with Frangipane and Black Pepper.* TOP RIGHT: *Champagne Grape Tart with Filbert Praline and Mascarpone.* MIDDLE, CLOCKWISE: *Eight Tartlets—Eight Fruits. Green Grape, Raspberry, Poached Kumquats, Cherry, Kiwi, Blueberry, Blackberry, and Strawberry.*

Whole Cherry Dumplings with Cherry Kirsch Sauce.

Two-Tone Terrine of Citrus and Cranberries with Lime and Campari.

Nectarine Mousse with Blueberries and Strawberry Rose Geranium Sauce.

Sicilian Orange Espresso Cheesecake.

CLOCKWISE: *Poached Oranges with Green and Red Grapes and Grenadine Orange Peel; Poached Pears and Pistachio Nuts Stuffed with Mascarpone; Baked Glazed Figs with Crème Anglaise.*

Chocolate Tartlets with Tangerine Cream and Tangerines.

CLOCKWISE: *Pink Grapefruit, Mint and Gin Sorbet with Honey Poached Kumquats and Vanilla Cigarettes; Blueberry Sorbet Heart with Papaya Balls and Red Currants; Pomegranate Sorbet with Kiwi Sauce and Hazlenut Thins.* CENTER: *Frozen Parfait with Three Fruit Sauces.*

Blackberry Flummery with Gin.

Strawberry Cheese Bombe with a Sauce of Blackberries and Crème de Cassis.

Mango, Strawberries, and Kiwi in Passion Fruit Sauce with Lemon Balm.

A Tribute to Tarts

The Queen of Hearts
She made some tarts,
All on a summer's day;
The Knave of Hearts
He stole the tarts,
And took them clean away.

Nursery Rhyme
Anonymous

As most Americans, we were latecomers to the glorious colors and tastes of summer-fresh fruit tarts. Being partial to pies for so much of our lives, we were thus quite overwhelmed by these dessert jewels when we finally did discover them, and now we can fully understand the Knave of Hearts stealing them away! There are other delights that come with the baking of tarts, aside from their taste and their visual treat.

Since they're prepared in stages rather than all at once, they are perfect for warm weather entertainment. And, with a 15 to 20 minute baking time, tarts are a natural for dinners that must be critically timed. Not only is the pastry prebaked and completely cooled, but it can also be wrapped and immediately frozen after it has been made, or it can be frozen after it is rolled and pressed into the tart pan. In any case, tart pastry is always baked in its frozen state so that it retains its rigid shape while baking.

Thus, the bottom of a tart is never soggy, as pies sometimes are. The only time that a tart might become damp and soggy is when it is assembled too far in advance and the juices have a chance to seep into the crust. Other than that, when made properly, the pastry crust has a quality that is similar to cookie dough. Thus, it doesn't suffer through overhandling as pie pastry does. The end result is a short, crisp, delicate, rigid container.

The filling can also be prepared well in advance, but as we previ-

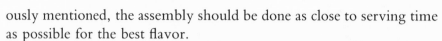

ously mentioned, the assembly should be done as close to serving time as possible for the best flavor.

These advantages, plus the fact that tarts can be quite costly when purchased at the local pastry shop, might be reason enough to make them at home. But there is yet another plus: the creative satisfaction of arranging the fruit right out in the open, and the fact that the finished tart becomes a small, pleasurable, and edible work of art.

As home cooks, having made pies for many years, we used a trial-and-error method with the making of tarts, teaching ourselves not only how to make them, but also storing a great many tricks in our recipe files. We pass along these hints—as well as some of the pitfalls—to our readers in the pages that follow. They'll help save you precious time. And just as in any endeavor, especially in the discovery of new culinary treats, practice will help you whip up a tart with very little effort. We have gotten to love them, both for the way they look as well as for their very special taste.

Some Tricks and Pitfalls: General Tips for Preparing and Baking Tart Pastry

Of the eight different tart pastries that we tried, the Basic Orange Tart Pastry (page 184) with variations of vanilla and lemon flavoring and the Chocolate Tart Pastry (page 186) won hands down as the favorites of our friends and neighbors in Fire Island, where we tested them all.

Our local police chief, Jim LoDuca, was one of our favorite tasters, since he is on the island all year round. After tasting the recipes mentioned above, he left a note tacked to our front door, along with the empty plate on which the sample had rested. The note read simply, "Yum, Yum, Yum!"

TART PANS

As we have mentioned in the section of pies, we prefer the black tart and tartlet pans with removeable rims. We always prime them before using. These pans come in a variety of sizes, including the round 8-inch, 9-inch, 10-inch tart pans, and the 4-inch tartlet pan. They also come in an assortment of depths and shapes—rectangles, squares, ovals.

CHILLING THE PASTRY

After the pastry is blended in a food processor, slam it down on the work surface to get rid of air pockets. Then divide the pastry into the amounts you'll need to correspond with the size of the tart pan. Allow roughly one ounce of pastry per inch of tart pan. (i.e., 9 ounces for a 9-inch pan.)

Wrap the pastry in foil and chill in the refrigerator for at least one hour. Freeze the remaining pastry for another time. It will keep in the freezer for several months.

Our Basic Orange Tart Pastry makes 1¾ pounds (28 ounces).

ROLLING OUT THE PASTRY

When ready to roll out, bring the pastry to a workable temperature. Lightly wet the work surface and place a sheet of waxed paper on top. The dampness helps the waxed paper adhere to the work surface. Sift a bit of flour over the waxed paper and flour the rolling pin. Pound the pastry dough down with the rolling pin to flatten it a bit more before rolling out from the center in all directions. As we mentioned in the pie and pastry section, until you get the hang of it, the pastry may tear. If it does, don't worry about it. Small tears can be easily repaired. Just dampen your fingers and press a small scrap of pastry over the tear. It will never show after it's filled.

Roll out the pastry to a thickness of between ⅛ inch and ¼ inch. (We make a quick toothpick gauge to check the thickness of our pastries: just mark off ⅛ inch, ³⁄₁₆ inch and ¾ inch on the toothpick and stick it into the pastry in 2 or 3 different places to measure the depth.) After a while, you'll learn by feel just how thick and even the dough should be. One of the reasons for testing for eveness is that the dough will brown more quickly in the thin places.

Roll the pastry 2½ inches wider in diameter than the tart pan you've selected. (A 10-inch pan would need a 12½-inch circle.) The extra width will prevent you from stretching the pastry when you place it in the pan, causing it to shrink too much during baking. As it is, tart dough will shrink away from the outside rim when it bakes, but this is entirely normal.

Roll the pastry loosely around the rolling pin, center it and unroll it over the tart pan. Let it slip into the pan naturally of its own weight. Trim the edge, allowing enough pastry to turn in along the rim. This gives additional support to the sides of the crust. The outer rim should be about ⅜-inch thick. Make a walnut-size ball of pastry out of the scraps, flour it, and press the sides of the pastry against the fluted rim of the tart pan. This will prevent you from making little nicks in the pastry as you firmly press it into the pan.

FREEZING

Handle the tarts by the rim so that you don't dislodge the pastry. Put the tart pans on a 12-by-18-inch jelly-roll pan with a rim so that it doesn't slip off. (The first time we ever tried this, we used a rimless cookie sheet and the tart pans slipped right off.) Freeze the tart on the jelly-roll pan for at least 20 minutes before baking. This is an absolutely essential step to make pastry as crisp as possible. If you tightly wrap the entire pan, the pastry can be stored in the freezer at this stage and kept for several months. (When the pastry is firm, you can take the tart pan off the jelly-roll pan.)

PREBAKING THE CRUST

Bake the tart directly from the freezer in a preheated oven. Although different pastries may require different baking temperatures (see the Chocolate Tartlet recipe for example) the Basic Orange Tart Pastry needs a preheated 350 degree oven. Hold the rim of the tart pan and place it on another jelly-roll pan. Put the entire thing in the oven on the lowest rack from the bottom. Prebake the tart for 12 to 15 minutes. Check after 5 minutes to see if the dough is bubbling up. If so, prick it with a toothpick to deflate the bubbles and continue to bake, checking from time to time for more bubbles.

After 10 minutes, the pastry is usually set and it should not puff up again. Bake until golden. With capricious ovens, this can mean anywhere from 13 to 20 minutes. So watch carefully and check the color of the pastry after about 10 minutes. When baked, let the pastry cool completely on a wire rack.

If you plan to use a runny filling such as a custard that will be baked in the cooled shell, beat 1 eggwhite with 1 teaspoon of water and brush this glaze over the bottom to seal it. Then bake it again in a 350 degree oven for 3 to 5 minutes. This will prevent the bottom crust from getting damp.

You are now ready to assemble the tart. Keep the ring on for support until just before serving. Then, either remove the ring alone and keep the tart on its base or slide the tart off onto a flat serving plate.

ASSEMBLING THE TART

Filling: As a rule of thumb, Vanilla Pastry Cream (page 188) is the traditional filling used in a tart as a first layer. Spread on the baked tart shell before the fruit layer is assembled, it gives the tart a lovely moistness that it would not otherwise have. It is also perfect for fruits that are not too juicy, i.e., grapes or fresh strawberries. However, many renegade bakers do break this so-called rule by making superb tarts with ripe juicy fruits such as peaches while using a base of pastry cream or a baked frangipane or a custard.

If a fruit is particularly moist, drain the liquid, blot the fruit with a paper towel, and consider using a base other than the pastry cream (or other baked filling). We occasionally use a mixture of ground walnuts, hazelnuts, or almonds, mixing them with sugar and a bit of cinnamon. This is sprinkled over the pastry shell in a thin layer to absorb some of the juice, while still keeping the bottom crust crisp.

There is a third option. Simply brush the tart shell with the same glaze that will cover the fruit on top, or make a sweetened purée of the same fruit that will eventually form the top layer of the tart.

The Fruit Layer: Our first choice, wherever possible, is to use fresh fruit, uncooked, and at the peak of its flavor. This also gives us the brightest colors and makes for sparkling tart desserts. However, many of us live in areas where this is not always possible, and some of the winter fruits that are imported from South America are generally shipped before they are fully mature. In that case, we poach the fruit in a simple syrup, draining and blotting it on paper towels before arranging it on the tart.

Arranging the Fruit: Here is where the most rewarding and artistic challenge begins. Try to arrange the fruit as close together in the shell as you can without crushing it. Small fruits such as whole strawberries,

raspberries, grapes, or blackberries should be set stem side down for the most appealing appearance.

Medium-size fruits such as apricots or plums can either be halved and set cut side down or sliced thinly and arranged in an attractive circular pattern.

Larger fruits such as apples and pears can be cut in half, then cut partially through in a cross-hatch pattern. They can also be sliced thinly and fanned out, or sliced and placed in overlapping rows of radiating quarters or slices.

Whatever fruit is chosen for your tart, always begin by arranging it starting from the outside edge and working toward the center in ever diminishing circles. This is, without doubt, one of the most rewarding of the steps in the process, for it is here that you finally begin to see the masterpiece take shape.

Glazes: Glazes not only enhance the flavor of the fruit but also the appearance of the tart. The three glazes that we've recommended have the truest colors and flavors most compatible with the different fruits. We make all three in advance, keep them refrigerated in covered plastic containers, and reheat just a few spoonfuls as we need them. (See page 201 for glaze recipes.)

Simple Embellishments: It is not only the color of the fruit and the shine of the glaze that brings on the accolades at presentation of a tart. Sometimes a simple embellishment proves that more is better.

Try a veiled border of finely chopped nuts, such as pistachios, on your strawberry tart. Or, center a paper circle smaller than the circumference of the tart and dust around the paper with a light shower of confectioners' sugar on the surface. Discard the paper circle and the white rim contrasts beautifully with the glazed fruit topping. (See Raspberry Tart with Brown Butter Filling, page 192.)

If you were raised on Mom's pies like we were (as well as the pies in the corner grocery store and bakery), we think you're in for a treat the very first time you try your hand at baking a fruit tart.

Basic Orange Tart Pastry

This recipe makes 1¾ pounds of dough, enough for three 9-inch tarts or a 10-inch tart plus one 9-inch tart, or eight 4-inch tartlets, all about 1 inch deep.

Our taste buds tell that a delicate vanilla or citrus-flavored pastry seems to complement fruit tarts even more than an unflavored pastry. This basic orange-flavored pastry can be adapted with lemon or vanilla flavoring. At the end of the recipe, we have suggested some variations.

> *2⅓ cups flour*
> *¼ teaspoon salt*
> *4 tablespoons fine sugar*
> *14 tablespoons butter (1¾ sticks), cut into ¼-inch pieces*
> *2 egg yolks*
> *4 to 5 tablespoons orange juice (1 medium orange)*

In the bowl of a food processor, blend the flour, salt, and sugar for a few pulses until combined. Add the butter and process only until crumbly, about 5 or 6 pulses.

In a small cup whisk the egg yolks with 4 tablespoons of the orange juice. With the processor on, slowly add the liquid and process only until the pastry begins to hold together. (On humid days you may need only 4 tablespoons orange juice but on a dry day you may need the additional tablespoon.) With lightly floured hands gather up the pastry, push it together, and knead it with the heel of your hand for 1 or 2 strokes. Slam the pastry down on the work surface to get the air bubbles out, and flatten it into a disc.

Divide the pastry and weigh the amounts needed for the size of the tart pans you will be using. As mentioned, we allow approximately an ounce of pastry per inch of pan. Wrap each piece separately in aluminum foil and chill in the refrigerator for at least one hour, or freeze what you will not be using for another time.

Lemon Tart Pastry
Substitute 1 tablespoon of lemon juice mixed with 4 tablespoons of water for the orange juice.

Vanilla Tart Pastry
Replace the orange juice with 2 teaspoons of vanilla mixed with 4 tablespoons of iced water.

Note: 9-inch tart pans, when measured, range from 9¼ inches to 9½ inches and the depths may vary from 1 inch to 2 inches.

Chocolate Tart Pastry

*Makes one 9-inch tart
or six 4-inch tartlets*

This chocolate tart pastry is compatible with vanilla pastry cream as well as with poached pears or fresh raspberries. It is also delicious with the Tangerine Cream (page 190) topped with poached pears or fresh raspberries.

> *1½ cups flour*
> *¼ cup sugar*
> *¼ cup unsweetened cocoa powder*
> *¼ teaspoon salt*
> *½ cup (1 stick) chilled butter, cut into small cubes*
> *1 egg yolk*
> *½ teaspoon vanilla extract*
> *2 tablespoons chilled orange juice or water*

In the bowl of a food processor, mix the flour, sugar, cocoa, and salt together for a few pulses until combined. Add the butter and process only until the texture is crumbly. Beat the egg yolk lightly with the vanilla and add the cold orange juice to the egg mixture. Pour over the flour mixture and process just until the pastry begins to hold together.

Gather the pastry into a ball and slam it down on the work surface to release the air bubbles, wrap it in aluminum foil, and chill for 1 hour.

Remove the pastry from the refrigerator and bring it to a workable temperature. *For the tartlets,* divide the pastry into six even pieces. Pound each piece into a disc with a rolling pin, then roll each piece separately into ⅛-inch-thick circles.

For a 9-inch tart, flatten into a rough disc by pounding with a rolling pin. Then roll into an ⅛-inch-thick circle, 12 inches in diameter.

Fit the rolled dough into the tart pan, fold over the edge and press against the sides to make a slightly thicker supporting rim. Carefully place on a jelly-roll pan with a rim. Freeze for 15 minutes while pre-heating the oven to 350 degrees.

Bake for 10 to 15 minutes on the jelly-roll pan. After 5 minutes and again after 10 minutes, prick any bubbles with a toothpick. Let the tart cool completely on a wire rack before removing the rim and carefully sliding off the base. While the tart cools, prepare the filling.

Crème Pâtissière
(Vanilla Pastry Cream)

Makes 1½ cups

This is a basic crème pâtissière that can be used with any of the pre-baked pastry crusts and your own choice of fresh, seasonal fruits. You can make this pastry cream in advance and keep it in the refrigerator for 3 to 4 days before baking the tart.

> *1 cup heavy cream*
> *1 1-inch piece of vanilla bean*
> *3 tablespoons sugar*
> *2 egg yolks*
> *1½ tablespoons cornstarch*

In a double boiler, warm ¾ cup of cream over simmering water. Split the vanilla bean and scrape the seeds into a medium-size bowl. Add the vanilla bean pod to the cream. Combine the sugar and egg yolks with the vanilla seeds and whisk until thick and light in color. Sift the cornstarch into this mixture and whisk until blended. When the cream is warm, remove from the heat and slowly add the egg yolk mixture, whisking constantly, and return to the top of the double boiler. Continue to whisk and cook over simmering water until thickened, about 4 to 5 minutes. (The whisk will form a ribbon when lifted.)

Remove from the heat and whisk in the remaining ¼ cup cream. Remove the vanilla bean pod. Press a piece of plastic wrap directly onto the surface of the pastry cream to prevent a skin from forming. Refrigerate until needed.

Eight Tartlets—Eight Fruits

Makes eight 4-inch tartlets

A sampling of fresh fruit tartlets, using your choice of seasonal fruits. We have suggested color variations, mostly because of their dramatic presentation, though any combination of these dark and red berries is equally appealing. Prepare the components ahead of time and assemble them an hour or two before serving.

Crust and Filling
> 1 recipe prebaked Basic Orange Tart Pastry (page 184)
> 1 recipe Crème Pâtissière (page 188) (allow 1½ tablespoons
>   filling per tartlet)

Fruit for Each Tartlet
> 1 small kiwi, peeled and thinly sliced
> 5 medium strawberries, stemmed and thinly sliced
> 4 Honey Poached Kumquats (page 15), cut in half and seeded
> 2 tablespoons blueberries
> 2 tablespoons ripe cherries, pitted
> 14 to 16 seedless green grapes
> 2 to 3 tablespoons raspberries
> 2 to 3 tablespoons blackberries

Glazes
> Red Currant Glaze (page 201) for strawberries, raspberries,
>   blackberries, blueberries, and cherries
> Clear Orange Glaze (page 201) for kiwi, kumquats, and
>   green grapes

When you are ready to assemble the tartlets, spoon 1½ tablespoons of the Crème Pâtissière into each prebaked tartlet shell. Cover with the kiwi in overlapping slices, arrange the strawberries like the spokes of a wheel, and place the kumquats (skin side up), the blueberries, and cherries in an appealing way. Spoon the appropriate glaze over the fruit.

Chocolate Tartlets with Tangerine Cream and Tangerines

Makes 6 4-inch tartlets

For a very special occasion, the initials of each dinner guest can be marked in chocolate on the tops of these festive tartlets.

Filling *Makes 2⅓ cups*
   1 6-ounce can frozen, defrosted tangerine juice concentrate
   ½ cup sugar
   Pinch of salt
   1 envelope unflavored gelatin
   ¼ cup cold water
   1 teaspoon finely minced tangerine or orange peel
   1 teaspoon lemon juice
   1 cup heavy cream

Crust
   1 recipe prebaked Chocolate Tart Pastry (page 186)

In a medium-size saucepan, combine the tangerine juice with the sugar and salt, stirring for about 5 minutes over low heat, until the sugar is dissolved. Meanwhile, sprinkle the gelatin over the cold water in another small saucepan and let sit for 5 minutes. Remove the tangerine-juice mixture from the stove and stir in the citrus peel and lemon juice.

Heat the gelatin over low heat, stirring until dissolved, about 1 minute. Add to the tangerine mixture. Cool for 10 minutes, stirring occasionally. Whip the cream until it holds stiff peaks and add the cooled tangerine mixture to the whipped cream. Chill in the refrigerator for 15 to 20 minutes, or until the edges begin to set. Stir the mixture well and spoon into the cooled tartlet shells. Refrigerate until set. While the tangerine cream is setting, prepare the fruit and glaze.

Fruit
   4 to 5 tangerines

Peel the tangerines, removing as much of the white membranes as possible. (You will need about 5 to 6 tangerine segments per tartlet.) Hold each segment up to the light to locate the seeds and remove them with the point of a knife before arranging them on the tangerine cream. When the tartlets are decorated, brush the fruit with the Clear Orange Glaze (page 201).

Note: To personalize the tartlets, dip the point of a knife into Chocolate Orange Sauce (page 334) and trickle a chocolate initial onto each tartlet.

Raspberry Tart with Brown Butter Filling

Serves 8 to 10
Makes one 10-inch tart

The subtle filling in this luxurious, festive tart can be prepared as many as 3 to 5 days in advance and kept refrigerated. However, it must be brought to room temperature before using it. The tart itself, with a sweet vanilla pastry crust, relies on the flavor of ripe raspberries. Truly an orgy for raspberry lovers—and we have yet to meet someone who is not!

Brown Butter Filling   *Makes 3 cups*
 3 eggs
 1¼ cups sugar
 1 tablespoon finely minced orange peel
 ½ cup flour
 1½ sticks butter (12 tablespoons)
 ½ vanilla bean, split

In the bowl of a food processor, add the eggs, sugar, and orange peel. Process until thick and light. Add the flour and process again until blended. Keep the mixture in the bowl of the food processor.

 In a medium saucepan, heat the butter over medium heat. Scrape the seeds from the inside of the vanilla bean into the butter and add the split bean pod. Continue to cook the butter, stirring occasionally, until foamy, dark brown, and bubbly. Remove from the heat and let the bubbles subside. Remove the vanilla bean with a slotted spoon. Turn on the processor and pour the hot butter in a stream through the feed tube, continuing to process until well beaten. Spoon into a covered container and refrigerate until needed.

Crust
 1 recipe prebaked Vanilla Tart Pastry (page 185)

The Fruit and Glaze
  4 cups fresh raspberries
  Red Currant Glaze (page 201)
  Confectioners' sugar

Preheat the oven to 350 degrees. Arrange one cup of the raspberries evenly on the bottom of the prebaked pastry. Spoon the room temperature brown-butter filling evenly over the berries and bake for 35 minutes or until the top is smooth and crisp. Cool completely on a wire rack before removing the rim of the tart pan.

Using a pastry brush, brush a thin layer of Red Currant Glaze on top of the cooled filling. Carefully arrange the remaining 3 cups of raspberries, very close together and stem side down, over the entire surface of the tart. Just before serving, cut out an 8-inch circle of waxed paper and place it in the center of the tart. Sift confectioners' sugar over the surface and then remove the circle, leaving a snowy border around the bright red center. Brush additional red currant glaze over the raspberries in the center of the tart. Serve at once before the confectioners' sugar melts.

Peach Tart with Frangipane and Black Pepper

Serves 8 to 10
Makes one 10-inch tart

In southern France, it is a Gascon tradition to use ground black peppercorns over fresh fruit to enhance their flavor. That is exactly what we do here, with pepper sprinkled on fresh peaches that rest on a bed of baked frangipane.

Frangipane
>*1¼ cup whole skinned almonds (6 ounces)*
>*½ cup confectioners' sugar, sifted*
>*1 egg white*
>*1 whole egg*
>*2 tablespoons butter, melted and cooled*
>*½ teaspoon almond extract*
>*1 tablespoon dark rum*
>*½ teaspoon finely minced lemon peel*

Preheat the oven to 350 degrees. Spread the almonds in a single layer on a pan and toast for 5 to 10 minutes. Cool and grind the almonds very fine in an electric blender. To the bowl of a food processor add the ground nuts and confectioners' sugar and process for a few pulses to combine. Add the egg white and the whole egg and process until thick. With the processor still on, pour the melted butter through the feed tube and add the almond extract, rum, and lemon peel. Process until combined and thick. Scrape out with a rubber spatula into a covered container and chill until ready to use. The filling will keep for 1 to 2 days chilled.

Crust
>*1 recipe prebaked Lemon Tart Pastry (page 185) (Use 12*
>*ounces of pastry for the 10-inch tart pan.)*

Preheat the oven to 375 degrees and fill the prebaked tart shell with the frangipane. Place the tart on a 12-by-18-inch jelly-roll pan and bake for 20 minutes. Remove to a wire rack to cool completely before adding the fruit.

Fruit and Glaze
> *1½ pounds ripe peaches, peeled and pitted*
> *1 teaspoon lemon juice*
> *Apricot Glaze (page 201)*
> *Fresh ground pepper*

Slice the peaches thinly into a large bowl and then mix with the lemon juice to prevent discoloration. Drain and dry the fruit on paper towels. Arrange the slices artfully over the frangipane by overlapping them slightly. Start from the outer rim of the tart pan and work in toward the center. Brush with the apricot glaze and grind a very light sprinkling of fresh black pepper over the surface.

Champagne Grape Tart with Filbert Praline and Mascarpone

Makes one 9-inch tart

Champagne grapes are extremely sweet and delicious and they contrast beautifully with the silky, cheese filling spiked with orange liqueur. Unfortunately, they are in season for only a short time in the fall. Red and green seedless grapes are available during most of the year, however, and can be substituted in this recipe. To add drama to the dessert, present the tart on a bed of grape leaves.

Filbert Praline Cheese Filling
> ½ cup sugar
> ¼ cup toasted filberts
> 3 ounces mascarpone or cream cheese
> 2 tablespoons Cointreau or other orange-flavored liqueur

Crust
> 1 recipe prebaked Basic Orange Tart Pastry (page 184) (Use
> ⅓ of the recipe.)

Lightly spray a 9-inch cake pan with vegetable oil spray and set aside. In a small heavy skillet, melt the sugar slowly and cook until it turns golden brown. Stir in the filberts, immediately remove from the heat, and pour into the prepared cake pan. Let the praline cool completely until it hardens.

Turn the praline out onto a paper towel and place another piece of paper towel over it to blot up any excess oil. Break into pieces, then grind in an electric blender until it is powdery. You should have ½ cup of praline or enough for 2 recipes. Store the rest in an air-tight container. Process 2 tablespoons of the praline powder in a food processor with the mascarpone and the Cointreau until smooth. Spread in the prebaked pastry shell, using a rubber spatula.

Fruit and Glaze
    ¾ pound champagne grapes or ½ pound each green and red
        seedless grapes
    Clear Orange Glaze (page 201)

Stem the tiny grapes and arrange them as closely together as possible, covering the surface of the filling. If using green and red grapes, start at the outer edge of the tart and work toward the center. Use double rows of alternating green and red grapes, as closely packed together as possible. Brush with the Clear Orange Glaze.

Pink Grapefruit and Caramel Tart
with Pine Nuts

Makes one 9-inch tart

Try this totally refreshing fruit tart in the winter when citrus fruits are at their best. Fresh, pink grapefruit sections rest on a thick, intensely flavored orange filling. Warm, sweet caramel is drizzled over to temper the fruit and then a small handful of toasted pine nuts is scattered on top for a very Italian-influenced dessert. This tart *must* be assembled no more than one hour before serving so the crust stays crisp.

Crust
>   1 recipe prebaked Basic Orange Tart Pastry (page 184) (use 9
>   ounces of pastry)

Orange Filling   *Makes 1½ cups*
>   1 cup juice (from 1 to 2 navel oranges)
>   Zest from 1 orange, minced (2 tablespoons)
>   ⅔ cup light brown sugar
>   Pinch of salt
>   3 tablespoons ground quick-cooking tapioca
>   1½ tablespoons Grand Marnier or other orange-flavored li-
>   queur

Place the juice, orange peel, sugar, salt, and tapioca in a small saucepan. Stir and slowly bring to a boil. Lower the heat and cook for 5 minutes, stirring until very thick. Cool completely and keep at room temperature.

Grapefruit
>   3 medium-size pink grapefruits

When ready to assemble the tart, prepare the grapefruit. Working over a bowl to catch the liquid, cut off the ends of the grapefruit with a very sharp knife. Peel them right down to the flesh so that no white pith is visible. Cut out the sections from each side of the supporting membrane and remove. Lay the fruit segments on a double layer of paper towels to blot excess juice before assembling the tarts.

Caramel
    ⅓ cup light brown sugar
    1 tablespoon water
    2 tablespoons soft butter

In a small saucepan, stir the sugar and water together, add the butter and cook over low heat, stirring until the butter is melted and sugar is dissolved, about 3 minutes. Let cool slightly.

Topping
    2 tablespoons pine nuts

Toast the nuts in a 350 degree oven for 5 to 8 minutes. Let cool and set aside.

To assemble: Spread the orange filling carefully over the prebaked pastry with a spatula. Arrange the drained grapefruit sections attractively over the filling. Drizzle the caramel and sprinkle the toasted pine nuts over the surface.

Red Plum and Apricot Tart

Makes 1 rectangular tart,
8-by-10½-by-1 inch
Serves 6 to 8

The Crème Pâtissière in this tart is enriched and lightened with an additional egg and a bit of cream. It makes a custardlike filling, which is lightly baked in a rectangular pan along with stripes of red plums and golden apricots shimmering under their glaze.

Crust
>   1 recipe for prebaked Lemon Tart Pastry (page 185)
>   (Use ¾ of the pastry.)

Custard Filling
>   ¼ cup heavy cream
>   1 egg
>   ¼ cup Crème Pâtissière (page 188)

Blend all ingredients together and spoon evenly over the prebaked and cooled rectangular tart shell.

Fruit and Glaze
>   ½ pound apricots (about 5 medium)
>   ½ pound red plums (about 3 large)
>   Apricot Glaze (page 201)

Preheat the oven to 350 degrees. Cut the fruit in half and remove the pits. Cut into thin slices and arrange over the custard filling, overlapping the pieces and alternating the fruit. Place the tart pan on a jelly-roll pan and bake for 15 minutes. Let cool completely on a wire rack. Remove the rim, but if you do not have a flat, rectangular serving plate, keep the tart on its base for support. When completely cool, brush the fruit with the Apricot Glaze.

Three Glazes:
Red Currant, Apricot, and Clear Orange

These glazes are simple to make, yet they add a most elegant touch to any tart. We usually prepare the glazes ahead and keep them ready for use in small jars in the refrigerator. That way, we have the right flavor and color at our fingertips. Just remember to warm before glazing.

Red Currant Glaze   *Makes ½ cup*
    ½ cup red currant jelly
    1 tablespoon kirsch, brandy, or water

Melt the jelly in a small saucepan and add the kirsch, brandy, or water. Cook for 1 to 2 minutes, or until it is thick and syrupy. Cool the glaze slightly before using.

Apricot Glaze   *Makes ¾ cup*
    ½ cup apricot preserves
    1 tablespoon sugar
    1 teaspoon lemon juice
    1 tablespoon Cointreau or other orange-flavored liqueur

In a small heavy saucepan, combine the apricot preserves with the sugar and cook until dissolved. Force through a sieve and return to the saucepan. (The remains in the sieve can be used as a thick preserve—don't discard them.) Add the lemon juice and liqueur and heat. Remove from the stove and cool slightly before brushing on the fruit.

Clear Orange Glaze   *Makes ⅔ cup*
    ½ cup orange marmalade
    1 tablespoon water

Mix the marmalade and water together in a small saucepan over medium heat, stirring until melted, about 1 to 2 minutes. Strain and cool slightly before brushing over the fruit.

Sweet Simplicities

In Praise of Puddings

Though fortune frown and skies are drear,
And friends are changing year by year,
One thing is always sure to please,
Just give 'em puddings such as these.

Susan Ann Brown
The Book of 40 Puddings
(1882)

The pudding is another dessert that evokes childhood memories. Some, like bread puddings, were (and still are) a way to use up yesterday's stale loaf. Yet the bread pudding can be, at once, both the most naive and the most sophisticated of desserts.

Bread pudding was reputedly a favorite of the late Duchess of Windsor, who gave it a certain cachet some years back when she ate it at the glorious and now sadly defunct Le Pavilion Restaurant in New York, the domain of the much honored Henri Soulé.

On the other hand, puddings have also been given a bad name through a dismal era of packaged mixes, and supermarket quick specials saturated with cornstarch and gelatin, flavored with chemicals, and colored with artificial dyes. However, we think that here, as in much of the cuisine of America, there has been a gradual return to the making of smooth, sweet, and simple puddings at home using fresh ingredients and seasonal fruits, puddings that can once again soothe the soul while completing a meal with simplicity and elegance.

Most puddings throughout the world are derived from the tradition of farm cooking. The frugal farm wife used what was seasonal and combined it with what was on hand—usually leftover grains or cooked porridge, bread, rice, or stale cookies—all combined with seasonal fruits and sweetened with honey, maple syrup, molasses, or sugar.

They were then sparked with the sweet spices such as cinnamon, mace, nutmeg, or cloves and enriched with what the cows and chickens provided—eggs and milk.

As puddings began to take their place in the traditions of the regions in which they evolved, they also began to take on whimsical names. The old English and the colonial American cooks dubbed one *spotted dick* (or *spotted dog*). This was a boiled or steamed suet concoction with "spots" of dried currants and raisins. The *kickshaw* was a sixteenth- to seventeenth-century English corruption of the French *quelque chose* or *something,* obviously referring to any mixture of many things put together. This is very much the same as the pudding made of whatever leftovers are on hand in the North Carolina version called *sonkers*. And, there is a simple New England *plum duff,* a name given by sailors to a stiff, flour dough pudding with fruit, nuts, and spices that is boiled in a bag.

In fact, most puddings from medieval England were tied in a cloth with a long wooden spoon pushed through the knot, allowing the spoon to rest on the pot as the puddings were lowered into boiling water to be simmered for great lengths of time. The result was a congealed and heavy, hard-to-digest mass.

We are probably most familiar with the very Victorian *English Christmas plum pudding,* served at the conclusion of the holiday feast, decked out with a sprig of holly, and set aflame with brandy. It is then carried ceremoniously to the table accompanied by an additional rich, buttery brandy or rum Hard Sauce. This quintessential pudding, the richest of all, sometimes takes an entire day to prepare with its myriad list of ingredients and the nine-hour cooking time. It is difficult to believe that it started out as a humble mixture of cooked grains with fruit and spices!

As its name indicates, the Christmas plum pudding is to be a once-a-year indulgence. And, fortunately for our health, our contemporary tastes now run to much lighter alternatives. Actually, it was during the Victorian era that many of the lighter puddings evolved. Some were enclosed in a mold or "pudding basin," a cloth tied under the rim with string, allowing the cloth to be pushed aside as the pudding began to rise during steaming.

Puddings tend to elude precise definition and the name is given to a great number of sweet and savory dishes—in fact many more than there are true puddings. There are, however, several categories of puddings that can be identified by their cooking methods or techniques: boiled or steamed, stirred or baked. As we've mentioned, the oldest types of puddings were inspired by the English, and their boiled and steamed puddings came with them to colonial America. Our own *roly-poly* was a fruit pudding that was originally wrapped in cloth and boiled. However, these have generally fallen from grace in America, no doubt because of the long cooking time involved.

Even though "merrie auld England" provided the historical development of the pudding, every country in the world boasts a traditional pudding that is made with some combination of grains and fruit. The old English *flummery* was based on oatmeal and wheat (frumenty), and thickened with *isenglass,* a gelatin made from fish bladders. And it is that same flummery that can be found in old cookbooks as *flammeri, flamri, flumery, flomery, kisel, kissels,* or *Middle Eastern apricot flummery.* Even the French have one called *flamri de semoule aux fruites,* simply a semolina flummery with fruit. And so, a flummery by any other name is still a flummery, and all continue to have universal appeal.

The *Danish Rødgrod med Fløde* (page 230) is the counterpart of the *German Röte Grütze* (page 228), both of them simple flummeries. The word *grütze* or *grød*—translates loosely into *grits* or coarsely milled cereal grains such as buckwheat, oats, barley, and our native southern corn grits. As we began to mill whole grains more finely, these grits were used to thicken fruit juices and fruit purées and became a sort of poor man's main course, many of them still eaten in parts of the world. The use of more refined grains as a method of solidifying hot fruit liquids and purées also allowed for a shorter cooking time.

Eventually, finely milled and more delicate thickening agents were used only minimally so that the delicate fresh flavors of fruits and berries would not be lost. These include arrowroot, sago, ground tapioca, cornstarch, semolina, ground rice, and potato starch. Even the illustrious chef, Antonin Carême, a gastronomic artist sometimes known as the founder of classic French cookery, used ground rice to thicken his soufflés.

Actually, what had begun to happen was that the *balance* in these desserts had changed. Formerly cereal flavored with fruit was the norm, and this evolved into fruit that was thickened with cereal. During the late 1930s and early 1940s, around the time of World War II, the simple, slightly thickened flummery, the so-called "poor man's pudding" had a revival both here and in Europe.

These puddings were easy to prepare. They used very little sugar, butter, eggs, or milk due to wartime shortages so that the tart taste of the fruit was unobscured. We think that simple fruit desserts are due for a revival during the 1990s, for they are desserts that are right in line with our lighter eating patterns and a prime candidate for the diet of cholesterol-watchers. We think, too, that they will win popularity contests with those of us who go to work every day, since they are not at all time consuming to make.

Some of the most popular puddings are the spongelike concoctions, very easy to combine, with the oven heat transforming them into especially appropriate home-style informal desserts that are virtually foolproof. Here, too, the heavy fare of yesteryear has evolved into the most airy, delicate, fluffy morsels, all of which have the texture of a soufflé, but which are much more sturdy. Desserts such as the Baked Lemon Sponges with Lemon Sauce (page 222), unlike soufflés, do not carry a sense of immediacy in getting them to the table before they collapse. And yet, they are as impressive as their delicate cousins and equally as tasty.

Baked puddings, bound by custards, have been popular for centuries, both here and abroad. Composed of egg and milk or cream with the addition of bread and fruit or rice, they have been in the category of the most ubiquitous desserts of our childhood and our travels. There probably isn't a roadside diner in the United States that doesn't serve some kind of rice pudding. And even here, this dessert can be made in a number of variations and interpretations—some creamy, some the texture of baked custard, some molded, and some made cloudlike with beaten egg white and served hot, warm, or cold.

At the other end of the recipe spectrum are rice pudding desserts such as the elaborate French classic, *riz à l'imperatrice,* taken out of its fanciful mold and decorated with fruit. And, bread pudding, too, has its range of recipes, from the ordinary to the sublime. At its simplest, it is prepared with bread slices, cubes, or crumbs, and sometimes slices of cake. However, when it is made with lady fingers or a sweet brioche, the French call it *pouding de cabinet* or *diplomate*. Technically, it might not be a *bread* pudding but the basics are very much the same. The popular English *chancellors* or *cabinet pudding* is but a combination of cake and custard, sort of a baked version of an English trifle, made with the very same ingredients assembled in a glass bowl. And yet another English bread pudding is *Queen of Puddings,* distinguished by a layer of jam and topped with baked meringue.

All of these puddings have left their indelible imprint on our culinary history, and all of them have been time-tested, revised, and adapted. Whatever their name, or their history, whether simple and basic or elegant and complex, they seem most appropriate for gracing our tables on any occasion, be it grand or humble.

Pineapple and Raisin Bread Pudding
with Buttered Rum Hard Sauce

Serves 6

This dessert is a gift from the Menehune, the legendary elves of Hawaii. However, this is a contemporary, pared down version. It was originally made with almost one pound of butter and a quart of heavy cream, no doubt delicious, but unconscionable for the way we eat today.

1 recipe Buttered Hard Rum Sauce (page 331)
1 small pineapple, peeled and cut into ¾-inch chunks
½ pound Italian or French bread
¾ cup dark raisins
3 eggs
½ cup light brown sugar
¼ cup white sugar
1 cup milk
2 tablespoons vanilla extract
½ teaspoon nutmeg
Pinch of salt

Preheat the oven to 350 degrees. Butter an 8-by-11-inch baking dish and set aside.

Slice the bread and tear into pieces roughly about the same size and put them into a large bowl. You should have about 3 cups of bread. Cover with water and soak the bread for one minute. Squeeze out the water between the palms of your hands. Add the bread to the pineapple along with the raisins and stir to distribute the fruit. Set the bowl aside.

In another large bowl, beat the eggs and add both sugars, milk, vanilla, nutmeg, and salt. Beat well and pour over the bread and fruit mixture. Stir to combine and spoon into the baking dish. Bake for 50 to 60 minutes, or until the top is golden. Serve warm with 1 teaspoon of Buttered Rum Hard Sauce melting on each portion.

Orange Bread Pudding with Gratinée Oranges

Serves 6

This is a bread pudding that is made with very little bread. It's more like a thickened baked orange custard with sweet navel oranges. It is slipped under the broiler at the last moment to caramelize the top.

4 eggs
⅓ cup sugar
¾ cup heavy cream
⅛ teaspoon cardamom
2 slices of egg bread (such as challah) with crusts trimmed, and
*   cut into ½ inch cubes (1 cup)*
2 medium-size navel oranges, plus the peel of 1 orange
1 tablespoon dark brown sugar
1 tablespoon butter, cut into tiny pieces
Cinnamon

Butter a 9-by-1½-inch round baking dish, preferably ovenproof earthenware. In a medium-size bowl, beat the eggs with a whisk until foamy. Add the sugar and beat until thick and pale. Add the cream and the cardamom and set aside. Peel the zest off one orange. Mince and add 1 teaspoon of the peel to the egg mixture. Remove the white part of the orange and slice crosswise, paper thin. Set aside.

Squeeze the juice from the other orange, measuring ⅔ cup. Add to the egg mixture along with the bread crumbs. Stir and pour into the pan. Place the orange slices gently over the top. Sprinkle with dark brown sugar and dot with butter. Bake 40 to 45 minutes, then broil for 2 minutes. Dust the top with cinnamon and serve warm.

Individual Brioche Apple Pudding
with Currants and Walnuts

Serves 10 to 12

This is really Momma's apple bread pudding, the one we fought over at the dining room table when we were kids. This version, however, is lightened with an eggy, yeasty brioche and presented individually, baked in minibread loaf pans and showered with a snowfall of powdered sugar.

> *½ cup currants*
> *2 tablespoons Cointreau or other orange-flavored liqueur*
> *1 brioche (about ½ pound) torn into small pieces (about 6 cups)*
> *2 eggs*
> *½ cup sugar*
> *⅓ cup milk*
> *Pinch of salt*
> *1 tablespoon plus 1 teaspoon vanilla extract*
> *1 teaspoon finely minced orange peel*
> *6 medium-size flavorful apples (Golden Delicious or Granny Smith)*
> *½ cup coarsely broken toasted walnuts*
> *4 tablespoons butter, cut into small pieces*
> *Confectioners' sugar*

Butter 12 individual miniature bread pans or other ½-cup molds or custard cups. In a small cup, soak the currants in the Cointreau. Put the brioche pieces in a large bowl and set aside. In another bowl, beat the eggs lightly with a wire whisk, and add the sugar, milk, salt, vanilla, and orange peel. Beat well and pour over the brioche. Stir and set aside.

Squeeze a wedge of lemon into a large bowl of water, and peel and slice the apples into small thin pieces, dropping them into the acidulated water so they do not discolor. Drain the apples in a colander and add to the brioche mixture along with the reserved currants, the Cointreau, and the toasted walnuts. Combine well and spoon into the prepared pans or a 2-quart buttered baking dish. Bake for 45 minutes for individual pans and increase baking to about 1 hour and 15 minutes for the larger baking dish. Cool for 15 minutes, run a knife around the inside of each mold and invert onto a serving plate. Turn over again, right side up. Before serving, dust with confectioners' sugar sifted through a small strainer. If you have used the larger baking dish, serve directly from the dish without inverting.

Individual Bread and Chocolate
Puddings with Clementines

Serves 6

A cloud of golden meringue tops each of these puddings, while hidden beneath is the surprise of chocolate and tiny pieces of clementine oranges.

> *4 to 5 clementines (see note)*
> *2 teaspoons finely minced clementine peel plus 1 tablespoon peel for garnish*
> *3 cups bread cubes made from a yeasty egg loaf (such as challah or brioche)*
> *3 ounces bittersweet chocolate, chopped in an electric blender (½ cup)*
> *1⅔ cup milk*
> *3 tablespoons butter*
> *2 eggs, separated*
> *Salt*
> *5 tablespoons sugar*
> *1 teaspoon vanilla extract*
> *Cream of tartar*

With a paring knife, remove the peel from 2 or 3 clementines and mince finely. There should be 2 teaspoons. Using the zester tool, shred the peel of the remaining clementines for garnish and set aside. Remove any white membrane from the fruit, divide into segments, and cut the segments into small pieces. Mix with the bread in a bowl and set aside.

Preheat the oven to 325 degrees. Butter, or spray with vegetable oil spray, six ¾-cup ovenproof custard cups and arrange on a jelly-roll pan. Distribute the bread and clementine mixture between the 6 cups, pressing the mixture down with a spoon. Sprinkle 2 teaspoons of the chopped chocolate over the tops and gently press down again.

In a small saucepan, scald the milk and butter together over medium heat. Do not boil the milk. Remove the saucepan from the heat and set aside. Beat the egg yolks with a whisk in a small bowl, adding a pinch of salt and 3 tablespoons of the sugar. Continue beating until pale yellow and thick. Whisk one tablespoon of the scalded milk mixture into the yolks, then slowly pour this mixture back into the scalded milk in the saucepan. Cook, whisking over very low heat for 1 minute. Add the minced clementine peel and vanilla to this custard mixture. Distribute the custard evenly among the prepared cups. Bake for 20 to 25 minutes. After 20 minutes, beat the egg whites, using a rotary hand beater. Add a pinch of salt and cream of tartar, beating until foamy. Then gradually add the remaining sugar, beating until the whites hold stiff peaks. Remove the puddings from the oven and lower the heat to 275 degrees. Spoon puffs of meringue over each cup and return to the oven for 5 to 10 minutes or until the tops are lightly browned. Cool to room temperature and sprinkle shreds of clementine peel over the meringue before serving.

Note: Tangerines or mandarine oranges can be used, but remember to remove the seeds from the fruit. Since they are also larger than clementines, you may need only 3 rather than 4 or 5.

Souffléed Orange Risotto Pudding
with Fresh Dates

Serves 6 to 8

Fresh dates and the subtle scent of orange peel enhance this baked souffléed rice pudding made with Italian short-grain rice.

1 quart milk
Pinch of salt
½ cup Italian short-grain rice, such as Arborio
2 2-inch pieces of orange peel
12 fresh dates
½ cup sugar
½ teaspoon cinnamon
1 teaspoon finely minced orange peel
1 teaspoon vanilla extract
½ teaspoon orange flower water
4 eggs, separated

In a large, nonstick saucepan, combine the milk and salt. Wash and drain the rice and combine with the milk. Add the pieces of orange peel and slowly bring to a boil, stirring occasionally. Then cover, lower the heat, and simmer for 12 to 15 minutes or until the rice is tender, stirring occasionally. Remove and discard the orange peel.

Cut the dates in half and remove the pits. Reserve 5 dates (10 halves) for garnish. Coarsely chop the other dates. (There should be about ¾ cup.) Add the chopped dates to the saucepan with the rice and milk. Then add the sugar, cinnamon, finely minced orange peel, vanilla, and orange flower water. Cook over low heat, stirring, for 10 minutes.

Preheat the oven to 325 degrees and butter a two-quart casserole. Remove the pot from the heat. Beat the egg yolks and slowly add to the milk mixture, stirring constantly. Return to the heat and cook, stirring,

until the mixture thickens slightly. Cool the mixture completely. When cool, beat the egg whites until stiff and gently fold into the rice mixture. Spoon into the casserole and bake for 25 minutes or until lightly browned. Remove from the oven and cool to room temperature.

Just before serving, arrange the reserved dates, cut side down, over the surface and garnish with additional shredded orange peel made with a zester tool. A pansy or two makes an attractive addition on top.

Caribbean Banana Pudding with
Warm Apricot Sauce

Serves 6

The Empress Josephine, who hailed from the Caribbean French island of Martinique, is reputed to have had an insatiable sweet tooth. This dessert was supposedly her favorite and is said to have satisfied that craving.

The Pudding
>   *1 medium-size lemon*
>   *½ navel orange*
>   *4 medium-size bananas, peeled and cut into small pieces (about*
>   *3 cups)*
>   *2 eggs*
>   *½ cup sugar*
>   *1 cup milk*
>   *1 cup bread crumbs, preferably made with challah, trimmed*
>   *(about 3 slices)*
>   *2 tablespoons butter, melted and cooled*

Cut off the peels of the lemon and orange with a vegetable parer and mince finely. There should be 1 tablespoon of each. Squeeze the juice from the lemon and orange. There should be a total of ½ cup. Pour the juice into a large mixing bowl and add the minced peels. Add the 3 cups of diced bananas, mix well and set aside. Boil a large kettle of water and preheat the oven to 300 degrees.

Butter and sugar a 1½-quart mold and set aside. In the bowl of a food processor, beat the eggs and then add the sugar and process until light in color. Add the milk and process for a few pulses. Add the bread crumbs and process again. Spoon the egg mixture into the bananas and citrus mixture in the bowl. Stir and add the melted butter. Stir lightly and scrape into the prepared mold with a rubber spatula. Place the mold in a larger pan and pour enough boiling water into the pan to reach halfway up the sides of the mold. Bake about 1 hour and 20 minutes, adding more boiling water to the larger pan as it evaporates to keep at the halfway level. Test the center of the pudding with the point of a knife. It should come out clean. Cool for 15 to 20 minutes and then refrigerate for 2 to 3 hours.

Warm Apricot Sauce
   1 cup apricot preserves
   3 tablespoons kirsch
   2 teaspoons lemon juice

Just before serving, prepare the Apricot Sauce. In a small saucepan, cook the preserves slowly until bubbles form around the edge, about 5 to 10 minutes. Remove from the heat and add the kirsch and lemon juice. Strain, forcing the solids against a sieve and scraping the bottom (see note).

Run a knife around the inside of the mold to loosen the pudding. Invert onto a serving dish and spoon the warm apricot sauce around the base and trickle some on top.

Note: Use the remaining solids in the sieve for toast at breakfast.

Spiced Almond and Persimmon
Pudding with
Ginger Cream Chantilly

Serves 6 to 8

One of the joys of autumn is a really ripe persimmon, that sensually textured fruit that glows with a rich orange-gold—the color of changing leaves. This homey baked persimmon pudding is moist and dense with a few almonds for contrasting texture and flavor. It's served warm, then sparked with a biting ginger-flavored whipped cream.

The Pudding
> 2 large, ripe, soft persimmons, about ½ pound each
> 4 tablespoons melted butter
> ⅔ cup light brown sugar
> ¼ teaspoon almond extract
> 1 cup milk
> 1 cup flour
> Pinch of salt
> 1 teaspoon baking powder
> ½ teaspoon baking soda
> ½ teaspoon freshly grated nutmeg
> 1 teaspoon ground cinnamon
> ¼ cup plus 2 tablespoons toasted, slivered almonds
> Ginger Cream Chantilly (page 323)

Preheat the oven to 400 degrees. Butter a 7-by-9½-inch rectangular baking dish, preferably earthenware, and set aside. Cut off the stem end of the persimmon with a sharp knife, split the fruit in half lengthwise, and cut out the thin whitish core that runs down the length of the fruit. (There is no need to peel the fruit for this recipe.) Cut the fruit into small pieces and purée in a food processor. There should be 1⅔ cups purée. Add the melted butter and brown sugar to the purée and blend.

In a measuring cup, combine the almond extract with the milk and set aside. In a bowl, mix together all the remaining ingredients except the nuts and sift on a piece of waxed paper to blend. Return the sifted ingredients to the bowl. Alternate adding the dry ingredients and the almond-extract mixture into the fruit purée with the processor on. When well blended, stir in ¼ cup of the slivered almonds. Scrape into the prepared pan with a rubber spatula and bake 40 to 50 minutes or until the pudding comes away from the sides of the baking dish. Sprinkle the reserved toasted almonds over the surface. Serve warm with the Ginger Cream Chantilly spooned over each portion.

Baked Quince with Toasted Pecans and Nutmeg

Serves 4 to 6

The quince is an ancient fruit, quite popular in medieval Europe, and one that has been enjoyed for centuries. However, it became a victim of food fashions, and for a while its popularity declined. Now, with its appealing and haunting flavor, it has once again found favor with chefs who seek out the unusual for their dessert recipes.

2 large quince (about 1½ pounds)
2 teaspoons butter, softened
¾ cup fine dry bread crumbs
½ cup toasted pecans, coarsely chopped, plus 12 halves as garnish
3 tablespoons light brown sugar
1 teaspoon nutmeg
Pinch of salt
1 teaspoon vanilla extract
2 tablespoons butter, cut into small pieces
1 small pitcher of cream for topping (optional)

Preheat the oven to 350 degrees. Wash and dry the quinces and rub the surface of each with 1 teaspoon of butter. Place the quinces in a small baking dish and bake for 30 minutes. Remove from the oven and let cool, then cut each fruit in half lengthwise. Using a small sharp knife, cut out the tough core and seeds and discard. There is no need to peel the fruit—the peel adds flavor. Cut into pieces and chop coarsely in a food processor. Scrape the fruit into a large bowl and mix with the remaining ingredients except the butter and pecan halves.

Butter and fill a shallow, 12-inch-long oval ovenproof baking dish with the fruit. Arrange the pecan halves evenly over the surface and dot with the butter. At this point, you can cover with plastic wrap and refrigerate until you are ready to bake the dessert.

Bake for 15 minutes and serve warm with a pitcher of cream to pour at the table, if desired.

Puffed Banana Ramekins

Serves 4

A "hand" or bunch of bananas is always plentiful year round. In addition, new varieties are being introduced and marketed all year long. If you are a banana aficionado, this banana soufflé should delight you.

4 ripe but firm bananas
1 teaspoon lemon juice
⅓ cup dark raisins
3 tablespoons dark rum
1 tablespoon confectioners' sugar
1 tablespoon cornstarch
½ cup milk
Pinch of salt
2 egg yolks
3 egg whites
Freshly grated nutmeg

Peel and cut the bananas into chunks and process for 5 or 6 pulses in a food processor. Transfer to a bowl and sprinkle with lemon juice. Stir and set aside. There should be 2 cups.

In a small cup, mix the raisins and rum and set aside. Combine the sugar, cornstarch, milk, and salt in a medium nonstick saucepan and cook over medium-low heat, whisking constantly until thickened, about 1 or 2 minutes. Add the bananas and continue to whisk for 1 minute. Add the egg yolks and cook, whisking for 5 minutes, until very thick. Stir in the raisins and rum and set aside to cool for 20 minutes.

While the mixture is cooling, preheat the oven to 350 degrees and butter four ¾-cup ovenproof ramekins. Beat the egg whites with a pinch of salt until stiff, but not dry. Fold into the puréed banana mixture and spoon into the ramekins. Grate fresh nutmeg over the tops of each and bake for 15 to 20 minutes, or until puffed and golden. Sprinkle with some confectioners' sugar if you wish and serve at once.

Baked Lemon Sponges with
Lemon Sauce

Serves 6

Part pudding, part cake, this dessert forms its own lemony custard sauce hidden at the bottom of each tiny soufflé dish when baked. Topped with a lavender crystalized violet or a fresh violet and a few shreds of lemon peel, it takes on an aura of elegance.

> *3 tablespoons butter, softened*
> *1 cup sugar*
> *1 cup milk*
> *Salt*
> *2 eggs, separated*
> *3 tablespoons sifted flour*
> *¼ cup lemon juice*
> *2 teaspoons finely minced lemon peel (about 2 lemons)*

Preheat the oven to 350 degrees. Boil a kettle of water and butter six ½-cup ovenproof soufflé or custard cups. Cream the butter until fluffy in a food processor. Add the sugar slowly while the processor is on and process for a few minutes. The sugar will still be grainy, but will dissolve later. Add the milk and a pinch of salt and continue to process until smooth. Add the egg yolks separately while the machine is on and continue to process for a few pulses. Add the flour and process again for a few strokes. Then add the lemon juice and peel.

In a deep bowl, beat the egg whites until stiff with another pinch of salt, using a hand beater. Fold the mixture from food processor into the beaten egg whites and spoon into the prepared soufflé cups. Fill to the top and place the cups in a larger pan. Pour enough boiling water into the bottom of the pan so that it reaches one inch up the sides of the soufflé cups. Bake for 25 to 30 minutes, until the tops are puffed and golden. Remove from the water bath to a wire rack and cool.

Garnish
> *Confectioners' sugar*
> *Shreds of lemon peel, if desired*
> *A crystalized or fresh violet, if desired*
> *A sprig of mint, if desired*

Serve the sponges in the baking cups while warm. Sprinkle with confectioners' sugar and, if you desire, a few shreds of lemon peel, a crystalized violet, fresh violet, or a sprig of mint to give this dessert a festive air.

Arabic Milk Pudding with
Pomegranate and Pistachio Nuts

Serves 5

The mottled skin of the pomegranate encloses countless small seeds that are surrounded by garnet, tart, sweet-fleshed kernels. When eaten, they veritably burst their red juices upon contact. This simple, rose-scented pudding with a touch of the Middle East relies upon the color and the flavor of the pomegranate kernels in contrast with green pistachio nuts. The result of red and green is a Christmas-colored dessert.

Pudding
    2 tablespoons rice
    3½ cups milk
    3 tablespoons cornstarch
    4 tablespoons sugar
    Pinch of salt
    1 teaspoon vanilla extract
    Rose Water Syrup (recipe follows)

Grind the rice in a blender or spice grinder until pulverized. There should be 3 tablespoons. Put ½ cup of the milk into a small measuring cup and add the ground rice and cornstarch. Mix well to combine and set aside.

In a medium-size nonstick saucepan, add the remaining milk, the sugar, and pinch of salt. Bring the mixture slowly to a boil, then lower the heat to medium and add the rice-cornstarch mixture in a steady stream, stirring constantly while the milk gently boils. Lower the heat and cook 3 minutes more, stirring well. Add the vanilla and pour into individual serving cups that have been rinsed in cold water and left damp. Chill in the refrigerator for at least 6 hours. While the pudding chills, make the rosewater syrup, and prepare the pomegranates.

Rose Water Syrup
    ¾ cup cold water
    4 tablespoons superfine sugar
    2 tablespoons rose water (see note)
    Pistachio nuts, skinned and lightly toasted for garnish

Boil the water with the sugar for 5 minutes. Remove from the heat and add the rose water. Chill.

Pomegranate
    Kernels from one pomegranate

Lay a sheet of foil over a cutting board since the juices of a pomegranate will stain. Cut the pomegranate in quarters from blossom end to stem, grasp the corners, and turn each section inside out. The whole kernels will pop out. Loosen the other kernels with the tip of a sharp knife and remove any white pith.

Just before serving, pour 1 tablespoon of the syrup over the top of each serving. Sprinkle with coarsely chopped pistachio nuts and pomegranate kernels.

Note: Rose water is available in specialty stores and Middle Eastern and Indian food shops.

Rhubarb Kissel with Cardamom

This is one of those desserts that has many spellings. For instance, this Russian version is known as *kisyel, kisel* and *kissel*. There is a common denominator, however, for no matter how it's spelled, it's always thickened with potato starch to give it a glossy, translucent look. Originally, in the Soviet Union, it was made with soured cereal water and then prepared with stone fruits such as peaches and plums. The skins and the pits were kept as a part of the recipe in order to extract as much flavor from the fruit as possible. Here, we have used rhubarb, a plant from the Volga region, and it makes a pale, rose dessert that is dusted with cardamom.

> *¾ cup sugar*
> *2 cups water*
> *1½ pounds trimmed rhubarb, cut into one inch pieces (about 6 cups)*
> *Pinch of salt*
> *¼ teaspoon ground cardamom*
> *2 tablespoons potato starch (see note)*
> *¼ cup cold water*
> *Whipped cream*

In a large saucepan, dissolve the sugar in the 2 cups of water and then bring slowly to a boil without stirring. Boil for 2 minutes. Add the fruit and salt and bring to a boil again, lower the heat, and simmer uncovered for 10 minutes, or until the fruit is very soft. Press the fruit against a nonreactive nylon or stainless steel sieve until only a bit of pulp is left. Discard the pulp. There should be 3 cups of purée. Return to the saucepan and add the cardamom and simmer. Mix the potato starch with the ¼ cup cold water and slowly add while stirring constantly. Cook, stirring, over medium heat for 2 to 3 minutes, or until thickened and glossy.

Pour the mixture into four individual serving bowls, cool, and then cover with plastic wrap and refrigerate for 2 hours or more. Before serving, dust the surface lightly with additional ground cardamom and drop five small ¼-teaspoon drops of whipped cream in a "polka dot" pattern on the surface. Pull the tip of a paring knife through each dot to form tiny hearts.

Note: Potato starch can be purchased at health food stores and specialty shops.

Röte Grütze

Serves 4 to 6

This is a German version of a red berry flummery and it is typical of those that are made with berries as well as the addition of fruit juice. It is thickened and then poured into a ring mold, served with whipped cream and additional berries to decorate.

⅓ cup sugar
3 tablespoons water
Pinch of cream of tartar
½ cup dry red wine
1 cup cranberry-raspberry juice
1 cup cranberries or red currants
1 cup strawberries, fresh or frozen, plus 3 or 4 extra berries
3 cups raspberries, fresh or frozen, plus ½ cup extra berries
Pinch of salt
¼ cup quick-cooking tapioca (see note)
1 teaspoon lemon juice
1 tablespoon kirsch
1 cup heavy cream, whipped

In a medium-size saucepan, combine the sugar and water until the sugar dissolves. Add the cream of tartar and bring to a boil. Boil for 2 minutes, then add the wine and cranberry-raspberry juice. Reduce the heat and add all the berries. Simmer for 10 minutes, or until the berries are tender and purée in a food processor. Force the purée through a strainer and discard the seeds and skins. Return the purée to the same saucepan over medium heat. Whisk the tapioca into the purée and cook for 5 minutes, until thick and translucent. Then, using a rubber spatula, spoon into a 3-cup ring mold dampened with water. Cool for 20 minutes, cover with plastic wrap, and chill for at least 4 hours.

When ready to serve, run a thin knife around the edge of the mold and invert onto a serving dish. Spoon whipped cream into the center of the ring and sprinkle the reserved berries over the cream and around the base of the ring.

Note: Tapioca is an excellent thickening agent with both density and body. Its viscosity increases as it cools, leaving a transparent product that does *not* change, as cornstarch does, if you add it after sugar and lemon juice.

Danish Rødgrød Med Fløde
(Red Fruit Pudding)

Serves 6

We have taken some liberties with this Danish red berry pudding. Traditionally, it's made with red currants and raspberries with a lot of water. The juice is then strained and thickened with potato starch and flavored with vanilla. Our version uses almost no water and relies on strawberries which are more readily available than red currants. As most things Danish, this dessert reflects the spare elegance of the country. Honor it by serving it in your best crystal goblets.

> 1 pound ripe hulled strawberries (or a 20-ounce package of
>   frozen, defrosted, unsweetened strawberries, reserving 4
>   ounces for garnish)
> ¾ pound ripe raspberries (or a 12-ounce package of frozen,
>   defrosted raspberries, reserving 4 ounces for garnish)
> 4 tablespoons sugar
> 2 tablespoons arrowroot or potato starch (see note)
> ¼ cup cold water
> 2 teaspoons lemon juice
> 1 teaspoon vanilla extract
> Sliced almonds for garnish
> 1 cup light cream

Purée the berries in a food processor and force through a fine sieve into a nonreactive medium-size saucepan. Stir in the sugar and bring to a boil over medium-high heat, stirring constantly. Mix the arrowroot and water until dissolved, then lower the heat to medium and stir it into the purée. Cook, stirring constantly until thickened, about 1 to 2 minutes. Do not allow it to boil again. Remove from the heat and stir in the lemon juice and vanilla. Let cool for 10 minutes and spoon into crystal goblets or a glass dessert dish. Cover with plastic wrap and chill for at least 2 hours or longer.

Serve topped with a whole berry and sliced almonds on each serving and pass a pitcher of cream to be poured at the table.

Note: Both arrowroot and potato starch are translucent thickening agents. They attain their maximum thickening power *before* boiling temperature is reached. High sustained heat and stirring will cause thinning. Potato starch is translucent but it also gives a sparkling quality to the finished dessert. With both, the viscosity increases as they cool.

Middle Eastern Apricot Flummery
(Mishmush Pudding)

Since perfectly ripe, fresh, ambrosial apricots are hard to come by these days, we have chosen to use the whole, dried variety for this recipe. A considerable amount of the world's apricot crop is actually picked for drying, and the intense flavor required for this simple flummery is best obtained from the dried fruit rather than from the inferior flavor of the fresh fruit. *Amradin,* or *apricot leather* is sometimes used to make this dessert. The "leather" is made by rubbing fresh apricots through a sieve and leaving them on trays to be sun dried.

> *¾ pound pitted, dried apricots*
> *4½ cups water*
> *3 tablespoons cornstarch (see note)*
> *¼ cup fine sugar*
> *1½ teaspoons orange flower water*
> *1 cup heavy cream, whipped*
> *Sliced almonds*

In a 2½-quart nonstick saucepan, soak the apricots in 2 cups of the water overnight. Add 1 more cup of water and bring it all to a boil. Lower the heat, cover the saucepan, and simmer for about 45 minutes, or until the fruit is very soft. Let cool for 10 minutes and then purée in a blender. (Do *not* use a food processor.)

There should be about 2⅔ cups of purée. Scrape back into the saucepan with a rubber spatula. Stir in 1¼ cups of water and cook over medium heat for 1 to 2 minutes. Mix 3 tablespoons of cornstarch with the remaining ¼ cup of water and slowly stir it into the purée. Cook, stirring constantly until the mixture starts to boil. When it begins to boil, cook, stirring, for only 1 or 2 minutes more, then stir in the sugar. Remove from the heat and add the orange flower water. Let cool 10

minutes, then distribute among 6 glass serving bowls or goblets. Chill for at least 2 hours. When ready to serve, top with a dollop of whipped cream and scatter a few sliced almonds over the cream.

Note: Cornstarch is a thickening agent that leaves a shiny transparent finish. Do not boil more than 2 minutes. Add sugar and any acidic ingredient such as lemon juice, only *after* it coagulates. If heated for too long, cornstarch will lose its thickening power.

Blackberry Flummery with Gin

In this simple recipe, the gin brings out the flavor of the blackberries.

> 2 cups blackberries
> Pinch of salt
> 2 cups water
> 3½ tablespoons cornstarch
> ½ cup fine sugar, or to taste
> 1 tablespoon lemon juice
> 2 tablespoons gin
> Heavy cream

In a medium-size nonstick saucepan, combine the blackberries, salt, and 1⅓ cups of the water. Simmer the berries without stirring for about 10 to 15 minutes. Dissolve the cornstarch in the remaining water and add slowly to the berries, stirring constantly. Simmer, stirring, for 2 minutes.

Remove from the heat and add the sugar, lemon juice, and gin. Taste to see if any additional sugar is needed. Cool for 10 minutes then spoon into individual glass serving bowls or wine goblets. Serve at room temperature or chilled. If you like, trickle 3 or 4 stripes of cream over the surface and run a knife through the stripes for a decorative surface effect.

Note: We did not sieve the berries in this flummery. We thought that the seeds added a bit of crunch. However, if you wish to remove the seeds and make a smoother dessert, do so *after* the flavorings are added.

Sweet Symbiosis

Cheese and Fruit Marriages

Some time back, and for a period of well over five years, we were lucky enough to have had an office in Rome, a glorious base from which we traveled on our film trips, making documentaries for Alitalia Airlines. And, along with millions of other travelers to that delicious country, we brought back memories of long, leisurely lunches during the sultry days of summer, our table shaded by colorful umbrellas or the swelling grape vines draped over secluded arbors. To say the least, we—as any other traveler who has had that experience—were usually loathe to finish eating and to get back to the bustle and the hysteria of our favorite European city.

We remember quite vividly the feeling of ease and good spirits that overwhelmed us as the dessert courses were served. The Italian (and French) custom is to serve a course of cheese, followed by a bowl of fresh fruit bathing in icy water. And, though we do not fault their way, we have noticed that Americans tend to combine the two courses into one serving—a wedge of some sort of cheese along with a piece of fresh fruit on the same plate. Cheese and fruit for dessert, along with a crusty loaf of bread and some wine is an irresistible combination. What better way to delay the return to reality than to peel or slice a ripe peach slowly. It is the very essence of summer.

Cheese and fruit can constitute an entire light meal or they can marry to make a wide range of desserts from compotes to rich, creamy cakes, bombes, pies, and tarts. Colorful grapes and creamy goat cheese make a good contrast both visually and in taste. Pears and Stilton cheese have been happily married for many years in Great Britain. Cascos de guayaba and salty South American white cheese are another marriage made in Heaven. The French *coeur à la crème,* the traditional white cheese heart surrounded by fresh red strawberries will probably not seek a divorce for centuries to come. And, here in our own country, many of us think that a slice of apple pie is incomplete without a wedge of aged golden Cheddar cheese. In fact, the nineteenth century poet, Eugene Field, took it a step further. He was convinced that it was actually good for you:

> No matter what conditions
> Dyspeptic come to feaze,
> The best of all physicians
> Is Apple Pie and cheese.

Cheese and fruit, no matter how we combine them, make a truly felicitous combination, and in this section of the book, we have tried to offer a whole new world of surprising, yet compatible relationships. Separately, they give pleasure. Together, they are perfectly paired.

Layered Raspberry Almond Cream

Serves 4

If you use a food processor, this is an extremely easy-to-prepare dessert. The almond cream is a tangy cream cheese base sandwiched between layers of jewellike raspberries.

4 ounces cream cheese, cut into pieces
2 tablespoons Amaretto
½ cup fine sugar
½ cup heavy cream
1½ to 2 cups fresh raspberries
4 sprigs fresh mint

Put the cream cheese, Amaretto, and sugar into the bowl of a food processor and process until combined. Slowly pour the cream through the feed tube while the processor is on. The mixture should have the consistency of stiffly whipped cream.

Using wine goblets or glass dessert dishes, distribute 1 cup of the raspberries among the 4 glasses, and spoon in equal amounts of the almond cream. Stud the surface with the remaining raspberries and garnish each portion with a sprig of fresh mint.

Guava Shells Stuffed with
Lime Ricotta Cheese

Serves 4

Guava trees—actually more like shrubs than trees—grow profusely in Mexico and Hawaii. Their oval-shaped, thin-skinned fruits are becoming more available now that they are also being cultivated in Florida and California. At one time, they were only available canned and were cloyingly sweet. They were plunked down with a wedge of cream cheese and saltine crackers as the ubiquitous dessert in every Mexican restaurant. Gratefully, the fresh guava bears no resemblance to its canned cousin, nor does this delicate, fresh dessert.

4 fresh guavas
1 cup water
3 tablespoons sugar
1 cup ricotta cheese
1 tablespoon lime juice
1 tablespoon finely minced lime peel plus a few extra shreds for
*   garnish*
Sprigs of mint for garnish
Coarse salt

Wash, dry, and slice the ends off the guavas. Cut each fruit in half horizontally. There is no need to peel the fruit. With the tip of a sharp knife, make a circle in the center of each half and scoop out the parts that contain the tough seeds. Discard the seeds. The remaining half fruit will be a cuplike container. Set aside.

In a saucepan, boil the water and sugar together for 2 minutes. Add the fruit and poach over medium high heat for 3 to 4 minutes. Lift out with a slotted spoon and place on a serving platter and chill.

Boil down the remaining syrup over high heat for 3 to 4 minutes, or until it is reduced to only 2 tablespoons, and set aside to cool.

In a small bowl, mix together the cheese, lime juice, and lime peel and spoon into the center of the shells. Trickle a ribbon of syrup over the cheese and scatter a few shreds of additional lime peel on the surface. Garnish each with a mint leaf. Just before serving, sprinkle with coarse salt to bring out additional flavor.

Lemon Ricotta Cheese with Rosemary and Glazed and Frosted Red Grapes

Serves 6

The flavors of Tuscany are beautifully blended in this baked cheese and lemon mold, redolent of rosemary and wreathed in clusters of glazed red grapes.

Lemon Ricotta Cheese
   3 eggs
   ¾ cup sugar
   2½ teaspoons finely minced lemon peel
   ½ teaspoon vanilla extract
   1 tablespoon finely minced fresh rosemary
   1 pound ricotta cheese

Preheat the oven to 350 degrees and boil a kettle of water. Spray a 3-cup brioche mold lightly with a vegetable oil spray or butter the mold lavishly with soft butter and set it aside. Put the eggs into the bowl of a food processor and process for a few pulses. While the processor is on, slowly add the sugar through the feed tube and continue to process until the mixture is thick and pale yellow. Add all the remaining ingredients and continue to process until well combined. Pour into the prepared brioche mold and place the mold in a larger pan. Pour enough boiling water into the large pan to reach halfway up the sides of the mold.

Cover the top of the mold with a piece of aluminum foil and bake in the water bath for 45 to 50 minutes. The center of the mold will firm up later as it cools. When baked, remove the mold from the water bath and cool completely on a wire rack. Then chill the mold in the refrigerator for at least 3 hours. One hour before serving, prepare the fruit.

Fruit

    30 red seedless grapes
    1 egg white, beaten lightly until foamy
    Granulated sugar
    1 recipe Clear Orange Glaze (page 201)
    Rosemary sprigs

Dip half the grapes into the egg white and then roll them in sugar. Air dry them on a wire rack until ready to serve. Dip the remaining grapes in the warmed orange glaze and dry on a wire rack.

When ready to serve, dip the mold in warm water and invert onto a serving plate. Alternate the glazed and frosted grapes in clusters of 3 or 5 in a wreath around the base of the mold. Tuck in a few sprigs of fresh rosemary between the grape clusters.

Stilton Cheese Tartlets with Ruby Port Glazed Pears and Roasted Walnuts

Serves 6

What could be more British than a dessert of Port, Stilton and walnuts? Here is an embellished version: a crustless tartlet using only a minimum amount of the intensely flavored Stilton, baked into a rich, savory mold and served with Ruby Port–glazed pears and a few roasted walnuts.

Tartlets
> 2 eggs
> 2 tablespoons heavy cream
> 3 ounces cream cheese, cut into small pieces
> 2 teaspoons fine dry bread crumbs
> ¼ pound Stilton cheese, crumbled

Preheat the oven to 300 degrees. Brush ¼ cup tartlet pans lavishly with melted butter or spray with vegetable oil. (The tartlet pans should *not* have a removable base or the filling will leak out.) Process the eggs and cream in a food processor until well blended. Add the cream cheese and bread crumbs and process until smooth. Add the Stilton and process for just a few pulses (the mixture should have tiny pieces of Stilton in a smooth base.)

Spoon 3 tablespoons of the cheese mixture into the prepared pans and set the pans in a larger pan. Pour one cup of boiling water around the tart pans and bake for 20 to 25 minutes. Remove the pans from the water bath with tongs, and cool for 30 minutes before unmolding. Tap smartly upside down on a wooden board to unmold.

Pears

    3 Bartlett or Anjou pears, peeled, cut in half, and cored
    1 small wedge lemon
    3 tablespoons light honey
    ½ cup Ruby Port
    ⅛ teaspoon cinnamon
    18 roasted walnut halves

Preheat oven to 375 degrees. Butter a baking dish large enough to accommodate the six half pears in one layer. Squeeze a few drops of lemon juice over the pears. Mix the honey and Port and pour over and around the pears. Sprinkle with cinnamon and bake for 20 to 25 minutes until tender but firm, basting occasionally. Cool and transfer the pears to individual serving dishes. Pour the sauce into a small saucepan and reduce until glossy and syrupy, and spoon the sauce over the pears.

Using a wide spatula, transfer the cheese tartlet to the serving plate with the pears. Arrange 3 roasted walnut halves between the tartlet and the pears.

Sicilian Orange Espresso Cheesecake

Serves 10

This is a coffee-flavored cheesecake in a crisp, almond cookie crust topped with glazed oranges, cream, and almonds. It is a truly Sicilian, voluptuous extravaganza!

Crust

   36 single Amaretti cookies
   ¼ cup fine, dry bread crumbs
   6 tablespoons butter, melted

Preheat the oven to 400 degrees. Butter a 9-inch springform pan. Put cookies in a food processor and process to make fine crumbs. Reserve ¼ cup of the cookie crumbs. Transfer to a mixing bowl, add the bread crumbs and stir in the butter. Press the mixture on the bottom of the pan and one third of the way up the sides. Bake for 5 minutes and cool completely.

Filling

   4 tablespoons sugar
   3 tablespoons Cointreau or other orange-flavored liqueur
   2 envelopes unflavored gelatin
   ¾ cup boiling water
   2 tablespoons Medaglia D'oro instant espresso powder
   2 15-ounce containers of ricotta cheese
   1 teaspoon vanilla extract
   1 cup heavy cream

Mix the sugar and Cointreau in a small saucepan, sprinkle the gelatin over them, and let stand for 5 minutes. Combine the boiling water and espresso and pour into the gelatin mixture. Stir over low heat for 1 to 2 minutes. Remove from the heat and chill the coffee mixture in the

refrigerator for 30 to 40 minutes, or until slightly thickened to the consistency of raw egg white.

Beat the ricotta cheese and vanilla in a food processor until smooth. Add the coffee mixture and process until combined. Transfer to a large mixing bowl and set aside. Beat the whipped cream until stiff, using a hand or electric beater, and gently fold into the cheese mixture. Spoon into the prebaked crust. Cover tightly with plastic wrap and chill for several hours, preferably overnight.

Topping
   1 navel orange, peeled and thinly sliced, and cut into halves
   ½ cup Clear Orange Glaze (page 201)
   Whipped cream
   Sliced almonds for garnish, if desired

Loosen the sides of the crust with a thin spatula. Place the cake on a serving plate, keeping it on its metal base. Remove the springform ring. Arrange overlapping orange halves on top in the center of the cake, leaving a 1-inch border. Spoon warm orange glaze over the oranges. Sprinkle the reserved ¼ cup of Amaretti crumbs around the outside border of the cake, pipe a few rosettes of whipped cream over the crumbs, and sprinkle a few sliced almonds over the oranges.

Wild Maine Blueberry and Cottage Cheese Pudding with Blueberry Orange Sauce

Serves 8

If you have ever been privileged to be in Maine during the wild blueberry season, and you've sampled these tiny black pearls of flavor, you may well have glimpsed the portals of culinary heaven. The tiny, extremely flavorful wild Maine blueberries have a short local season when freshly picked. However, they are now available in 15-ounce cans, packed in syrup and can be substituted for the fresh berries.

Pudding
> 2¼ cups cream-style cottage cheese (1½-pound container)
> ½ cup sour cream
> ¼ cup sugar
> Pinch of salt
> 2 teaspoons vanilla extract
> ½ teaspoon ground cardamom
> 3 eggs
> 1 cup coarsely broken, toasted walnuts
> 1 15-ounce can drained wild Maine blueberries, or 1 cup fresh
>   blueberries

Preheat the oven to 300 degrees and butter a 1½-quart soufflé dish. In a food processor, process the cheese until smooth, then add the sour cream, sugar, salt, vanilla, and cardamom. Continue processing and add the eggs, one at a time, until they are well combined. Spoon the mixture into a mixing bowl and add the toasted walnuts. Fold in drained blueberries. If you are using fresh blueberries, cook them lightly in ¾ cup water with some sugar; reserve the liquid in both cases.

Pour into the prepared baking dish and bake for 1 hour and 15 minutes. Turn off the oven and keep the door of the oven ajar for 5 to

10 minutes before removing. Serve warm with Blueberry Orange Sauce spooned over the pudding.

Blueberry Orange Sauce
 1 cup reserved blueberry liquid
 Pinch of salt
 2 teaspoons cornstarch
 ½ teaspoon vanilla extract
 1 teaspoon finely minced orange peel

Combine ½ cup of the reserved blueberry liquid with the salt and the cornstarch in a small nonstick saucepan. Stir constantly over low heat until thickened and dark, about 3 to 4 minutes. Remove from the heat and add the remaining ½ cup blueberry liquid, vanilla, and orange peel. Keep warm, or reheat before serving.

Strawberry Cheese Bombe with
a Sauce of Blackberries and Crème de Cassis

Serves 8

A "bombe" actually refers to the dome-shaped mold used for making a layered ice cream dessert. Before modern refrigeration, the round bottom made it easier to keep ice cream cold when buried in shaved ice. This bombe is not made of ice cream; rather it is a year-round dessert made of cheese and frozen strawberries in a bombe-shaped stainless steel mixing bowl. We also think that it's a more appropriate winter dessert than ice cream.

Fruit and Cheese Mold
> 2 cups frozen unsweetened strawberries or fresh, ripe straw-
> berries, hulled
> ½ cup sugar
> 3 tablespoons kirsch
> 2 envelopes unflavored gelatin
> ⅓ cup cold water
> 3 tablespoons lime juice
> 1 pound cream-style cottage cheese
> ½ cup milk
> 8 ounces cream cheese, softened and cut into cubes
> 3 egg whites
> Pinch of salt
> ¼ cup fine sugar

Defrost the frozen strawberries completely, combine with the sugar and kirsch, and let stand for 20 minutes. Purée in a food processor; there will be 1¾ cups purée. Sprinkle the gelatin over the cold water in a small saucepan and let stand for 5 minutes. Heat over low heat, stirring to dissolve the gelatin. Remove from the heat, add the lime juice to the gelatin and add to the strawberry purée. Set aside.

The strawberry purée must not be cold, but served at room temperature, or the gelatin will make the purée stringy when added.

Combine the cottage cheese and milk in the bowl of a food processor and process until very smooth. Add the cream cheese and continue to process until smooth. Add the strawberry gelatin mixture and process until just blended. Scrape into a bowl with a rubber spatula and refrigerate for 15 to 20 minutes, stirring often, until the mixture thickens and mounds slightly.

Using a rotary hand beater, beat the egg whites and salt until foamy. Gradually add the sugar and continue to beat until soft peaks form, and fold into the strawberry-cheese mixture. Spray a 6-cup stainless steel bowl or mold with vegetable oil spray and spoon the mixture into it. Cover with plastic wrap and refrigerate for at least 4 to 5 hours.

Prepare Blackberry Sauce with Crème de Cassis while the mold is chilling.

Blackberry Sauce with Crème de Cassis   *Makes 1¼ cups*
    1¼ cups blackberries (frozen, unsweetened blackberries can
        also be used)
    ¼ cup cold water
    Pinch of salt
    1¼ cups sugar
    2 teaspoons lemon juice
    1 tablespoon crème de cassis

In a medium-size nonstick saucepan, combine 1 cup of the blackberries, water, salt, and sugar and bring to a boil. Lower the heat and simmer for 3 to 4 minutes. Let cool 5 minutes and add the lemon juice and crème de cassis. Purée in a food processor and force through a strainer to remove the seeds. Add the remaining whole blackberries.

When ready to serve, run the tip of a knife around the edge of the mold and unmold onto a chilled serving plate. Spoon some of the sauce over the top of the mold and let it trickle down the sides of the mold. Spoon the rest of the sauce with the whole blackberries around the base of the bombe.

Poached Pears and Pistachio Nuts Stuffed with Mascarpone

Serves 6

A most attractive combination—a glazed pear with a cache of mascarpone cheese showered with vibrant green crunchy pistachio nuts.

2 cups dry white wine
½ cup sugar
1 2-inch piece of cinnamon stick
1 1-inch piece of vanilla bean
1 2-inch piece of lemon peel
6 large, firm wide-based Comice pears (about ½ pound each)
¼ pound mascarpone cheese, at room temperature
⅔ cup coarsely chopped pistachio nuts, toasted

Using a nonreactive Dutch oven, or wide-based skillet, mix the wine and sugar until the sugar is dissolved. Add the cinnamon stick, vanilla bean, and lemon peel. Bring slowly to a boil, then reduce the heat and cook for 5 minutes.

Meanwhile, peel the pears with a vegetable parer, leaving the stems intact. Cut a thin slice off the bottom of each pear to steady them and place the pears upright in the simmering poaching liquid. Cover the pot tightly and cook over low heat, basting occasionally, for 15 minutes or until the pears are tender but firm. Remove the pears carefully with a slotted spoon and place them on their sides on paper towels to drain and cool. Bring the poaching liquid to a boil, then lower the heat to a low boil and reduce to ⅔ cup of syrup. Remove and discard the lemon peel, cinnamon stick, and vanilla bean. Pour syrup into a bowl and refrigerate for 15 minutes, or until it has thickened.

While the syrup is cooling, use a melon baller to remove a round cavity at the core of the base of each pear. Mash the softened cheese with a fork and put about 1 teaspoon of cheese into each pear cavity. Brush the base and about one inch of the bottom side of the pears with the glazed thickened syrup and press the pistachio nuts into the glaze. Arrange the pears upright on a serving dish and brush the tops of the pears with the remaining glaze. Sprinkle only a few more pistachio nuts over the top, spooning any remaining glaze around the bottom of the serving dish.

New York Style Cranberry and Orange Cheesecake

This is a flagrant indulgence—a rich and dense yet light and crustless cheesecake, the kind that New Yorkers prefer when breaking good diet principles. It's a shared intemperance we all feel we've earned at various moments in our busy lives.

The Cheesecake
> 3 8-ounce packages cream cheese at room temperature, cut into
>   large pieces
> ¾ cup sugar
> 5 eggs, separated
> Salt
> 1 cup sour cream
> 3 tablespoons flour
> 1 tablespoon vanilla extract
> 2 teaspoons finely minced lemon peel

Preheat the oven to 325 degrees and butter a 9-inch springform pan. In a food processor, beat the cheese and sugar until smooth. Add the egg yolks one at a time and process until well blended. Add the flour, vanilla, and lemon peel and continue to process until smooth.

Beat the egg whites in a bowl with another pinch of salt, using a rotary hand or electric beater, until the whites are stiff, but not dry. Fold 2 cups of the cheese mixture into the egg whites, using a rubber spatula. Add the remaining cheese mixture and continue to fold until no white shows. Pour into the prepared pan and place the pan on a piece of aluminum foil with the edges turned up to catch any drippings while the cake bakes.

Bake for one hour and 10 minutes, or until the top is lightly golden. Turn off the oven, leaving the cake in it for 1 hour or longer with the door slightly ajar. Remove and cool at room temperature before chilling in the refrigerator overnight. The cake will shrink a bit from the sides and will also sink somewhat in the center.

Cranberry Topping   *Makes 1 cup*
    2 cups cranberries, fresh or frozen
    ¼ cup orange or tangerine juice
    ¾ cup sugar
    1 tablespoon arrowroot
    1 teaspoon finely minced orange or tangerine peel
    Long shreds of orange or tangerine peel for garnish, made with
        a zester tool.

Combine the cranberries, orange or tangerine juice, and sugar in a saucepan. Cook 3 to 4 minutes, or until the cranberries just begin to pop. Add the arrowroot, stir, and continue cooking for 1 to 2 minutes, or until the mixture thickens. Stir in the minced orange peel, cook, and then chill. This topping can be prepared a day in advance and kept in the refrigerator.

When ready to serve, run a warm, damp knife around the edge of the cake and remove the springform ring, leaving the cake on the metal base for support. Spoon the cranberry topping evenly over the cake and sprinkle long shreds of orange or tangerine peel over the cranberries.

Gingered Figs with Cream Cheese

Serves 4

Tiny explosions of ginger burst pleasantly on your tongue, soothed by cool white cream cheese to temper the tingle. The delicate violet pulpy-centered fig with its mottled chartreuse and purple exterior contains and controls it all.

8 large fresh figs
1 3-ounce package softened cream cheese
2 tablespoons finely minced preserved stem ginger
1 tablespoon sugar
2 tablespoons water
2 tablespoons preserved ginger syrup

Cut each fig crosswise one quarter of the way down the length. Using a small demitasse spoon, make a well in the bottom half of each fig by scooping out the soft center containing the tiny seeds. Add this pulp to the cream cheese in a small bowl along with the minced ginger. Mash well with a fork until the ginger is incorporated. Spoon the cheese back into the bottom halves of the figs and replace the tops. Put 2 stuffed figs in each of four separate serving dishes.

In a small saucepan, dissolve the sugar in the water over medium heat. Add the ginger syrup and bring to a boil. Boil hard for 2 to 3 minutes. Let the bubbles subside, then baste the figs with the syrup to glaze them. Serve with a sharp knife and fork.

Note: If you have access to a fig tree, slip one fig leaf under each portion before serving.

Sweet Seductions

Light, Airy, and Elegant

We might say that this chapter is devoted to "puffy witchcraft," for all the recipes are based on the adaptable egg combined with fruit and on the techniques that turn them into light, airy concoctions. They are all quite different, yet they are all related. And, they are all puffy.

The magic ingredient is the foamy, beaten egg white and we rely upon it for many of the desserts that follow. Add some sugar to the egg white and the resulting meringue can be turned into a tempting display of kitchen wizardry. However, here again we must let our imaginations expand, for when we think of meringue, the American reaction is *Lemon Meringue Pie,* and fortunately that is but a small part of the tale.

The meringue on the above-mentioned pie is actually what pastry chefs call *soft meringue* or *pie topping.* But when the French speak of it, they are thinking of *Swiss meringue* or a *hard meringue* that is then used as the base or container for the rest of the dessert. For example, a *Vacherin* (page 258) is a recipe that uses a classic Swiss meringue with the addition of ground nuts. The meringue requires more sugar, more beating of the egg whites, and a lower baking temperature for a longer period of time than the American pie meringue.

The *Pavlova* is another Swiss meringue that contains fresh fruit and is topped by whipped cream. The classic of all meringue might well be the dessert made in the finest Viennese Baroque tradition, The *Spanish Wind Torte,* an elaborately piped decorated meringue with swirls and curlicues, rosettes, candied violets, and silver dragées, an extravaganza that no home cook would dare try for dinner guests!

To simplify is sometimes to confuse, for there is yet another entry, the *Italian meringue.* This one does not require any baking, although it is sometimes lightly browned for color. The stiffly beaten egg whites are "cooked" by the addition of a hot sugar syrup that is beaten in. It's used to frost cakes and is sometimes mixed with fruit purées.

As with most other basic ingredients, meringues can be handled in a number of ways, each one delivering a variation in texture, taste, or presentation. In *Oeufs à la Neige* (Snow Eggs), the meringue is poached, while in *Petites Iles Flottantes* (page 270) it is baked. The Hungarian inspired *Witches' Froth* is a dessert that combines a mixture of apple purée or other fruit purées, beaten together with egg white, as it gathers more and more volume.

The adaptable egg can also be fashioned into the fragile, but intimidating *hot soufflé,* an airy, baked sweet dish with a base of milk, butter, flour, egg yolks, sugar, and flavoring. Steam forms, created by the liquid in the mixture, and the air beaten into the egg white expands until the soufflé rises. If the air cells do not expand sufficiently, the soufflé will be unstable and much flatter than it should be. If the whites are overbeaten, the cell walls will break down and lose their elasticity, resulting in a dry, lumpy soufflé that will probably collapse like a deflated balloon.

Because a properly made soufflé must be served without delay, a great many expensive restaurants have the terrible habit of requiring that you order your soufflé dessert even before you have managed to select the hors d'oeuvres! Then, as you sit back and try to relax, the creation is rushed to your table by a waiter who might well use a pair of roller skates, so that this crowning achievement will not deflate before you sink a spoon into it.

It is a practice that we must admit we abhor, for who really wants to choose a dessert *before* selecting the rest of the meal? On the other hand, having attempted soufflés at home, we can thoroughly sympathize with the chef, for timing is so very critical. Luckily, for those of us who entertain in our homes, there is a solution, that of the *Cold Soufflé,* which is more like a mousse or a bavarois and which does not have that sense of urgency since it can be made as far in advance as the day before.

Sometime back, when we lived in Salzburg, Austria, for a period of two years, we fell in love with the *Salzburger Nöckerl* (page 268), a delightfully airy egg dessert that also relies on volume under a delicate, lightly golden crust. The center of these creamy poufs are soft and, unfortunately, they collapse quickly, just like a soufflé. However,

unlike a soufflé, which needs more elaborate prepreparation and at least 30 minutes baking time in order for it to rise, the *nöckerl* needs less than 15 minutes in the oven to firm it up. It might well be described as "creamy baked air."

There is also an interesting egg-base dessert called a *Dutch Baby* (page 266), and though we have done our research quite diligently, we cannot find the origin of its name. Basically it's similar to a large popover batter, which whimsically and capriciously changes its shape each time it's baked. It puffs up like magic, and then the center falls, leaving a depression that is just the perfect container for fresh fruit.

The *clafouti* (of which we have included five), is another bit of egg and fruit wizardry. This rustic, puffed spongelike cross between a pancake and a soufflé is of French origin, and the easiest fruit and egg combination to make. When the *clafouti* is served warm right from the oven in an earthenware dish, and dusted with a light shower of confectioners' sugar, it conjures up visions of a French farm kitchen with rough stone walls somewhere in the Limousin, where this dessert originated.

Cervantes wrote in *Don Quixote,* "As one egg is like another," probably because the author was just not a cook. The pure, simple egg, used in a variety of ways, offers a vast range of elegant desserts. And though working with eggs can sometimes be a tricky test of kitchen competence, we have always found the results worthwhile.

Vacherin Heart with
Blueberry Curd and Fraises Des Bois

Serves 4

The base is a nutty, sweet and crisp ivory-colored heart with a navy blue border of blueberries that surrounds the prize of tiny wild or woodlands strawberries. Unfortunately, the tiny strawberries are sometimes difficult for Americans to find since they come from Europe, and are terribly expensive when they do appear at the greengrocer or the farmer's market. However, they are quite easy to cultivate yourself anywhere that is sunny, in either a large container or directly in your garden, as we have done for some years. The berries have a subtle scent and the flavor of roses, and their compact, bushy, and very productive plants will yield their treasure throughout the summer. Of course, if you cannot find or grow these delicious wild strawberries, you can substitute others in the recipe.

Blueberry Curd
>   *1 cup blueberries*
>   *2 tablespoons water*
>   *¼ teaspoon finely minced lemon peel*
>   *2 tablespoons sugar*
>   *1 tablespoon butter*
>   *1 egg*

In a small saucepan, bring the blueberries, water, and lemon peel slowly to a boil and cook for 5 minutes. Purée in a blender, strain, and return to the saucepan. Add the sugar and butter, stirring until dissolved. Whisk the egg and add some of the hot purée to it, whisking all the while. Return the mixture to the saucepan and cook, whisking constantly, until thickened. Transfer to a small bowl, cool, and refrigerate.

Vacherin Heart

> *3 tablespoons whole blanched almonds*
> *2 tablespoons confectioners' sugar*
> *⅔ cup superfine sugar*
> *2 tablespoons cornstarch*
> *4 egg whites, at room temperature*
> *Pinch of salt*
> *¼ teaspoon cream of tartar*
> *A few drops white vinegar*
> *½ teaspoon pure almond extract*

Preheat the oven to 350 degrees. Place the whole almonds on a cookie sheet and toast for 5 minutes. Cool the almonds and lower the oven temperature to 225 degrees. When the almonds are cool, grind them very fine in a blender. Sift the confectioners' sugar over the nuts and stir gently to combine. Set aside.

On a piece of parchment paper cut to the size of a cookie sheet draw a heart measuring 8 inches across the widest part and 8 inches from tip of the heart to the center top where the heart indents. Trace the outline with a permanent marking pen and turn the paper over so the heart is visible but the ink will not come off onto the Vacherin. Tape the parchment down at the corners of the cookie sheet. Spray very lightly with vegetable oil spray and sift flour over the heart. Tap the cookie sheet to remove any excess flour and set aside.

Mix the superfine sugar with the cornstarch and sift together into a measuring cup; set aside. In a deep, stainless steel or copper bowl, beat the egg whites until foamy with an electric hand beater on low speed. Add the salt and cream of tartar and continue to beat until soft peaks form. Increase the speed of the beater and gradually add the sugar-cornstarch mixture, ¼ cup at a time, beating continuously. Add the vinegar and almond extract, beating until stiff peaks are formed, and the mixture is satiny white in color. Do not overbeat or the mixture will collapse.

(continued on next page)

Vacherin Heart (*cont.*)

Using a rubber spatula, fold the confectioners' sugar and ground nuts mixture into the meringue. Spread one half of the meringue in an even layer, covering the inside area of the heart. Drop the meringue by tablespoonfuls around the rim of the heart, pushing off the meringue with your fingers, smoothing it a bit so that the edge of the heart is built up to form a low wall. Bake for 2 hours, turn off the heat, and leave in the oven for 2 hours or longer with the door closed (overnight, if you can). The heart should be thoroughly dry and ivory colored. When cooled completely, turn the meringue upside-down onto your hand, and peel off the parchment paper. Then store in an airtight container until ready to use.

Topping
 ½ cup fraises des bois or 10 to 12 small strawberries
 Mint leaf or rose geranium leaf (optional) for garnish

Just before serving, spoon the blueberry curd into the center depression of the heart, smoothing it to fill completely. Arrange the fraises des bois close together in the center in a triangular shape, leaving a border of blueberry curd visible. Add a green leaf of mint at the top or a rose geranium leaf, if desired.

Note: It is also possible to make three individual hearts with this recipe. However, if you do, shorten the baking time to one hour, plus one hour with the oven off. Use 1 tablespoon of the blueberry curd and 1 tablespoon of the fraises des bois for each heart.

Strawberry Witches' Froth

Serves 8

You may call it *Hexenschaum* like the Austrians do, or *Witches' Froth,* but we call it "easy magic." Just 10 minutes with an electric hand beater, some fruit purée, flavoring, and egg whites, and dessert is ready for 8 people!

2 cups very ripe, juicy strawberries, plus a few for garnish
½ cup confectioners' sugar
Pinch of salt
1 teaspoon Chambord liqueur
A few drops of lemon juice
3 egg whites, at room temperature
Mint sprigs or rose geranium leaves for garnish, if desired

Purée the strawberries, sugar, salt, liqueur, and lemon juice in a food processor. Transfer to a large deep bowl and add the egg whites. Beat the mixture at high speed with an electric hand beater for 10 to 15 minutes, or until the mixture is stiff enough to hold its shape and is tripled in volume. Pile large mounds into small wine glasses and decorate each glass with a few slices of strawberry and a sprig of mint or rose geranium leaf.

"Tarte" Citron

Serves 6 to 8

For those who have a fear of pastry, this "tarte" is a perfect compromise. It is crustless with paper thin slices of lemon sandwiched between a ground almond and egg cake and a cloud of glossy meringue.

> *4 eggs, separated*
> *⅔ cup sugar*
> *6 ounces blanched almonds*
> *1 tablespoon flour*
> *2 medium-size lemons*
> *4 egg whites*
> *Pinch of salt*
> *⅓ cup fine sugar plus 1 tablespoon*

Preheat the oven to 350 degrees and butter a 10-inch quiche pan. In a bowl, beat the egg yolks and sugar with an electric hand beater until very thick and pale. Set aside.

Wash and dry the beater. Grind almonds finely in a blender. There will be 1⅓ cups. Mix 1 cup of the ground almonds with the flour and set aside. With a vegetable parer, peel the zest of one lemon and mince finely. There should be 2 teaspoons. Stir into the almond-flour mixture.

Drop the 2 lemons into boiling water, turn off the heat, and let stand for 1 minute. Then rinse in cold water, remove the peel and white pith with a sharp knife, and cut the lemons horizontally into paper thin slices. Place on a flat plate and set aside. Beat the egg whites with the salt until stiff peaks form. Alternately fold the yolk mixture and almond-flour mixture, a bit at a time, into the beaten egg whites. Pour into the prepared pan and bake for 20 minutes or until golden. Leave the oven on and remove the cake. Let cool for 10 minutes, then place lemon slices over the entire surface. Sprinkle the one tablespoon of fine sugar over the lemon slices. In a bowl, beat the 4 extra egg whites, adding the remaining fine sugar, a few tablespoons at a time, until stiff glossy peaks form. Fold in the remaining ground almonds. Spoon the meringue over the lemon slices and with a rubber spatula dipped in cold water (to prevent the meringue from sticking), spread the meringue over the top. Return to the oven and bake for 10 to 12 minutes, or until the meringue is lightly browned.

Warm Rhubarb and Orange Soufflé

Serves 6 to 8

This is not a true soufflé, rather it is a dessert with a bit more holding power. A piquant orange custard forms at the bottom with a light delicate cakelike pudding on the surface. Between the two layers is tart, rose-colored rhubarb.

The Fruit

    1 pound trimmed, thin rhubarb stalks, cut into diagonal
        one-inch pieces (about 4 cups)
    1 tablespoon Grand Marnier, or other orange-flavored
        liqueur
    ⅓ cup sugar
    1 teaspoon cornstarch

Preheat the oven to 350 degrees and butter a 1½-quart soufflé dish. Toss the rhubarb in a medium-size bowl with the Grand Marnier. In a small cup, mix the sugar with the cornstarch and sprinkle over the rhubarb. Toss well and spoon into the prepared soufflé dish. Cover with foil and bake for 15 minutes. While the rhubarb is baking, prepare the soufflé.

The Soufflé

    2 tablespoons butter, softened
    ½ cup sugar
    2 eggs, separated
    1 tablespoon shredded orange peel made with a zester tool
    ½ cup orange juice (from 1 large navel orange)
    ½ cup milk
    ¼ cup flour
    Salt

In the bowl of a food processor, cream the butter and sugar until light in color. Add the egg yolks and process until thick and light. Add the orange peel, orange juice, and milk and process until combined. Sift the flour over the mixture and process for a few more pulses. In another bowl, using a rotary hand beater, beat the egg whites with a pinch of salt until stiff but not dry peaks form. Fold some of the egg-yolk mixture into the whites, then fold in the rest. Remove the rhubarb from the oven, take off the foil and pour the soufflé batter over it. Return to the oven and bake, uncovered, for 30 minutes until the soufflé has risen and is golden brown. Sprinkle the surface with a dusting of confectioners' sugar and serve warm.

Note: This dessert can also be made in individual 1-cup soufflé ramekins and baked for a total of 35 to 40 minutes.

Dutch Baby Filled with
Mixed Fruit

The dutch baby is a puffed, crisp, popoverlike baked pancake. The sides blow up, and the center remains hollow forming a natural container which is just perfect for holding an assortment of fresh fruit. Drain the fruit in advance and have the batter ready to slip into the oven just 30 minutes before you want to serve the dessert.

The Filling
> 1 cup small whole strawberries, hulled
> ½ cup blueberries
> 1½ cups peeled, pitted, and thickly sliced peaches
> 1½ cups peeled and thinly sliced pineapple
> ½ cup raspberries
> 2 tablespoons fine sugar
> 1 teaspoon lemon juice
> 2 tablespoons kirsch

In a large bowl, mix together the fruit, sugar, lemon juice, and kirsch and let stand for 30 minutes. Drain in a sieve and set aside.

Dutch Baby
> ¼ pound butter
> ½ cup flour
> ¼ teaspoon salt
> ⅛ teaspoon nutmeg
> 3 eggs
> ½ cup milk
> 1 tablespoon lemon juice
> 2 tablespoons confectioners' sugar

Preheat the oven to 425 degrees. Melt the butter slowly in a 9-inch black iron skillet with an ovenproof handle until the butter is hot and begins to bubble. Do not let it brown.

Sift the flour, salt, and nutmeg together in a small bowl. In another medium-size bowl, beat the eggs lightly with a whisk, add the milk, and add all the dry ingredients at once, whisking lightly. The batter should be slightly lumpy. Pour into the skillet with the hot butter, place on the bottom rack of the oven, and bake for 15 minutes without opening the oven. Pierce the bottom of the dutch baby with a knife in a few places, sprinkle the lemon juice on the bottom, and return to the oven. Lower the heat to 375 degrees and continue to bake for 10 to 15 minutes more, or until the sides have puffed up and browned and the center is only slightly moist.

Remove from the oven and pour the drained fruit into the center of the dutch baby. Sift confectioners' sugar over the fruit and serve from the pan at once.

Salzburger Nöckerl with Red Plum Purée

The French word *souffler* means to breathe, inflate, or puff up, hence the derivation of the term soufflé. This dessert is a traditional Austrian specialty, and though similar to a soufflé, is a much faster and easier version than the French. Mounds of airy, soft, and creamy soufflé puffs are covered with a delicate brown crust and are accompanied by a fruit purée rather than the fruit as a part of the soufflé itself.

Red Plum Purée
- ¼ *cup sugar plus 1 to 2 tablespoons fine sugar*
- ¼ *cup water*
- 6 *soft flavorful plums (about 1 pound), pitted and quartered*
- ½ *teaspoon kirsch*
- ½ *teaspoon vanilla extract*

In a medium-size saucepan, bring ¼ cup of the sugar and water to a boil. Boil for 1 minute, add the plums, and lower the heat. Simmer, covered, 15 to 20 minutes, stirring occasionally. The plums should be very soft. Cool for 10 minutes and purée without removing the skins in a food processor for a few pulses. The mixture should not be too smooth. Add the kirsch and vanilla, and add the remaining sugar to taste.

Salzburger Nöckerl
- 2 *tablespoons butter*
- 2 *tablespoons milk*
- 3 *eggs, separated*
- 2 *additional egg whites*
- ¼ *cup sugar*

268   FRESH FRUIT DESSERTS

1 teaspoon finely minced lemon peel
1 teaspoon vanilla extract
⅛ teaspoon salt
1 teaspoon flour
Confectioners' sugar

Preheat the oven to 450 degrees and butter the sides of a shallow ovenproof 10-inch oval baking dish with 1 tablespoon of the butter. Place the other tablespoon of butter and the milk in the baking dish and melt the butter in the oven. Remove, stir, and set aside.

In a medium-size bowl, add the egg yolks. In another larger bowl, place the 5 egg whites and set aside. Using an electric hand beater, beat the egg yolks until foamy, add the sugar, and beat until thick and pale yellow. Add the lemon peel and vanilla, and beat again. Set the mixture aside and wash and dry the beaters. In another bowl, beat the egg whites until frothy, add the salt, and sift the flour into the whites, beating until stiff and glossy. Fold the egg whites into the yolk mixture with a large rubber spatula. Scoop up four large, tall mounds of the mixture with the spatula and arrange in the prepared pan. Bake in the oven for 7 minutes, or until lightly brown. Sift confectioners' sugar over the surface and serve immediately along with the plum purée.

Petites Iles Flottantes with
Raspberry Purée and Starfruit

Serves 8

Oeufs à la Neige (or Snow Eggs) and L'Ile Flottante (or Floating Island) are different but similar and frequently confused. Traditionally prepared, the Oeufs à la Neige are *poached* in milk and the milk is then used for the preparation of a crème anglaise, in which they float. The dessert is then topped with golden threads of spun caramel (Angel's Hair) (certainly not an undertaking for damp weather or for the cook who gets flustered by last minute preparations!). For L'Ile Flottante, the meringue is *baked* in a large mold and also floats in a lake of crème anglaise. Here our sauce is an uncooked purée of fresh raspberries perfumed with kirsch rather than a crème anglaise and the meringue is baked in individual molds. We think it's a delightful variation.

Raspberry Kirsch Purée   *Makes 2½ cups*
    2 cups puréed raspberries (about 2 pints), seeds strained out
    ½ cup superfine sugar, or to taste
    1 tablespoon lemon juice
    ⅓ cup kirsch

Mix the raspberry purée with the sugar until the sugar dissolves. Stir in the lemon juice and kirsch. Taste to adjust the sweetness again after chilling in the refrigerator for 2 hours.

Baked Meringues
    4 to 5 large egg whites (about ¾ cup)
    Pinch of salt
    Pinch of cream of tartar
    ½ teaspoon cornstarch
    ½ cup superfine sugar
    1 teaspoon vanilla extract
    4 tablespoons coarsely chopped almonds

Garnish
   1 starfruit or peeled kiwi

Boil a kettle of water and preheat the oven to 300 degrees. Spray the insides of eight ¾-cup ovenproof custard cups or dariole molds with a vegetable oil spray, or brush them with melted clarified butter (page 67).

Using an electric hand beater, beat the egg whites with the salt, cream of tartar, and cornstarch until very foamy. Gradually add the sugar, one tablespoon at a time, beating until the meringue is stiff and glossy. When the last of the sugar has been added, add the vanilla and fold in the nuts. Spoon into the prepared cups. Place the cups in a larger pan and add enough hot water to the pan to reach 1½ inches up the sides of the molds and bake for 15 to 20 minutes, or until the tops appear golden and puffed. (Meringue will puff up as it bakes, but then shrink back a bit.)

Remove the cups from the oven and let cool. Cover the cups with waxed paper and chill in refrigerator for one hour. When ready to serve, gently invert onto individual serving plates. Spoon some raspberry purée around the base and arrange thin slices of starfruit or kiwi over the sauce.

Iron Skillet Apple Pancakes

Makes 16 to 18 pancakes,
serving 4

These pancakes may be a dessert, but they can also serve as the focal point for a weekend brunch. Crisp and surprisingly full of flavor, these simple little pancakes transcend the ordinary into the extraordinary.

1 egg
½ teaspoon vanilla extract
¾ cup pineapple-orange juice made from concentrate, or ½ cup
*   pineapple juice and ¼ cup orange juice combined*
1 cup flour
½ teaspoon baking powder
Pinch of salt
2 tablespoons sugar
¼ teaspoon cinnamon
1 large Granny Smith apple, peeled, cored, and quartered
1 small wedge of lemon
Corn oil for frying
Confectioners' sugar

In a small bowl, whisk the egg and vanilla together. Add the pineapple-orange juice and set aside. In another bowl, combine the flour, baking powder, salt, sugar, and cinnamon. Grate the apple using the shredding blade in a food processor or grate by hand. Squeeze the lemon over the apple and toss to coat. Heat a thin layer of corn oil in a heavy iron skillet. While the oil is heating, pour the egg-juice mixture over the apple then add to the dry ingredients, stirring well to mix.

Allow 1 rounded tablespoon per pancake and slide batter off the spoon into the hot oil with the push of a finger. Cook until the edges are golden brown and bubbles form on the surface, about 2 to 3 minutes. Turn and cook 2 to 3 minutes. Drain on paper towels and keep warm in the oven. Sprinkle with confectioners' sugar before serving.

Maple Peach Clafouti with Walnuts

Serves 8

The original recipe is of peasant origin from the Limousin region of France and is classically made with dark, sweet ripe cherries. The substitution of peaches and a maple-walnut flavor is our own variation on this traditional clafouti.

3 large ripe peaches, peeled, pitted, and thickly sliced (3½ cups)
1 tablespoon finely minced lemon peel
½ cup real maple syrup
4 eggs
1 cup milk
¼ cup heavy cream
Pinch of salt
1 teaspoon vanilla extract
1¼ cups flour
⅓ cup sugar
⅓ cup coarsely chopped toasted walnuts
¼ teaspoon cinnamon

In a large bowl, mix the peaches, lemon peel, and maple syrup. Let stand for 30 minutes. Preheat the oven to 350 degrees, butter a 10-inch-by-1½-inch nonstick tart or quiche pan without a removable base.

In the bowl of a food processor process the eggs, milk, cream, salt, and vanilla until well combined. Add the flour and sugar and process until smooth. (There will be 3 cups of batter.) Pour 1 cup of the batter into the baking dish and bake for 10 minutes, or until slightly firm.

Using a slotted spoon, remove the peaches from the accumulated liquid, reserving the liquid, and arrange them closely together over the partially baked batter. Sprinkle the walnuts and the cinnamon over the peaches and slowly pour the remaining 2 cups of batter over the fruit. Spoon the reserved liquid gently over the surface and bake for 35 to 40 minutes more or until the center is firm to the touch. Broil for a few minutes to brown the top. Let cool for 5 minutes before serving.

Italian Plum Clafouti with Cognac

Serves 6

This dessert takes advantage of the season from August to October when the small ink-blue plum brushed with its smokey haze graces our fruit stands and wayside markets. As the height of the season peaks and the prices drop, buy some to pit and freeze for year-round pleasure.

1 cup milk
⅓ cup heavy cream
3 eggs
2 teaspoons vanilla extract
2 tablespoons cognac
⅓ cup sugar plus 4 tablespoons
2 teaspoons finely minced lemon peel
¾ cup flour
Pinch of salt
15 ripe Italian plums, quartered
Whipped cream, if desired

Preheat the oven to 375 degrees and butter a 10-by-1½-inch tart, quiche or pie pan (without a removable bottom). Add the milk, cream, eggs, vanilla, and cognac to a food processor and process until combined. Mix ⅓ cup of the sugar, 1 teaspoon of the lemon peel, the flour, and salt in a small bowl, add to the food processor, and process until smooth. There should be about 3 cups of batter. Pour 1½ cups of the batter into the prepared pan. Arrange the plums on top in one layer. Sprinkle with the remaining lemon peel and gently pour the rest of the batter over the plums. Bake 15 minutes and remove from the oven. Sprinkle with 4 tablespoons sugar and bake for 45 minutes more, or until the center is set and the top is browned and puffed. If the top is not browned, but the center is set, put the clafouti under the broiler for about 1 to 2 minutes.

Let cool on a wire rack for 5 minutes. (The clafouti will fall as it cools.) Cut into wedges and serve warm with softly whipped cream.

Raspberry Almond Clafouti

Serves 4 to 6

Ruby-colored raspberries are drenched in port. A scattering of slivered almonds sit on the bottom of a ground almond-based batter in this simple and very flavorful dessert.

2 cups raspberries (1 pint)
2 tablespoons slivered almonds
2 tablespoons ruby port
¼ cup whole blanched almonds
2 tablespoons flour
¾ cup milk
2 eggs
⅓ cup plus 2 tablespoons sugar
Pinch of salt
2 tablespoons cold butter, cut into bits
Confectioners' sugar

Preheat the oven to 400 degrees and butter an 11-by-1½-inch deep (5 cup) oval ovenproof gratin pan. Arrange the raspberries in the bottom of the pan and sprinkle with the slivered almonds and the port wine. In a blender or food processor, grind the whole almonds with the flour until fine. Add the milk, eggs, sugar, and salt and mix well. Pour this mixture slowly over the fruit and nuts in the prepared pan. Dot with the butter and sprinkle the surface with the remaining 2 tablespoons of sugar. Bake in the middle of the oven for about 30 minutes, or until the clafouti is set, puffed, and the top is golden. If the top is *not* golden, broil for 1 to 2 minutes.

Let cool in the pan on a rack for 15 minutes. The clafouti will shrink somewhat. Sprinkle the surface with confectioners' sugar and serve warm.

Cherry Clafouti with Kirsch

Serves 6

Although pitting cherries is a labor-intensive job, doing them in advance, preferably with a friend or lover, makes the time go by more quickly. If you are pressed for time, frozen pitted cherries can be used as a substitute.

1½ pounds (about 4 cups) dark, sweet cherries, stemmed and pitted (see note)
4 tablespoons butter
⅔ cup flour, sifted
¼ teaspoon salt
3 eggs, beaten lightly
½ cup sugar, or to taste
1 cup milk
2 tablespoons kirsch
½ teaspoon vanilla extract

Preheat the oven to 425 degrees. Melt 4 tablespoons butter in the bottom of a 10-inch quiche pan and reserve 2 tablespoons of it. Arrange the pitted cherries on the bottom of the buttered pan and set aside.

In a small bowl, mix the flour and salt together. Set aside. In a large bowl, beat the eggs with the sugar, then add the milk, kirsch, and vanilla and beat until well blended. Add the reserved melted butter and the flour and salt, and beat again. Pour the batter slowly and evenly over the cherries so that they are not dislodged. Bake for 5 minutes, reduce the heat to 350 degrees, and continue to bake for 45 to 50 minutes, or until the clafouti is firm, puffed, and golden brown. Serve warm with a sprinkle of confectioners' sugar if you wish.

Note: Make a small slash in the cherry with the point of a sharp knife and lift out the pit.

Cranberry and Orange Clafouti

Serves 6

Garnet-colored cranberries made fragrant with orange peel are the basis
for a special brunch pancake—a clafouti for a crisp, fall Sunday morn-
ing, served with steaming mugs of coffee.

2 cups cranberries
1¼ cups sugar
1 cup water
1 tablespoon finely minced orange peel
⅓ cup flour
Pinch of salt
1⅓ cups milk
3 eggs
1 teaspoon vanilla extract
⅛ teaspoon cinnamon
Confectioners' sugar

Preheat the oven to 400 degrees. Butter a 10-inch quiche pan that does
not have a removable bottom and set aside. Mix the cranberries with ½
cup sugar and water and cook over medium heat for about 5 minutes,
until they just begin to pop. Drain the berries, reserving the liquid, and
scatter them on the bottom of the prepared pan. Put the reserved liquid
in a nonstick saucepan, add the orange peel, and cook for 5 to 8 minutes, or until reduced to ¼ cup. Cool slightly and set aside.

In a food processor, combine the flour, salt, remaining sugar,
milk, eggs, and vanilla. Blend well and add the reduced cranberry-
orange liquid. Slowly pour the batter over the cranberries. Sprinkle the
top with the cinnamon and bake for about 40 minutes or until the
clafouti is puffed and golden. Let cool for 5 minutes before serving.
Then dust with confectioners' sugar.

Frozen Assets

Cool and Refreshing

If you grew up as we did, spending the hot, humid summers on the streets of an urban jungle, then you no doubt also remember the welcome evening ding-a-ling of the ice cream wagon as it came down the steaming streets at dusk. In our day, there were the bungalow-shaped minitrucks (with their aptly named Bungalow Bars) and the squat Good Humor trucks, both of which would be urgently flagged down by small hordes of children, all clutching just enough money to buy a refreshing ice cream treat—either a flat, delicious bar on a stick or a small cup of cooling ambrosia.

There were 22 flavors, we remember, but the stimulus for our continued loyalty was more than just the ice cream. In those days, a certain number of the ice cream sticks were stamped as prizes, and when the luscious, dripping bar was devoured, we might well be the recipients of a *free* one on the driver's next trip through the neighborhood. There are two other things that we remember: the paper that covered the stick was always difficult to get off, and making the poor driver list the 22 flavors in all their delectable glory only to choose the same one each time—vanilla!

The trucks are gone, but even today we still see little carts in some urban neighborhoods, both here and in other countries, with a cake of ice melting in the sun and twelve or more syrupy liquids in long-neck bottles. The ice is shaved into a paper cup, the syrup poured on, and it is handed to the little ones clutching their coins tightly in their hands. Called *snow cones* or *water ices,* or *sharbat* in Asia, they all have one thing in common: They are the most welcome of simple foods when the sun hovers mercilessly overhead and both the tongue and the spirits are parched.

Many years have passed, and we no longer search the long list of flavors only to order vanilla. Our experience of buying Italian ices from the little stands outside the corner grocery store has been broadened by the marvelous discovery of *granita* in Italy. We have taken these ices a step further with our discovery of *sorbets* and *sherbets,* made all the more delicious when they are made with fresh, ripe fruits in season. And when it comes to commercially manufactured products such as ice milk, frozen yogurt, and frozen fruit bars, we, as most Americans, have become more and more calorie-conscious and cholesterol-aware, and are reading the labels on these products ever so carefully.

For those of us who love to make and eat desserts, the most rewarding part is that *we* have control over the ingredients, the calories, and above all, the flavor. By making our own, we can intensify the taste, we can control the sweetness, the calories, and fat, and we can invent flavors that do not exist in the commercial world of lemon, orange, and raspberry sorbet. This past season the grape sorbet made from the harvest of our own small arbor was something that we had never tasted before, and the flavor has been commented upon enthusiastically by every one of our guests.

We have designed this chapter for those who want to break what some have called "the ice-cream addiction." For a product to be called ice cream, the butterfat content must be a minimum of 10 percent, and many premium products now in the marketplace run as high as 15 to 16 percent. When we add such taste "bonuses" as chocolate, butterscotch, and other toppings, the fat content and the calorie count can rise astronomically.

For those who have no guilt, and for those who feel, as we do, that dessert time is a special time, we have included some tempting rich and caloric frozen desserts in this section of the book, all of them made with fresh fruits of course. We have also added a short section devoted to recipes for cookies to accompany the desserts. They make a marvelous contrast to a frozen dessert, but they are not overpowering embellishments. For the most part, we have concentrated on sorbets, made only with fruit, sugar, water and, sometimes, a small amount of liqueur. Occasionally, they contain a beaten egg white to give them a fluffier

texture. We prefer sorbets because the simple ingredients bring out the most vivid flavor of the fresh fruits.

A sherbet includes milk or cream, but follows almost the same procedure as a sorbet. *Granités* are a bit rougher in texture than sorbets and sherbets since they contain less sugar than either and the ice crystals that form are larger. In addition, they are generally made in ice trays or in metal bowls rather than in ice-cream makers.

Sorbets: The Rules of the Game

Sorbets are easy to make. And there is practically no limitation to your inspiration once you understand the basics. Home-grown raspberries, an abundance of grapes, blueberries in season (or frozen for the winter months), pineapple, pomegranates, oranges, grapefruit, pears, rhubarb, cranberries—we have tried them all. The most delightful part is that they can be whipped up within half an hour with an ice-cream maker. If you make them in ice cube trays or a metal bowl, they need very little tender loving care while they convert from liquid to a lush, fruit-filled frozen dessert.

Though we have given specific instructions in the recipes that are included in this chapter, there are a few rules that will allow you to strike out on your own and make any number of fresh fruit sorbets, depending on the ingredients on hand or the season of the year.

THE SUGAR SYRUP

All sorbets are based upon the use of a sugar syrup, not only for determining the sweetness but also to provide the base on which the texture and freezing time is determined.

- The smaller the amount of sugar, the less time to freeze and the icier the result.
- The larger the amount of sugar, the longer it takes to freeze and the smoother the texture.
- *Too much sugar,* however, can keep the sorbet from freezing.

We have suggested a basic sugar-syrup recipe of 1 cup of water and ½ cup of sugar, boiled slowly for no more than 5 minutes and then chilled in the refrigerator before using. You can use your judgment from that point on, since some citrus might warrant a little extra sugar. You can't really go wrong, as long as you don't use too much sugar. Begin with the basic recipes and work from there. You can make a large amount of sugar syrup in advance and store it in the refrigerator.

THE BASIC SORBET RECIPE

This very basic sorbet recipe will allow you to experiment with amounts, flavors, sweetness, and texture. Depending upon what fruits are in season, your own preference for sweetness, and your imagination, you can take off from here. This recipe makes about one pint, or enough to serve 4 to 5 people.

The Sugar Syrup
Use amounts mentioned above for sugar syrups:

> *1 cup water*
> *½ cup sugar*

Boil for five minutes and chill thoroughly.

The Fruit Flavoring
> *1 cup fruit juice, pulp blended or strained, chilled*
> *1 tablespoon liqueur or other flavoring such as lemon juice, if*
> *desired*

Combine the fruit liquid with the sugar syrup and make the sorbet according to the method of choice.

The Methods

ICE-CREAM MAKERS

This is by far the easiest way to make your own sorbets. There are many ice-cream makers now on the market, and we would strongly suggest that you check either *Consumer Reports* or go to your local department store and take a look at them. You will decide on one according to the amount of sorbet you want to make—a pint or a quart—the amount of room in your freezer, and whether you prefer a hand-operated machine or a self-timing electric wonder. We strongly recommend a simple hand-cranked model, such as the one we use. It does a wonderful job.

Basically, the freezing unit is put into the freezer for somewhere between 8 and 10 hours or overnight. When you are ready to make the sorbet, all the cold ingredients are poured in, the cover is put on, and the handle turned. The best thing about making sorbet is that the handle is only turned to mix the forming ice crystals about once every five minutes. If it is turned too often, the ice does not have a chance to form. We find that we make sorbets while doing other things such as reading or cooking. Every once in a while, we go back to turn the handle and about 25 minutes later—voilà! The sorbet is ready!

METAL ICE CUBE TRAYS OR METAL MIXING BOWLS

Before buying an ice-cream maker you may want to try making the sorbet by using the standard metal ice cube trays with the dividers removed or a simple metal mixing bowl, preferably stainless steel. The trays or the bowl should be put in the freezer for several hours before beginning.

The sorbet mixture is put in the trays or bowl and placed in the freezer. After about 1 hour, stir with a wire whisk. Ice will have begun to form around the edges of the container. After another hour, stir

again, combining the slush that has formed. Keep the container in the freezer, and every hour or so, combine again.

Depending upon the amount of sugar used, it will take about 4 to 5 hours for the sorbet to completely form. It can be removed, put in a food processor, and blended slightly, then put back in the container to freeze again.

When the sorbet is ready, transfer it to a container and serve it that day if possible. If you plan to keep it for several days, place it in the refrigerator for 30 minutes before serving to soften it slightly.

Some Other Basic Tips

The most important thing to remember when making sorbets is that everything should be cold when you begin including the containers, sugar syrup, fruit juices or syrups, all utensils, and the container for the sorbet.

- Sorbets are generally at their best when served as soon after making them as possible. Their texture is perfect when they come right from the ice tray or the ice-cream maker. Flavors have a tendency to become weaker as time goes by.
- As we've suggested, if you *do* want to make them well in advance, take them out of the freezer about 30 minutes before serving and let them soften a bit in the refrigerator.
- Another method of bringing the sorbet to proper serving texture is to purée it in the chilled bowl of a food processor with a chilled blade. Generally, the sorbet will remain soft for about 2 hours. Put it back in the freezer and remove when ready to serve.
- All serving dishes, cups, or glasses should also be chilled. Sorbets have a tendency to melt quickly.
- The ideal freezer temperature for sorbets is somewhere between 10 and 20 degrees Fahrenheit. Once you get too far below that temperature, such as in a large chest freezer where temperatures generally drop to 0 degrees, the sorbet will end up as a solid block of ice. We know several restaurants that don't serve sorbets only because their freezer temperatures are too low.
- If you've used an ice cream maker, don't try to wash it out right after you've made the sorbet. Since it will still be frozen, paper and sponges will stick to the metal surface. Wait until it comes back to room temperature then rinse it in warm water. Dry it thoroughly and place it back in the freezer for future use.

Sorbets are not new. Even our childhood memories of "snow ice" are recent history. Stories have been told of Alexander the Great indulging in flavored snow and Nero partaking of granita. Even Marco

Polo is supposed to have been ecstatic about having discovered a combination of milk and frozen fruit on his trip to the Orient. The French, the Italians, and the Asians have all developed their own special variations. Closer to home, the Vermont treat "sugar on snow" comes to mind, topped with a large helping of pure maple syrup.

Today, when we decide to finish the meal with a sensible, light dessert, the sorbet once again comes into its own. Easy to make—even easier than we might have imagined when we first began to make them years ago—they are delicious, sparkling with the best of fresh, ripe fruits. They tempt not only our taste but our imagination. If you revel in instant gratification, we think sorbets are probably your answer.

Peach Slush with Blueberries

A cooling, remarkably easy treat for a light finale. Perfect year round.

> *1 pound ripe peaches (about 4 large), sliced, pitted, and peeled*
>   *(see note)*
> *½ cup sugar*
> *⅓ cup cold water*
> *2 teaspoons lemon juice*
> *1½ teaspoons vanilla extract*
> *½ cup sour cream*
> *2 cups blueberries*
> *4 sprigs mint*

Arrange the peaches in a single layer on a jelly-roll pan and freeze for about 30 to 45 minutes. When frozen, put in a food processor with the sugar, water, lemon juice, and vanilla and process until slushy. Add the sour cream with the machine running and process until smooth. Distribute ⅔ of the blueberries between four wine glasses. Spoon the peach slush over the berries. Scatter the remaining berries on top and add a sprig of mint to each glass. Serve at once.

Note: Frozen peaches can also be used in this dessert. Process them frozen with all the ingredients except for the blueberries, and then follow the procedure.

Frozen Kiwi and Green Tea Mousse

Serves 8

The kiwi—or the New Zealand gooseberry became the pampered darling of the chic, nouvelle cuisine chefs of the 1970s. Understandably so, for its gentle, sweet flavor and extravagant color make it irresistible. Thus, it has never really lost its popularity. It is paired here with the effervescent flavor of Japanese green tea, which underlines the ice-green cool color of a frozen mousse.

> *4 large kiwis, plus 1 small kiwi for garnish*
> *⅔ cup sugar*
> *1 tablespoon Japanese powdered green tea (Matsu-cha)*
> *¼ cup lime juice (1 large lime)*
> *1 cup heavy cream*
> *Sprigs of mint, for garnish*

Cut off both ends of each kiwi, peel with a vegetable parer, and cut into pieces. (There should be 2 cups.) Process in a food processor with the sugar, green tea, and lime juice until smooth and transfer to a medium-size bowl. Whip the cream with a rotary hand beater until it holds stiff peaks and fold thoroughly into the purée mixture.

Spray the inside of eight ½-cup molds with a vegetable oil spray and distribute the mousse evenly among them. Cover each one with a small piece of aluminum foil and freeze for several hours.

When ready to serve, run a knife around the inside of the mold and dip the bottoms of the molds in warm water for a few seconds to loosen. Invert onto individual serving plates. Peel and slice the reserved kiwi into 8 thin slices. Top each mold with a slice of kiwi, a rosette of whipped cream, and a sprig of mint if desired.

Raspberry Sorbet with Chambord

Makes 1 pint

The chambord makes a perfect addition to this lush, raspberry sorbet. However, you may want to try an orange flavored liqueur as a change. Hazelnut Thins (page 306) make a wonderful accompaniment.

Sugar Syrup
    1 cup water
    ½ cup sugar

Sorbet
    1 pint fresh raspberries
    2 tablespoons lemon juice
    2 tablespoons chambord

To make the sugar syrup, combine the water and sugar in a saucepan, boil slowly for 5 minutes, and chill in the refrigerator. Purée the raspberries in a blender and chill. If you prefer the purée without seeds, force the raspberries through a sieve. Add the lemon juice and chambord and combine everything with the sugar syrup.

Make the sorbet according to one of the methods described on pages 282–285.

Comice Pear Sorbet with Fraises Des Bois and Passion Fruit Sauce

Makes 1½ pints

We find that the most flavorful pears for this sorbet are the Comice. However, if they are not available, you may substitute Anjou pears, since you will need a juicy, sweet fruit for this dessert.

Sugar Syrup
    1 cup water
    ½ cup sugar

Sorbet
    3 ripe Comice pears (about 1½ pounds), peeled and thickly
        sliced
    ½ teaspoon vanilla extract
    2 tablespoons lemon juice (½ lemon)
    1 tablespoon Poire William

To prepare the sugar syrup, combine the water and sugar in a nonreactive saucepan and boil until the sugar is dissolved. Add the sliced pears, vanilla, and lemon juice, cover and poach the pears for 5 minutes, or until they are soft. Put the pears and poaching liquid into a blender with the Poire William and purée. (You will have about 3 cups.) Put the purée in a bowl or large measuring cup and chill in the refrigerator for about 3 to 4 hours.

Make the sorbet by choosing one of the methods described on pages 282–285. Serve with Fraises Des Bois and Passion Fruit Sauce (page 319) and Orange Almond Cookies (page 307).

Pink Grapefruit, Mint, and Gin
Sorbet with
Honey Poached Kumquats

Makes 1 pint

This is one of the most refreshing and tangiest of sorbets. The addition of little flecks of fresh mint adds a tempting color as well as an elusive taste. If you like, you can also serve it without the Honey Poached Kumquats (page 15), but we strongly suggest serving the "whole works." Brandy Snap Flutes (page 312) add a nice bit of contrast.

Sugar Syrup
> 1 cup water
> ½ cup sugar

In a nonreactive saucepan, combine the water and sugar and boil for five minutes. Chill in the refrigerator for several hours until very cold.

Sorbet
> 1½ cups pink grapefruit juice (from 2 to 3 grapefruits), strained
> 1 teaspoon finely minced fresh mint
> 2 tablespoons gin
> 2 tablespoons Campari

Combine the grapefruit juice, mint, gin, and Campari and chill. Then mix with the sugar syrup and make the sorbet using one of the methods described on pages 282–285. Serve with Honey Poached Kumquats.

Biscuit Tortoni

Serves 12

Signor Tortoni, an eighteenth-century Italian who opened a shop in Paris, was responsible for creating this frozen, creamy, almond-scented dessert that is traditionally served in little paper cups.

6 Amaretti cookies
2 cups peeled, pitted, and sliced ripe peaches (2 to 3 peaches,
*   depending upon size)*
1⅓ cups heavy cream
¼ cup confectioners' sugar
Pinch of salt
2 tablespoons dark rum
¾ teaspoon vanilla extract
¼ teaspoon almond extract
2 egg whites
12 raspberries, for garnish

Pulverize the cookies in a blender. There will be ½ cup fine crumbs. Reserve 2 tablespoons for the top, leaving the remaining crumbs in the blender. Add the peaches, ⅓ cup of the cream, confectioners' sugar, salt, rum, vanilla, and almond extract and blend until smooth.

In a medium-size bowl, beat the egg whites with a rotary hand beater until they hold stiff peaks and set aside. In another bowl, beat the remaining cup of cream until it holds stiff peaks. Fold the two mixtures together with a large rubber spatula and fold in the peach mixture.

Line a 12-cup muffin tin with foil liners. Spoon about 3 heaping tablespoons into each foil cup. Sprinkle with the remaining cookie crumbs and freeze for a minimum of 2 hours. Cover with foil after 2 hours if you are going to freeze them for a longer period of time. One hour before serving, soften them slightly in the refrigerator. Serve right from the foil liners on a plate covered with a paper doily. Top each with a fresh raspberry if desired.

Blueberry Sorbet Heart with
Papaya Balls and Red Currants

Serves 6

One way to make sorbet desserts look more festive is to serve them as individual portions, using molds of varying shapes. For this recipe, we have chosen heart-shaped molds, garnished with papaya balls as a vivid color counterpoint, completing the picture with fresh currants scattered on top.

Sugar Syrup
 1 cup water
 ½ cup sugar

In a nonstick saucepan, combine the water and sugar and boil for five minutes. Refrigerate until very cold. At the same time, put the ½-cup heart-shaped molds in the freezer to chill them.

Sorbet
 2 cups fresh blueberries
 1 tablespoon lemon juice
 1 tablespoon crème de cassis or kirsch
 1 egg white
 2 papayas, seeds removed and cut with a melon baller
 ½ cup fresh currants

Blend the blueberries in a food processor or blender. (If you are using frozen blueberries, let them thaw before blending.) Add the lemon juice, crème de cassis, and blend again. Combine the sugar syrup and the blueberry mixture in a bowl. Beat the egg white until it holds soft

peaks and fold it into the mixture. Make the sorbet according to one of the methods described on pages 282–285 and fill each chilled mold with the mixture. Cover with plastic wrap and place in freezer until ready to serve.

Remove the molds from the freezer, dip the bottoms in warm water just long enough to loosen the sorbet, invert them onto a chilled serving plate. Surround each sorbet with the papaya balls and sprinkle some fresh red currants on top. Serve at once.

Green Wine Grape Sorbet with Blackberries in Little Lemon Cup Cookies

Serves 6

This dessert is unusual in that we have chosen tart wine grapes for the base of the sorbet rather than the sweet table grapes sold at the green-grocer. If you happen to grow your own, as we do, so much the better, since we are always looking for ways to use the overabundance of grapes in a good growing year. To make it more special, we suggest that you fill the little lemon cups with blackberries and serve on the side.

Sugar Syrup
> 1 cup water
> ½ cup sugar

In a nonreactive saucepan, combine the water and sugar and boil for 5 minutes to make the syrup. Chill in the refrigerator.

Sorbet
> 1 pound green wine grapes
> The juice of 2 limes

In a blender, liquify the wine grapes, then strain through a sieve or strainer. You should have about 1½ cups of grape juice. Add the lime juice and chill. When all the ingredients are chilled thoroughly, combine the sugar syrup with the grape mixture and make the sorbet according to one of the methods suggested on pages 282–285.

Garnish and Cookies
   ½ pint fresh blackberries
   6 Little Lemon Cups *(page 308)*

When ready to serve, put the sorbet in chilled wine or small brandy glasses and top with a few blackberries. Place 3 or 4 blackberries in each Little Lemon Cup cookie and serve on the side.

Pomegranate Sorbet with Kiwi Fruit Sauce

Makes 1 pint

We loved pomegranates as kids, and we remember tearing them apart right out on the street and spitting the seeds in a contest of distance, our lips and tongues stained indelible red. The sorbet is a very special one, we think, but it might be wise to give you some tips about preparing the fruits, since they do stain anything and everything that they come into contact with. This sorbet is wonderful with Vanilla Cigarettes (page 310) accompanying it.

Preparing Pomegranates

Three pomegranates will give you about one cup of juice, just the amount you need for the recipe. Cut the pomegranates on a piece of aluminum foil to keep the juice from staining the counter. Cut each one into quarters and then take each quarter and bend it inside out over a blender. Keep the fruit below the top rim of the blender to minimize the scattering of seeds. Do not use a food processor. Using a teaspoon, scrape the kernels into the blender. Do not use any of the white pith. If some should drop in, remove it and discard. Blend on slow speed.

When the seeds have begun to cling to the sides, push them down with a spatula and blend again. Do this a third time until all the seeds have been liquified. Blend them at high speed for a few moments until you see pinkish juice.

When all the seeds have been blended, pour the juice into a cup and then strain through a sieve, pushing firmly with the back of a wooden spoon until all the juice is in the cup. Discard the seed residue.

The juice will keep in the refrigerator for about a week and about three months in the freezer. Don't let your red hands discourage you. It will wash off. And the taste is well worth it!

Sugar Syrup
>   1 cup water
>   ½ cup sugar

Make the sugar syrup by combining the water and sugar in a nonreactive saucepan and boil for 5 minutes. Chill in the refrigerator.

Sorbet
>   1 cup pomegranate juice (about 3 pomegranates)
>   Kiwi Fruit Sauce (page 324)

Combine the sugar syrup and juice and make the sorbet using one of the methods described on pages 282–285. When ready to serve, divide the sorbet among glasses or small plates and use a few spoonfuls of Kiwi Fruit Sauce to cover each portion.

Frozen Parfait with
Three Fruit Sauces

Serves 8 to 9

Three colorful fruit sauces arranged alongside one another are crowned with a creamy, frozen, molded parfait. All can be made well in advance and assembled just moments before serving.

Parfait
    ⅔ cup milk
    1 2-inch piece of vanilla bean
    3 eggs yolks
    ½ cup sugar
    2 tablespoons orange-flavored liqueur
    1 cup heavy cream

Put the milk into a small heavy saucepan. Split the vanilla bean, scrape the seeds into the milk, and add the vanilla pod. Bring the milk slowly to a boil. While the milk comes to a boil, beat the egg yolks in a stainless steel bowl with an electric hand beater, and add the sugar slowly, beating until the mixture is pale and thick. Place the bowl over a pot with 1½ inches of gently simmering water. Add the liqueur and continue to beat for one minute. Remove the vanilla pod from the milk and add ¼ cup of the milk and continue to beat. Add the remaining hot milk, beating constantly until the mixture is cooked and slightly thickened. Remove the bowl and continue to beat for about 10 minutes, or until the mixture has cooled. Chill in the bowl until cold. When cold, whip the cream until it holds stiff peaks, then fold into the egg mixture. (Both mixtures must be the same temperature.) Pour into individual ½-cup metal molds, such as a tall dariole mold, and freeze for 1 hour. Cover the molds with aluminum foil and continue to freeze for at least 5 hours more or overnight.

Three Fruit Sauces
Prepare the three fruit sauces ahead of time.

Blueberry Sauce (page 327)
Mango Sauce (page 321)
Kiwi Fruit Sauce (page 324)

When ready to serve, spoon a generous tablespoon of each sauce in a row on an individual serving plate, with the blueberry sauce in the center. Run a knife around the inside edge of the parfait mold and tap down smartly on a work surface. Transfer the parfait with a wide spatula and place it over the blueberry sauce. A sprig of mint is a nice garnish if desired.

Cranberry and Orange Sorbets in a
Melon Mold

Serves 6 to 8

Based on the principles of the ice-cream Bombe, this dessert surprises everyone when it's cut to reveal the cranberry exterior nestling an orange sorbet filling. When frozen in a melon mold, it makes a very special finale to a festive dinner. Best of all, it has very few calories—and no cholesterol at all. We think Green Tea Madeleines (page 314) make a lovely accompaniment.

Sugar Syrup
>   2 cups water
>   1 cup sugar

Chill a melon mold or any stainless steel mixing bowl in the freezer. Prepare the sugar syrup by combining the water and sugar in a non-reactive saucepan. Boil for 5 minutes and chill in refrigerator.

Cranberry Sorbet
>   1½ cups cranberries (see note)
>   2 tablespoons frozen apple juice concentrate
>   1 teaspoon lemon juice

Cook the cranberries until they pop and then purée them in a blender. Add the apple juice concentrate and the lemon juice and chill the mixture until cold.

When both the sugar syrup and the cranberry mixture are chilled, make the sorbet by combining half the sugar syrup and all the cranberries using one of the methods described on pages 282–285. Reserve the remaining sugar syrup for the orange sorbet.

Spoon the sorbet into the chilled melon mold and roughly form an oval depression in the middle by pushing the sorbet up against the sides

with a spoon. At this point, the sorbet will still be slightly softened so the mixture will not form a perfect oval. Don't worry; you'll get it later on.

Chill for about 3 hours then push the hardening sorbet more firmly against the sides to form a smooth, large oval. The entire process will take about 5 hours for the sorbet to become very firm. In the meantime, keep the mold in the freezer while making the orange sorbet.

Orange Sorbet
  Reserved sugar syrup
  The peel of 1 orange, finely minced
  1 cup orange juice (2 to 3 oranges)
  1 tablespoon orange-flavored liqueur

Mix the reserved sugar syrup with the orange peel, orange juice, and liqueur. Make the sorbet using one of the methods described on pages 282–285. Take the mold from the freezer and spoon the orange sorbet into the oval that you formed. Smooth with the bottom of a spoon. If there is any orange sorbet left over, freeze it in a container for another time.

Cover the mold with its cover, or if using a metal bowl, with aluminum foil and chill in the freezer for at least 3 hours more.

Chill the serving plate in the freezer. To unmold the dessert, use a towel that has been dampened with warm water and wrung out thoroughly. Apply the warm towel around the mold 2 or 3 times to loosen the dessert, but make sure you don't melt the sorbet. After each application, invert the mold onto the serving plate and shake it firmly. When it comes out chill the dessert on the plate in the freezer for about 15 minutes. Cut the mold with a serrated knife and place each portion on a chilled serving plate.

Note: If cranberries are not in season, you can make the sorbet by using frozen cranberries. They work rather well but the texture will be slightly different from the orange filling.

Rhubarb and Strawberry Sherbet

Serves 6

Transforming a sorbet into a sherbet is very simple. With the addition of a small amount of heavy cream, we not only change the name of the dessert but also its texture. You can do the very same thing with any of the sorbets that we've included in the book. Serve with Green Tea Madeleines (page 314) or Orange Almond Cookies (page 307).

Sugar Syrup
>   1 cup water
>   ½ cup sugar

In a nonstick saucepan, combine the water and sugar, bring to a boil for 5 minutes, then chill thoroughly in refrigerator.

Sherbet
>   1 cup water
>   1 2-inch strip of lemon peel
>   ½-pound trimmed rhubarb, cut into ½-inch pieces (about 2¼
>   cups)
>   1 pint ripe strawberries, hulled
>   1 tablespoon kirsch
>   3 tablespoons heavy cream

Bring the water and lemon peel to a boil, add the rhubarb, and cook, covered, over medium heat for 5 minutes, or until tender. Drain the mixture in a sieve, discarding the liquid. Remove the lemon peel and transfer the rhubarb to the bowl of a food processor. Add the strawberries, kirsch, and chilled sugar syrup and process until puréed. Force through a sieve using a rubber spatula and discard the seeds. There should be about 3 cups of purée. Stir in the cream and make the sherbet using one of the methods described on pages 282–285.

Sauce
  Strawberry Rose Geranium Sauce (page 320), optional
  Passion Fruit Sauce (page 318), optional

Serve with either the Strawberry Rose Geranium Sauce, or Passion Fruit Sauce and one of the suggested cookies.

Hazelnut Thins

Makes 32 to 34 cookies

These are tiny, crisp discs with toasted, chopped hazelnuts. Their plain round shape belies their delicious flavor. This simple drop cookie is a cinch to make and its sweet, nutty crunchiness is just right for any fruit dessert, frozen or poached.

2½ ounces hazelnuts
1 egg
½ cup light brown sugar
3 tablespoons butter
1 teaspoon vanilla extract
⅓ cup flour
Pinch of salt

Preheat the oven to 350 degrees and butter two baking sheets. Spread the nuts out in a pie plate and roast for 10 minutes. Wrap them in a kitchen towel and rub off the skins (if some skins still adhere, it doesn't matter). Chop the nuts coarsely and set aside. In the bowl of a food processor, process the egg until well beaten, then add the sugar, butter, vanilla, and flour and process until blended. Scrape the mixture into a large measuring cup for easy handling and stir in the chopped nuts. Raise the oven heat to 375 degrees. Drop the batter by the half tea-spoonful about two inches apart onto the baking sheet (they will spread while baking). Bake 4 to 5 minutes, or until the edges are golden. Loosen all the cookies with a spatula while hot and transfer to a wire rack to cool.

Orange Almond Cookies

Makes 40 to 42 cookies

These cookies, can be cut out into fanciful shapes—stars, flowers, hearts, or butterflies. They can be tucked into the top of an iced dessert or they can be served as nibbles when the desire for that "something sweet" just seems to overcome you.

¾ cup flour
Pinch of salt
2 tablespoons sugar
¼ cup ground almonds
4 tablespoons butter, cut into pieces
½ teaspoon finely minced orange peel
1 egg yolk combined with 1 tablespoon cold milk
Fine sugar

In the bowl of a food processor, process the flour, salt, sugar, and almonds until combined. Add the butter and process for a few pulses until the mixture is mealy in texture. Add the orange peel and egg yolk-milk mixture and process only until a soft dough forms. Gather together into a ball, flatten, and wrap in plastic wrap. Allow the dough to rest for 30 minutes at room temperature.

Butter two baking sheets and set aside. Roll out the dough onto a floured surface to a ⅛-inch thickness. Cut out shapes with small cookie cutters (we like to use small stars, hearts, flowers, and butterflies). Gather up the scraps, roll out, and cut more shapes until all of the dough is used. Arrange the cookies closely together on the baking sheets and chill in the refrigerator for 20 minutes. While the cookies are chilling, preheat the oven to 350 degrees. Bake the cookies for 10 to 12 minutes, or until they are golden but not browned. Transfer with a spatula to a wire rack to cool completely. When cool, dip them in fine sugar. Store in an airtight container.

Little Lemon Cups

Makes 30 to 32 cookies

These Little Lemon Cups are adorable, taste wonderful and are a perfect, crisp container for berries as an accompaniment to a sorbet. Served alone with a puff of whipped cream, a raspberry, and a sprig of mint in each makes a wonderful mouthful. Three tiny filled cups would make a portion.

> *3 tablespoons butter, melted*
> *1 egg*
> *1 egg white*
> *1 teaspoon finely minced lemon peel*
> *½ cup fine sugar*
> *½ cup flour*
> *Pinch of salt*

Butter two baking sheets and the underside of a 1¾-inch muffin pan with the melted butter. (You will be using the bottom of the muffin pan to mold the lemon cups later on.) You will need to have a wire rack and a pair of old white cotton gloves handy, since you may find the cookies too hot to handle when they come out of the oven.

Preheat the oven to 350 degrees. In the bowl of a food processor, combine the egg and the egg white and process until well beaten. Add the lemon peel and process. Sift the sugar, flour, and salt together and add while the processor is on. When well combined, transfer to a large measuring cup for easier handling. Warm the cookie sheets in the oven for 2 minutes. Spoon 2 generous teaspoons of batter onto the baking sheet at least 5 inches apart. The batter will spread out into 2-inch circles while baking. Bake the cookies for 5 minutes, or until only the edges of the cookies turn light brown. Remove from the oven and wait 10 to 12 seconds, then transfer the cookies one at a time with a wide spatula to the buttered inverted muffin pans. Place each cookie over the bottom of a muffin form, working quickly. Use your fingers to press and pinch the sides of the cookies gently against the form. They firm up very quickly. Slip the cookie off and place on a wire rack to cool completely. If the cookie becomes too firm before you get to mold it, return it to the oven for 30 to 40 seconds to soften up a bit. Put the next prepared cookie sheet into the oven and continue to bake two at a time until all the cookies are formed.

Vanilla Cigarettes

Makes 28 to 30 cookies

Delicate and luxurious, each batch of these cookies gets easier and easier to make once you get the knack of the timing.

¼ cup butter, softened
½ cup fine sugar
Pinch of salt
3 egg whites
1 teaspoon vanilla extract
½ cup flour, sifted

Measure parchment paper to fit two baking sheets. Cut a piece of cardboard into a 3-inch circle to use as a stencil, then draw 6 circles on the parchment paper. Spray the cookie sheets with vegetable oil spray. Place the paper, pencil-side down on the sprayed pan and spray the top of the paper with the vegetable spray. (You will be able to see the circles through the paper.) Set the pans aside.

Preheat the oven to 350 degrees. You will need to have six chopsticks ready and a wire rack for cooling the cookies (see note). In the bowl of a food processor, cream the butter until pale, add the sugar, and process until smooth and creamy. Gradually add the egg whites and vanilla to the food processor while it is on. Transfer the mixture to a bowl and, using a rubber spatula, gently fold in the sifted flour. Drop a generous teaspoon of the batter in the center of each circle. Using the back of a damp spoon, spread the batter evenly inside the circle, working in a circular motion from the center out toward the edges. Prepare both trays but bake one tray at a time for 5 to 6 minutes, or until golden.

Loosen the cookies by sliding a spatula underneath each one while they are still hot. Working rapidly, roll each cookie gently around a chopstick to shape it and place on a wire rack, seam side down, to cool. Remove the chopsticks as soon as the cookies can maintain their shapes.

Continue the procedure with the remaining batter using both cookie sheets. Wipe the surface of the parchment with paper towels and respray after each batch if necessary. Keep the spatula clean of crumbs. When the cookies are cool, store them in an airtight container.

Note: You may also roll the cookies around the handle of a wooden spoon for a slightly fatter cookie. If your hands are sensitive to the heat while you are rolling, wear an old pair of white cotton gloves for insulation.

Brandy Snap Flutes

Makes 20 to 22 cookies

Crackling crisp and shiny, these transparent amber, honey-comb-pattern flutes are a marvelously contrasting texture for a cooling, refreshing, frozen dessert.

> *2 tablespoons butter, melted*
> *¼ cup butter, softened*
> *½ cup light brown sugar*
> *⅓ cup light corn syrup*
> *2 teaspoons brandy*
> *2 teaspoons lemon juice*
> *½ cup flour*
> *½ teaspoon ground ginger*

Preheat the oven to 350 degrees and have a wire rack handy as well as several wooden spoons (see note). You will be using the handles of the wooden spoons, so make sure they're clean and dry. Cut a piece of parchment paper to fit a baking sheet. Brush the sheet with some of the melted butter, place the parchment on it, then brush the parchment with some of the melted butter.

In a nonstick saucepan, combine the softened butter, brown sugar, and corn syrup and cook over low heat, stirring occasionally, until combined and the butter is melted. Stir in the brandy and lemon juice, remove from the heat, and cool completely.

Sift the flour and ginger together and add to the mixture, stirring briskly until cooled. The mixture will be thick and sticky. Drop six scant teaspoonsful on the prepared baking sheet, spacing them well since they will spread while baking. Bake for 8 to 10 minutes, or until the edges darken. Cool about 2 to 3 minutes, turn the parchment paper upside down and peel it away from the cookie. (The paper may be used again; just keep it buttered and free of crumbs.)

Working quickly, wrap each cookie around the handle of a wooden spoon and roll it up to form a flute. Slip the handle out as soon as the cookies hold their shape. Let cool on wire rack. Repeat the process until all the batter is used. If the cookies should harden too much while rolling them around the handle, place them back in the oven for a few seconds to soften them. Store the cookies in an airtight container.

Note: You may also use wooden chopsticks to make the flutes. The cookies will be thinner than those wrapped around wooden spoon handles, but the process is the same.

Green Tea Madeleines

Makes 24 cookies

A classic Proustian treat with a Japanese touch. The result is a pale green cookie that serves as a color and flavor accent with sorbets or other simple fruit desserts.

>*2 tablespoons softened butter for buttering the molds plus 4*
>   *tablespoons butter*
>*2 eggs at room temperature*
>*Pinch of salt*
>*5 tablespoons fine sugar*
>*½ teaspoon vanilla extract*
>*½ teaspoon finely minced lemon peel*
>*Scant ½ cup flour*
>*1 teaspoon Japanese green tea powder (Matsu-cha)*
>*Confectioners' or superfine sugar for dusting*

Preheat the oven to 375 degrees and lavishly butter two madeleine forms with the softened butter. Melt the 4 tablespoons of butter over low heat and then cool completely. In a bowl, beat the eggs and salt with an electric hand beater until frothy. Gradually add the sugar, a few tablespoons at a time, beating well after each addition. Add the vanilla and lemon peel and continue to beat until thick ribbons form when the beater is lifted from the bowl and the mixture triples in volume.

Sift the flour and green tea together and sift again into the egg mixture, one tablespoon at a time. Fold in gently using a rubber spatula. Fold in the cooled butter, bit by bit, in the same manner. Spoon the mixture into each prepared madeleine form, filling each one about ⅔ full. Run a toothpick through each madeleine once or twice to break any large bubbles. Bake 8 to 10 minutes, or until lightly golden.

Loosen each madeleine immediately with the point of a paring knife, then remove from the molds. Place on a wire rack to cool, rounded side up. Before serving, dust with confectioners' or fine sugar.

Sauces

There once was a fad—thankfully, long gone—when sauces were made in public at the table for all to see and admire. With an enormous amount of flourish and swagger, the tableside performer (usually the captain or maitre d') would rapidly pour, stir, and add all sorts of ingredients without measuring any of them and then, in a burst of glory, ignite the whole concoction, totally intimidating the home cook with the dazzling spectacle. Never in their wildest dreams would the awed patrons ever attempt to duplicate these incendiary sauces at home without first increasing the premiums on their fire insurance! All of this was supposed to make eating out the equivalent of theater.

Nevertheless, one time many years ago, we decided in a naive, rebellious burst of enthusiasm to try this at home. Having been given a gift of a gleaming copper chafing dish, we thought that we might be adept enough to ape these tableside theatrics at home by making what was then the enormously popular, crêpes suzette. However, we never suspected that the disaster that followed would have a very happy ending.

At that time, we did not know that spirits had to be warmed before being ignited. Thus when the time came to add the cognac, we kept pouring more and more, standing back with each addition as we applied a long match, waiting for the sauce to ignite in the spectacular pyrotechnic display that we had seen at the restaurant. Niente. Nada. Nothing. By now we had some little folded soggy crêpes floating mournfully in a half bottle of very fine cognac. We threw away the crêpes and offered our guests the warm sauce alone in mugs, which made our dinner party quite a success anyway!

This was also part of an era where elaborate and overly rich sauces smothered *all* of our food and were, at least, partly responsible for our joining our ancestors much too prematurely.

In the first century, the Roman chef, Apicius (whom someone once called the "Mrs. Beeton of Rome"), gave us the Latin inklings of the functions of sauces and just what they should do. He wrote that they made a simple dish more appetizing. Essentially, this theory has not changed in 2,000 years. Although sauces have sometimes served as a disguise in order to hide something unpalatable, their true purpose is not to mask flavor but to add refinement to the flavor and to accompany it.

Today, sauces have become easier for the home chef, and though we frequently complain that there is nothing new in cookery, the advent of machines for the home, such as blenders and food processors, has inspired the preparation of still lighter and newer sauces. These machines have allowed the home cook to experiment and improvise quickly, using fresh ingredients, and with no more effort than the flick of a switch.

Gratefully, too, sauces now are as numerous and as varied as they are adaptable, and just a little bit of experimentation and imagination can develop flavor combinations that add new interest to the same dessert. Properly used, the flavors and the colors of these sauces complement and enhance the presentation as well as offer textural contrast.

There are however, several rules of thumb that can help you determine just what sauces go well with particular desserts. For example, cream sauces are never used with cream desserts. The effect upon our contemporary palates would probably be nauseatingly rich. Although we have included some rich sauces in this chapter, we have generally emphasized and stressed the fruit sauces because they are easy to prepare, simple, and colorful.

Fruit sauces are wonderful companions to fruit desserts since they adapt their flavors quite well and enhance rather than diminish the overall effect. When fruits are ripest, sauces made from them will have the most clarity of flavor and require the least amount of sugar. Most often, just a few lovely fresh, ripe peaches, for example, puréed with a touch of lemon juice and only a bit of sweetening, may be all that is required.

When fruits are not at their peak, a combination of a reduced sugar syrup with citrus juice will intensify the flavor of the fruit. With the addition of a bit of liqueur, the flavor will be further heightened and perked up. Liqueurs, however, should be used judiciously, since spirits can also be assertive and mask the other ingredients in the sauce when they are overused. Spices, such as vanilla bean, fresh ginger root, and

spirits such as wine, cognac, rum, or bourbon, and other compatible fruit juices can also be added for still more variety.

Sauces have been called "the soul of cooking" by the French chefs of the eighteenth and nineteenth centuries. Though we do not rely on them today as much for flavor enhancement, nor do we sauce our food as liberally as we once did, there is no denying that a bit of sauce with the proper dessert adds nuance and a complexity of flavor, as well as a most welcome addition of festivity.

Passion Fruit Sauce

Makes ⅔ cup

The passion fruit, a newcomer to our shores, is becoming more and more popular as chefs around the country are creating demand for new flavors. It's an odd looking oval fruit, pale yellow or purply brown, depending upon the variety. It's wrinkled when ripe and ready to use. Inside, the fruit harbors an intensely aromatic yellow-orange gelatinous pulp with edible seeds. Sounds strange but tastes just marvelous!

> *2 to 3 ripe yellow passion fruits (see note)*
> *2 tablespoons sugar*
> *½ cup water*
> *1 teaspoon arrowroot*
> *1 teaspoon Grand Marnier or other orange-flavored liqueur*

Cut the fruits in half on a plate, scoop out the soft pulp and seeds, and set aside. There should be ⅓ cup. In a small cup, dissolve the arrowroot with one tablespoon of cold water and set aside. In a small saucepan, dissolve the sugar and ¼ cup of the water. Bring the sugar and water slowly to a boil and boil for 2 minutes. Remove from the heat and let the bubbles subside for one minute. Add the arrowroot to the sugar syrup. Return to low heat and stir, cooking for about 1 minute, or until the mixture has thickened. Add the passion fruit pulp and Grand Marnier. Cover and cool.

Note: We tested this sauce with both the purple and the yellow passion fruits. The yellow, which we have used here, seemed to be more fragrant.

One fruit yielded one tablespoon of pulp so, depending on the size of the passion fruit and the yield of the pulp, you may need 3 fruits. We left the seeds in this version, since they are edible and add to the crunch and the interest of the sauce.

Fraises Des Bois and Passion Fruit Sauce

Makes about 1¼ cups

The mingled perfumes of tiny wild strawberries and passion fruit make an intensely flavorful sauce of pure ambrosia! It's wonderful over a pale sorbet, such as pear or grapefruit, or stirred into plain whipped cream to create a sensational fool.

¾ cup fraises des bois (*see note*)
2 tablespoons sugar
½ cup water
2 passion fruits
1 teaspoon arrowroot
2 teaspoons kirsch

Reserve ¼ cup of the berries whole and crush the remaining ½ cup. Set both aside. Dissolve the sugar and ¼ cup water in a small saucepan. Bring to a boil and boil for 1 minute. Add the crushed berries and simmer for 1 minute. Remove from the heat and force through a sieve into the saucepan. Halve both passion fruits, remove the pulp and seeds, and force through a sieve into the saucepan. Discard all the seeds.

In a small cup, stir the arrowroot with the remaining water and add to the saucepan. Return to the heat, and cook the sauce, stirring constantly over medium heat, for about 1 to 2 minutes or until thickened and clear. Stir in the remaining whole berries and the kirsch.

Note: Ripe strawberries may be used as an acceptable substitute for the *fraises des bois,* but the flavor will not be quite the same.

Strawberry Rose Geranium Sauce

Makes 1½ cups

This is an uncooked sauce with many uses, as can be said of most fruit sauces. It enhances any cream-based dessert. Prepare the sauce at least one hour before assembling the dessert so that the flavors will blend and mellow.

> *2 cups ripe strawberries, rinsed and hulled*
> *⅓ cup sugar*
> *1 tablespoon lemon juice*
> *1 tablespoon kirsch*
> *1 large scented rose geranium leaf*

Purée one cup of the strawberries with the sugar, lemon juice, and kirsch in a food processor. Transfer to a small bowl and add the rose geranium leaf. Slice the remaining cup of strawberries thinly and add to the purée. Remove the rose geranium leaf before serving.

Mango Sauce

A thickish apricot-colored sauce with just a hint of lime and honey. Mango sauce can be used over cream desserts or sorbets.

1 ripe mango
1 tablespoon lime juice (about ½ lime)
1 tablespoon light mild honey
Pinch of salt

Peel the mango and cut out the flat pit with a serrated grapefruit knife. Purée the fruit in a food processor, then force the purée through a nonmetallic sieve, pressing the pulp against the bottom of the sieve and scraping the underside into the sauce. Stir in the lime juice, honey, and salt.

Raspberry Sauce with Chambord

Makes 1½ cups

A simple berry sauce that can be used lavishly with any mousse or cheese dessert.

> 2 cups (1 pint) fresh raspberries (see note)
> 2 tablespoons lemon juice (about ½ large lemon)
> ¼ cup water
> ½ cup sugar
> ½ teaspoon arrowroot
> 1 tablespoon chambord

Combine the raspberries, lemon juice, and water in a food processor, purée until smooth, and strain through a fine sieve, pressing the raspberries against the sides of the sieve to remove all the seeds. Using a rubber spatula, scrape the raspberry mixture into a nonstick saucepan, scraping the underside of the sieve to get all of the raspberry purée into the pan. Discard the seeds. Add the sugar and bring slowly to a boil over moderate heat, stirring occasionally. Then lower the heat and simmer for about 15 minutes. Dissolve the arrowroot in the chambord and stir into the raspberry mixture. Cook, stirring, for 1 minute until thickened. Remove from the heat and transfer to a small bowl. Cover and refrigerate.

Note: Frozen unsweetened raspberries may also be used for this sauce.

Ginger Cream Chantilly

Makes 1 cup

A soothing cream that carries the zippy bite of ginger.

> *1½ tablespoons finely minced crystallized ginger*
> *1 teaspoon finely minced lemon peel*
> *1 cup heavy cream, softly whipped*

Mix the ginger and lemon peel with the softly whipped cream and refrigerate for 15 to 20 minutes to blend the flavors. Stir before serving.

Kiwi Fruit Sauce

Makes ¾ cup

This bright green sauce, sweetened with maple syrup and tempered with a few drops of lime juice, is an easy accompaniment to sorbets. You may also use it in combination with Red Currant Sauce (page 325) and Mango Sauce (page 321) for three of the brightest, most alluring combinations of colors and flavors.

2 large kiwis
2 tablespoons maple syrup
½ teaspoon lime juice

Cut both ends from the kiwis and peel with a vegetable parer. Cut into small pieces and purée in the bowl of a food processor until smooth. Add the maple syrup and lime juice and purée for a few more strokes until the mixture is well combined.

Red Currant Sauce

This sparkling, clear, shiny, and bright red currant sauce will enliven any fruit composée, cream dessert, or simple pudding.

>*1½ cups fresh, red currants (about ½ pound)*
>*3 tablespoons sugar*
>*½ cup water*
>*1 teaspoon arrowroot*
>*1 teaspoon lemon juice*
>*1 teaspoon kirsch*

Set aside ½ cup of the currants, preferably with the stems on. Pull the remaining currants off their stems. Set aside.

In a small saucepan, dissolve the sugar in ¼ cup of the water and boil for one minute. Add 1 cup of the currants and bring to a boil again, stirring with a wooden spoon and crushing the berries against the sides of the pot. Cook for one minute, then force through a nonmetallic sieve, scraping the underside until only the seeds remain in the sieve. Return the liquid to the saucepan and discard the seeds.

Mix the arrowroot with the remaining water and add to the saucepan. Cook gently, stirring constantly, until the mixture darkens and thickens, about 1 to 2 minutes. Remove from the stove and stir in the lemon juice and kirsch. Use reserved syrup of currants to garnish the sauce.

Three Berry Sauce

A lovely, colorful, and welcome addition to a cream dessert such as bavarois or a stirred or baked custard.

⅓ cup sugar
¼ cup light brown sugar
¼ cup water
1 slice lemon
2 tablespoons lemon juice
1 tablespoon framboise, kirsch, or orange liqueur
1 tablespoon butter, softened
½ cup blackberries
1 cup strawberries, hulled
1 cup raspberries

In an 8-inch sauté pan, combine the sugars and water, bring to a boil, and add the lemon slice. Cook over medium heat, stirring, for about 2 minutes. Remove from the heat and add the lemon juice, liqueur, and butter. Remove the slice of lemon, add the berries, and shake the pan to coat the fruit with the sauce. Return to low heat and simmer for one minute. Serve slightly warm.

Blueberry Sauce

Makes 1 cup

A dark and dusky sauce that tastes and looks lovely with any pale mousse, bavarois, or sorbet.

2 cups blueberries
1 tablespoon water
2 tablespoons light brown sugar
Pinch of salt
1½ teaspoons lemon juice
⅛ teaspoon cinnamon
¼ teaspoon vanilla extract
½ teaspoon arrowroot

In a nonstick saucepan, mix the berries with the water, sugar, and salt over low heat. Stir until the sugar is dissolved. Simmer 3 to 4 minutes, or until the berries burst. Add the lemon juice, cinnamon, vanilla, and arrowroot and continue to simmer the sauce, stirring for about 1 minute more, or until slightly thickened.

Crème Frâiche I

Crème frâiche is a cream that has been allowed to mature through natural fermentation. It thickens and becomes what the French also call *crème double*. This thickish, slightly soured, nutty-flavored cream sauce is a perfect accompaniment for both fresh fruits and fruit desserts.

> *1 cup heavy cream*
> *1 tablespoon buttermilk*

Pour the cream and buttermilk into a jar that has a screw top. Shake to combine. Remove the top, cover with a napkin, and let stand at room temperature for 8 to 12 hours. Screw the top on tightly, shake again and refrigerate. It can be kept for up to two weeks in the refrigerator.

Crème Frâiche II

Makes 1½ cups

For calorie watchers, here is a 25 calorie per tablespoon version of the true French crème frâiche. It keeps well when refrigerated in a covered container for up to two weeks. Although it can be used immediately, the taste improves after 24 hours of refrigeration.

> ½ cup heavy cream
> ½ cup low-fat plain yogurt
> ½ cup low-fat sour cream

In a medium-size bowl whip the heavy cream, add the yogurt and sour cream, and combine. Put in a covered container and refrigerate.

Snow Drift Sauce

Makes 1 cup

This old New England hard sauce does indeed resemble the snow drift for which it was named. By omitting the rose water and substituting one tablespoon of whiskey such as bourbon, you can create a whiskey hard sauce, which is traditionally served in the deep South with bread puddings.

> *¼ pound of butter (1 stick) softened*
> *⅔ cup confectioners' sugar*
> *Pinch of salt*
> *1 tablespoon heavy cream*
> *2 teaspoons rose flower water*

In a small bowl beat the butter with an electric hand mixer until pale. Sift the confectioners' sugar and salt gradually into the butter and add the cream. Beat and then add the rose flower water. Spoon softly into a bowl. If chilled, bring to room temperature to soften before serving.

Buttered Hard Rum Sauce

Makes 1 cup

This sauce marries well with bread or sponge puddings. For a festive touch, spread the sauce in a shallow pan lined with a piece of plastic wrap. Chill until stiff. Cut out 2-inch stars with a cookie cutter and place a small birthday candle in the center of the star. Place several stars around the pudding and light the candles when served.

> *¼ pound butter (1 stick) softened*
> *¾ cup light brown sugar*
> *3 tablespoons dark rum*
> *1 teaspoon finely minced orange peel*
> *¼ teaspoon ground mace*

In a food processor beat the butter until light in color, add the brown sugar gradually, and continue to process, scraping down the sides, until well beaten and fluffy in texture. Add the rum, orange peel, and mace and continue to process for a few more pulses, until the rum is well incorporated. Scrape out with rubber spatula into a small serving dish. Cover with plastic wrap and chill for one hour. Bring to room temperature before serving.

Crème Anglaise I

Makes 1¼ cups

This is a rich and slightly thick basic custard cream, which can be made even thicker and richer by using light or heavy cream instead of milk. This version is used for trifles, charlottes, and as a warm sauce for fruit. Using varied flavorings, it is easily changed to complement whatever fruit dessert you may choose to make.

3 egg yolks
3 tablespoons sugar
Pinch of salt
1 cup milk, light cream, or heavy cream
1 ½-inch piece of vanilla bean, split (see note)

In a food processor, beat the yolks, sugar, and salt until thick. In a small nonstick saucepan, combine the milk and split vanilla bean, scraping the seeds of the pod into the milk. Scald the milk over very low heat. With the processor on, pour ¼ cup of the milk into the egg yolk mixture, then slowly add the remaining milk through the feed tube.

Pour the mixture into the top of a double boiler over 1½ inches of barely simmering water. Stir constantly with a wooden spoon, scraping down the sides of the pan, for about 5 to 10 minutes, or until the custard coats the spoon lightly and is thickened. Do not overcook or it will curdle. Continue to stir for 2 minutes more after removing from the stove, so that the mixture will cool slightly. Strain into a small bowl. Rinse and dry the vanilla bean and save for another use.

Press plastic wrap directly onto the surface of the custard so a skin does not form while cooling. If serving warm as a sauce, serve at once or keep warm over hot water.

Note: For variations, instead of vanilla bean, stir in two tablespoons of sherry or rum, cognac, kirsch, or orange-flavored liqueur. Add the liqueur at the end, when the custard has thickened.

Crème Anglaise II

Makes 1 cup

This custard cream is a bit less sinful than Crème Anglaise I, since it has one less egg yolk and uses low-fat milk. It is, nonetheless, light and quite acceptable as a sauce for fruit.

> *2 egg yolks*
> *3 tablespoons sugar*
> *Pinch of salt*
> *1 cup low-fat milk*
> *Flavoring: either 1½ teaspoons vanilla extract or 2 tablespoons sherry, light rum, cognac, kirsch, or any orange-flavored liqueur. You may also use one teaspoon of rose flower water.*

Follow the same instructions as for Crème Anglaise I.

Chocolate Orange Sauce

Makes 2/3 cup

A versatile sauce with just the proper thickness to trickle over oranges, raspberries, or any desert that a chocoholic does not consider a dessert unless it has some chocolate in it.

2/3 *cup unsweetened Dutch process cocoa powder*
1/3 *cup sugar*
1/2 *cup water*
2 tablespoons butter, softened
1/2 *teaspoon vanilla extract*
1 to 2 teaspoons Cointreau, or other orange-flavored liqueur

Combine the cocoa and sugar in a nonstick saucepan and slowly stir in the water, whisking until smooth. Whisk constantly over medium heat until the liquid starts to boil. Lower the heat, whisking constantly for three minutes. Whisk in the butter and continue to cook for three minutes longer until slightly thickened. Stir in the vanilla and spoon into a covered plastic container. Refrigerate until ready to assemble the dessert. The sauce will thicken and should be diluted with the Cointreau for the proper consistency, just before serving.

Burnt Caramel Cream Sauce

Makes ¾ to 1 cup

This easy sauce adds an unusual dimension to simple poached fruit such as peaches, pears, apricots, or apples. A few lady fingers placed under the fruit or a thin cookie with the sauce makes the dessert even more special.

⅓ cup sugar
1 tablespoon water
1 cup heavy cream at room temperature
¼ teaspoon vanilla extract

In a small, heavy, nonstick saucepan, mix the sugar and water together and cook slowly until a dark caramel syrup forms. Remove the saucepan to the sink and add ¼ cup of the cream. (The mixture will sputter up and the sink will give you protection from the hot sauce.) Stir in the remaining cream and return the pot to the stove, cooking until the mixture is thickened, about 2 minutes. Remove from the heat and add the vanilla. Serve warm.

Warm Peach Caramel Sauce

Makes 1 cup

A golden caramel syrup is added to puréed peaches in a luxurious sauce that takes less than 10 minutes to prepare.

> *2 large ripe peaches, peeled, pitted, and cut into 1-inch pieces*
> *(about 1¼ cups) (see note)*
> *1 teaspoon lemon juice*
> *⅔ cup sugar*
> *5 tablespoons water*
> *1 teaspoon vanilla extract*

In the bowl of a food processor, process the peaches and lemon juice and leave in the bowl. In a small nonstick saucepan, stir the sugar and water together over low heat until the sugar dissolves. Increase the heat and boil for 5 to 8 minutes without stirring, until it is a rich, golden brown syrup. With the food processor on, pour the hot syrup through the feed tube and process. Add the vanilla and process 2 seconds more. Serve warm.

Note: In place of the peaches 2 to 3 peeled ripe pears can be used.

An Addendum

Making Life Easier

We'd like to add a few words at the end of this fruit-filled journey. Though we have enjoyed writing and testing every one of our cookbooks, this one gave us a particular exhilaration, for it was filled with the colors, shapes, and textures of some of nature's most rewarding harvests. It was not only joyful, it was also sensual, a double pleasure through the act of creating with beautiful new materials—plus, of course, the act of *eating* and *sharing* our creations.

But, as in any book, the creation and testing of recipes to be certain that they work properly in the kitchens of our readers, the accuracy of measurements, the simplification of explicit instructions, the very act of repetition, gives the authors a new insight into shortcuts and the clarification of time-consuming procedures. During the year of our testing, we also experimented with various flavorings, at times to barely heighten the exquisite natural perfumes of fresh fruit, and at other times to enhance out-of-season produce not at the peak of its perfection.

We also tried to refine some old techniques by experimenting with various thickening agents, gelatins, and sugar syrups. As in any long term investigative and repetitive process, we learned a lot and would like to share some of these results and discoveries with you. Since they made our lives easier and we have now included them in our voluminous recipe files, we hope they will do the same for you. Here are some of the results.

THICKENING AGENTS. Our favorite thickening agent proved to be ground quick-cooking tapioca, perfect because of its unobtrusive qualities. We ground a whole box of it in an electric blender and so had it on hand whenever we wanted to use it, rather than grinding a spoonful at a time.

CITRUS PEEL. Rather than constantly peeling lemons, limes, and oranges, we accumulated citrus peel at every opportunity and then froze them in a container for future use. When we needed them, we chopped them while frozen. They quickly defrost and retain their flavor.

CHOPPING. We invested in a minichopper, a small food processor and an invaluable gadget that chops citrus peels finely. It is also perfect to chop small amounts of nuts, ginger root, or fresh herbs. It's a marvelous time saver.

PASTRIES. We made batches of pastry for both pies and tarts and froze them to use quickly as fruits came into season.

FREEZING THE HARVEST. Our garden was bountiful, and so we froze our berry harvest at its peak in order to extend the seasons. As an added bonus, we found that our freshly frozen berries had more flavor and perfume when defrosted than any available out-of-season imported fruits. We have given hints for freezing fruits and berries in a separate section of this addendum.

USING NUTS. We came to love the combination of soft fruits and crisp, toasted nuts—marvelous textural opposites. There is a method by which you can toast them quickly and then peel them easily.

SHELLING AND PEELING. Preheat the oven to 350 degrees. Arrange the shelled nuts in one layer on a jelly-roll or pie pan and toast them for 5 to 10 minutes. Some nuts, like hazelnuts and pistachios, will require an additional procedure to get the skins off.

HAZELNUTS. Hazelnuts are toasted for 10 minutes, or until the skins blister and are lightly colored. Wrap them in a rough kitchen towel to steam for 1 minute. Rub the nuts back and forth on a flat surface to remove the skins.

PISTACHIO NUTS. For pistachio nuts, pour boiling water over the shelled pistachios in a heat proof bowl. Let them stand for 10 minutes, drain the water, rub off the skins, and dry them in a 300-degree oven for 10 to 15 minutes.

UNDERRIPE FRUIT. To increase the flavor and intensity of underripe fruit we learned to hasten the process by sealing the fruit in a plastic bag with a banana. The banana gives off ethylene gas which triggers the fruit enzymes to begin the ripening process.

VANILLA BEANS. We experimented with two kinds of vanilla beans: Tahitian and Madagascar. We prefer the Tahitian bean, which turned out to be stronger in flavor, plumper, and more moist. If you use the bean to steep in a sauce or syrup, but you do not split it, it can be rinsed, dried, and used again. Sometimes we put a used bean into a container of fine sugar and used the vanilla sugar in some of our recipes.

OLD-FASHIONED FLAVORINGS. We rediscovered and used some old-fashioned flavorings such as cassia buds and cassia bark, sometimes called Chinese cinnamon. We loved its smokey overtones. We also tried rose and orange flower waters instead of using vanilla in some recipes. These are flavorings that were lavishly used by American colonials as well as by the ancients in Asia and the Middle East. We thought they added a note of exotica and gave some fruit desserts a blissful distinction.

HERBS. We tried fresh green herbs combined with fruit such as piney rosemary with lemon, crisp refreshing mint with grapefruit, and scented rose geranium with stone fruits and berries.

SUGAR SYRUPS. We explored the use of simple, boiled sugar syrups and the stages that they enter as they cook. Although a complete description of sugar syrups for sorbets has been included in Frozen Assets (pages 282–283), we have expanded upon the instructions later on in this addendum for sugar syrups that are made into caramels.

GELATINS. Using gelatins with certain fruits gave us some problems at first, until our research turned up some clues that solved our difficulties. For gelatins, too, we have added a complete analysis later on.

On Using Frozen Fruits

There are times when frozen fruits and berries truly become "frozen assets," offering better quality and flavor than the fresh fruits that are available. Although our first choice is obviously the use of fresh fruit at the peak of flavor, we do not hesitate to use commercially frozen fruit; we also freeze our own when there is a bumper crop or when the greengrocer has an abundance of freshly harvested produce. (The first fruit that comes to mind is the Italian prune plum, and our freezer quickly fills with the moderately priced fruit at the height of its season.)

These days, some fresh fruit is either harvested too early or imported off-season. Much of it ripens before it gets to market, usually in a warehouse, or is offered for sale while not fully ripe. Much of the fruit shipped from South America falls into these categories, since shipping at flavor peak would probably damage the crop by the time it gets to us. On the other hand, commercially frozen fruit or home-frozen fruit are picked and frozen at peak flavor, thus extending the season and allowing us to enjoy them at any time of the year, no matter what the season.

Pitted, frozen cherries, peaches, strawberries, raspberries, and blueberries are commercially available and usually of excellent flavor. Frozen melon, however, which is also available on the supermarket freezer shelves, is really not a favorite of ours. We find that it's much too watery and quite flavorless.

In our small garden we grow currants, rhubarb, gooseberries, wild strawberries, and raspberries (the latter always threatening to overrun the property.) Fire Island, which is our retreat, also provides us with wild blueberries and cranberries. We freeze all the berries dry and unsweetened, cleaned, and frozen in one layer on a jelly-roll pan. When they are hard as marbles, we transfer the berries to a sealed container and store them in the freezer. That way they don't stick together and you can measure off just what you need. Rhubarb is washed, trimmed, and cut up before freezing. We also buy short season favorites such as the Italian prune plums, halve them, pit them, and freeze them.

We also freeze fruit purées, such as mango, kiwi, and red currant. When thawed, they can be used for sauces and sorbets as well as additions to many desserts.

On the Stages of Sugar Syrup Through Caramel

Granulated sugar and water are two simple ingredients that, when made into a liquid solution, become indispensible for many dessert recipes. They blend with other ingredients more easily, and as their properties change through the various stages of cooking, so do the uses to which they can be put.

The thickness and density of the syrup will vary with the proportions of sugar to water and the length of time that they cook together. As the water evaporates, the temperature of the syrup rises and the sugar goes through the various stages until it finally becomes caramel, just one stage short of being burnt. Caramel, incidentally, can also be made without water, but the addition of some water will allow you more leeway.

Everything seems to happen in the blink of an eye, usually in under 10 minutes of boiling time, and though the old adage says that "a watched pot never boils," it certainly doesn't apply when cooking sugar syrups.

EQUIPMENT

Equipment is simple. Although professional chefs prefer an unlined copper pan, we use a large, deep, nonstick pan for easier cleanup when making sugar syrups and caramel. The mixture will bubble as soon as it cooks and expands to an amazing volume.

COOKING

Cook the mixture of sugar and water over low heat, using a wooden spoon to stir. Metal conducts and holds the heat. Once the sugar has dissolved, do not continue to stir. If sugar is stirred while boiling, crystallization occurs and it will ruin the texture of the syrup. Add a candy thermometer to the pot at each stage. If, after stirring, any sugar remains on the sides of the pot, cover the pot for a minute or two to allow the steam to wash down the sugar crystals. Remove the cover and add a tiny amount of acid, such as a dash of vinegar or lemon juice or a small pinch of cream of tartar. The acid acts as an interfering agent to prevent crystals from forming.

Boiling 1 cup of water with ½ cup of sugar for about 4 to 5 minutes results in a *simple syrup,* used to sweeten drinks, uncooked fruit, sorbets, or as a poaching liquid. If you prefer, you can use more sugar for a medium or heavier syrup. Our own personal preference is the simple syrup ratio of 1 cup water to ½ cup sugar (as we have used in the chapter that includes sorbets), increasing proportionately for larger amounts of syrup.

As the syrup continues to cook, the sugar goes through a series of stages depending upon the needs of the recipe. Again, a good candy thermometer will help in telling you the proper temperature and the proper stage.

- 230 to 235 degrees forms the *thread stage.* When a fork is dipped into the syrup and then removed, threads will form as it trickles from the tines of the fork.
- 240 to 245 degrees is the *soft ball stage.* After a bit of syrup is dropped into a dish of cold water, a slightly gummy, soft ball is formed. If you roll it between your fingers you can feel that this is an apt description of the stage, usually used to sweeten Italian meringues.
- Increasing the cooking time will bring the syrup to the next stage at 255 to 260 degrees, the *hard ball stage.* The same test of dropping a small amount of syrup into cold water will result in a ball that is much harder when rolled between the thumb and forefinger and is usually used as a candy base.
- When the syrup registers 270 to 275 degrees and a bit is dropped into water, it will separate into threads, called the *soft crack stage.*
- At 290 degrees the water test produces brittle threads called the *hard crack stage.* Glazed or candied fruits are produced by immersing them in the syrup then placing them on an oiled rack to cool.

A crisp, shiny casing will form. This is also the stage at which we can produce "angel's hair," the wisps of fine, hardened sugar used to contrast with and garnish some creamy desserts.

· Finally, at 310 to 340 degrees, the *caramel stage* is reached. The sugar starts to color, going from a light gold to a dark amber. It loses some of its sweetness and takes on other subtle flavors. The bubbles which form while boiling become large and close together, and it is at this stage that the mixture can easily burn.

Tawny-colored caramel is used for making the traditional praline, a cooled, brittle blend of caramel and nuts, which is then ground to a powder and used for flavoring butter creams, whipped cream, and as a topping for many other desserts. It also acts as a kind of glue to fasten cream puffs together in the elaborate *croquembouche* and for lining the molds for crème caramel or flan. Warm, sticky caramel combined with cream also makes an exquisite sauce for poached or baked fruit. And we can all remember the street fairs and carnivals where the treat was an apple on a stick—dipped in caramel.

On Gelatin

Gelatin, extracted from animal skins and bones and then made into a water soluble protein, is indispensible in some dessert recipes. Gelatin gives support and lightly binds or stiffens desserts that need to keep their shape such as a molded bavarois, cold soufflés, and some mousses. Simply put, the gelatin molecules develop a supporting mesh of protein chains, and as the mixture cools, they align themselves into a network that sets quite firmly. When chilled, that network grows still firmer, bonding the dessert in its final form.

However, the amount of gelatin to use, the heating and cooling temperatures, and the addition of various other ingredients are all elements that must be considered. Since we are essentially trial and error cooks when we are not limited to making notes of specific recipe amounts for our cookbooks, the use of gelatin presented a few troublesome moments. On the other hand, there is a part of our personalities that loves the challenge of finding solutions to the unexpected situations that crop up in the kitchen. What follows are some of the results of the testing.

- Although European chefs favor "sheet" or "leaf" gelatin, our tests showed them to require a preliminary soaking of about 30 minutes in order to soften them. They were also difficult to obtain.
- The most popular brand of powdered, unflavored gelatin (Knox), which is easily attainable in any supermarket, is packed in individual envelopes. Each envelope contains 2¼ teaspoons of gelatin, enough for 2 cups of liquid. Other brands require one tablespoon of gelatin to jell the same amount of liquid.
- Gelatin, when softened, swells into a spongelike consistency. Just add about ¼ cup of cold liquid, let it stand for 3 to 5 minutes, stir, and melt it over low heat, just until it dissolves. It dissolves rather quickly, so don't allow it to overcook or it will not solidify when it cools.
- Add gelatin to mixtures that are at room temperature. If the

gelatin is added to a cold mixture, what results will be stringy and lumpy.

- After adding the gelatin, set the mixture over ice water and stir until the desired consistency is achieved. Or, refrigerate the mixture, stirring it frequently as it cools and then sets.
- If you are going to add additional ingredients such as berries or pieces of fruit, do so when the mixture is the consistency of beaten egg whites.
- For bavarois or mousse, the gelatin mixture should be partially chilled until it mounds slightly when dropped from a spoon. At that point, fold in the whipped cream or beaten egg whites and then chill again.
- Some mixtures may take 30 minutes while others can take several hours of refrigeration. The longer they set, the stronger the mesh structure becomes and the firmer your end result. Trying to expedite the chilling by placing the mixture in the freezer will only crystallize or separate it. Mixtures that contain cream or milk will slow down the setting time.

We also discovered in our testing that certain fruits prevented the gelatin from becoming firm. Research indicated that there is a chemical incompatibility with some fresh fruits, which contain an enzyme that disintegrates the protein chain and prevents jelling from occurring. These fruits include pineapples, kiwis, mangoes, passion fruit, guavas, figs, and papayas. These are the tropical fruits with which we were the least familiar when we started our testing.

A chemist friend finally told us that cooking tropical fruits to a temperature of 175 degrees would destroy the enzyme so that they can be used successfully with gelatin. However, we also learned that heavy cooking of most tropical fruits destroys the flavor as well, so we avoided combining them with gelatin when it was possible.

Certain acids that are found in fruit juices and desserts that use a large amount of fruit purée require the addition of more gelatin than the ratio of one envelope to 2 cups of liquid. Again, our chemist friend gave us the answer. The gelatin protein is weakened by certain acids, making the gelatin tender and thus varying its ability to set. The recipes in this book, therefore, are quite specific as to the proper amounts to use and the instructions to follow.

When it's time to unmold a dessert made with gelatin, you can anticipate the procedure by oiling the mold *before* any ingredients are poured into it. When the mixture has set and you are then ready to unmold it, gently push it away from the sides of the mold by running a knife around the inside, capturing any air bubbles between the dessert and its container. Then invert a serving dish over the mold and, holding both together, turn the mold upside down, give a firm shake, and the mixture should unmold. If it doesn't, repeat the process.

Index

About the Authors

Mel and Sheryl London are the authors of thirteen other books, including seven cookbooks as well as on subjects that range from travel to lifestyle, gardening, and film and videotape career guides. Their *Fish Lovers' Cookbook* was First Prize winner in its category in the Tastemaker Awards.

As documentary filmmakers, Mel and Sheryl have worked in over sixty countries on every continent, producing films for foundations and corporations on the environment, travel, energy, training, fund raising, and health. Mel's documentary on aging and chronic disease was a nominee for the Academy Award and together they hold over 250 other awards for their film work.

They make their home in New York's East Village, but create and test recipes at their house on Fire Island.